Rita Cheminais'
Handbook *for* SENCOs

SAGE was founded in 1965 by Sara Miller McCune to support the dissemination of usable knowledge by publishing innovative and high-quality research and teaching content. Today, we publish more than 750 journals, including those of more than 300 learned societies, more than 800 new books per year, and a growing range of library products including archives, data, case studies, reports, conference highlights, and video. SAGE remains majority-owned by our founder, and on her passing will become owned by a charitable trust that secures our continued independence.

Los Angeles | London | Washington DC | New Delhi | Singapore

Rita Cheminais'
Handbook *for* SENCOs

2nd Edition

Rita Cheminais

Los Angeles | London | New Delhi
Singapore | Washington DC

Los Angeles | London | New Delhi
Singapore | Washington DC

SAGE Publications Ltd
1 Oliver's Yard
55 City Road
London EC1Y 1SP

SAGE Publications Inc.
2455 Teller Road
Thousand Oaks, California 91320

SAGE Publications India Pvt Ltd
B 1/I 1 Mohan Cooperative Industrial Area
Mathura Road
New Delhi 110 044

SAGE Publications Asia-Pacific Pte Ltd
3 Church Street
#10-04 Samsung Hub
Singapore 049483

Editor: Jude Bowen
Editorial assistant: Miriam Davey
Production editor: Sarah Cooke
Copyeditor: Jane Fricker
Proofreader: Audrey Scriven
Indexer: Judith Lavender
Marketing manager: Dilhara Attygalle
Cover design: Wendy Scott
Typeset by: C&M Digitals (P) Ltd, Chennai, India
Printed and bound in Great Britain by Ashford
Colour Press Ltd

Library of Congress Control Number: 2014935420

British Library Cataloguing in Publication data

A catalogue record for this book is available from
the British Library

ISBN 978-1-4462-7418-7
ISBN 978-1-4462-7419-4 (pbk)

At SAGE we take sustainability seriously. Most of our products are printed in the UK using FSC papers and boards.
When we print overseas we ensure sustainable papers are used as measured by the Egmont grading system.
We undertake an annual audit to monitor our sustainability.

I would like to dedicate this book to every SENCO, experienced and newly appointed, who have found this 'bible' on leading and coordinating SEN provision invaluable in enabling them to get to grips with implementing a revised SEN system, designed to further improve the participation and achievement of children and young people with SEN and/or a disability, within the education setting in which they are working.

Contents

List of figures and tables

Figures

Tables

About the author

Rita Cheminais is a leading expert in the fields of special educational needs (SEN), nationally and internationally. With a background as a teacher, an SEN coordinator, an OFSTED inspector, a General, Senior and Principal Adviser in SEN and Inclusion, as a School Improvement Officer, and as a freelance education consultant, Rita has 37 years of practical experience.

She is a prolific writer and respected author of journal articles and books in the areas of SEN, inclusion, Every Child Matters, Pupil Voice and Partnership Working with Families and Multi-Agencies. Rita speaks regularly at national conferences on these topics.

Preface

The second edition of this book provides the essential practical guide for all experienced and newly appointed SENCOs, who are implementing the revised SEN system, in a range of education settings, for children and young people, aged from birth to 25.

In addition, the book acts as an invaluable resource to support newly appointed SENCOs, undertaking the National Award for Special Educational Needs Coordination. The book will also be relevant to training providers in teaching schools, brokering specialist leaders of education in SEN; to higher education institutions, to independent training organisations; and to local authorities. Each chapter focuses, in depth, not only on the key learning areas specific to the revised national SENCO training framework, but also on the six core aspects, relating to the role of the SENCO, in implementing the latest SEN changes.

These areas and aspects cover:

- the professional context of SEN and disability
- strategically leading improvement for SEN
- implementing an effective SEN system
- building capacity in other colleagues to respond to SEN
- productive partnership working with SEN pupils, their families and external agencies
- accountability for SEN policy and practice outcomes.

The SENCO in the twenty-first century undoubtedly faces a number of opportunities and interesting challenges, in implementing a new SEN system.

This handbook, referred to by many SENCOs as 'the bible', aims to guide all SENCOs, newly appointed and experienced, through a significant period of change in the field of SEN.

The resource includes downloadable materials, which can be tailored and customised accordingly, to suit the context of the education setting. It also includes useful points to remember and further activities for reflection, at the end of each chapter.

To all those SENCOs using the handbook, I do hope you find it invaluable in enabling you to ensure pupils with SEN receive the high quality educational provision they deserve.

Acknowledgements

Thanks are due to the reviewers of this second edition proposal, who helped to inform the revisions required in some chapters for the final manuscript. I wish to acknowledge the valuable feedback I have received from the many SENCOs I have been privileged to meet during my travels as a keynote conference speaker, across the country. These comments have identified the essential information needed in the book to equip SENCOs to meet the requirements of implementing a revised SEN system.

I wish to thank the DfE, OFSTED, the NCTL and the EEF for giving me permission to make reference to some of their key documents and resources, relating to SEN and disability, the pupil premium and to the professional development of middle and senior leaders. I also wish to thank Helen Sanderson for giving me permission to refer to some of her resources relating to the pupil profile, the person centred approach and the Education, Health and Care plan; and to Julie Starr, Shaun Allison and Michael Harbour, for allowing me to utilise some of their information relating to coaching.

Finally, my thanks go to Jude Bowen, Amy Jarrold and Miriam Davey for their patience, in guiding and supporting me throughout the production of the second edition of this book.

How to use this book

The coalition government's SEND reforms effective from the 1 September 2014 have been seismic. The period of transition permitted by the DfE, to phase out the old 2001 SEN framework, and move towards implementing the 2014 new statutory framework for SEND, is very much appreciated. While this may pose a huge challenge for all SENCOs, it is envisaged that this book will go some way towards enabling them to manage the change in the SEND system far more effectively.

Equally challenging, for all newly appointed SENCOs undertaking the National Award for Special Educational Needs Coordination, will be introducing the new SEN changes, while at the same time working towards completing their part-time study in one year.

However, whether the SENCO is new to their role, or an experienced veteran, this resource will enable all SENCOs to understand:

- the recent statutory and regulatory frameworks and developments in SEN and disability that inform the SENCO role
- the strategic leadership and development of SEN policy and provision
- how best to coordinate and manage additional provision, to ensure best value, in meeting high incidence SEN
- how to support the professional development of other colleagues, to help them to identify, assess and meet the needs of pupils with SEN
- how to strengthen pupil and parent participation in the EHC plan process, by using person centred planning and the structured conversation
- productive partnership working with external agencies to inform and support the joint commissioning and planning of SEN provision
- how to gather a range of evidence to demonstrate the impact of SEN policy and provision, on pupil outcomes
- how to meet the latest OFSTED requirements, in relation to SEN and disability.

The book can be worked through systematically in chapter order, or it can be dipped into, focusing on particular topics and aspects.

Each chapter provides a summary of what will be covered; key information; checklists offering practical tips; examples of good practice; photocopiable and downloadable resources which can be customised and adapted to suit the type of education setting; useful points to remember; further activities for reflection and professional development, as well as signposting to further resources and information.

Overall, the book provides an essential resource that can be used to:

- act as a quick point of reference for busy SENCOs, and others involved in the delivery of SEN provision and the training of SENCOs
- support professional development by enabling pages to be photocopied, within the purchasing organisation
- promote further discussion and encourage reflection on SEN policy, SEN provision and the SENCO role
- support the national modules of training for newly appointed SENCOs, undertaking the National Award for Special Educational Needs Coordination.

Online materials

This book is supported by a wealth of resources for use in your education setting that can be downloaded from:

www.sagepub.co.uk/cheminais2e

To access these resources:

1. Visit www.sagepub.co.uk/cheminais2e
2. Create a SAGE account
3. Once you have created a SAGE account, re-visit www.sagepub.co.uk/cheminais2e, and a zip folder including all the resources below will automatically download to your computer.

A full list of the downloadable resources is indicated below.

Chapter 1

Figure 1.1 How cyber-bullies hurt victims
Table 1.2 SEND Code of Practice 2014 – Improving outcomes for all
Table 1.3 Template for a risk assessment

Chapter 2

Figure 2.3 SEN development plan template
Figure 2.6 Emotional resilience survey
Figure 2.7 Time management self-review audit
Figure 2.8 Template for reporting on SEN to the governing body
Figure 2.9 Model parent SEN leaflet
Table 2.2 SENCO leadership survey
Table 2.4 Challenging questions for governors on SEN
Table 2.5 SEN budget summary template
Table 2.6 Example of an individual pupil's provision map for SEN Support
Table 2.7 SEN provision map template for a year group
Table 2.8 SEN/Pupil premium provision map for a year group and area of SEN

Chapter 3

Figure 3.2 Overview of the SEN graduated approach four stages
Figure 3.3 Model SEN pupil/student transfer passport
Table 3.1 Meeting the needs of pupils with high incidence SEN
Table 3.3 Pupil premium approaches and their effectiveness

Chapter 4

Figure 4.1 SEN training audit for staff
Figure 4.2 Model SENCO PowerPoint presentation for SEND INSET
Figure 4.4 Recording sheet for a coaching session

Chapter 5

Chapter 6

1

The professional context of SEN and disability in an era of change

> **This chapter covers:**
>
> - the laws and guidance on SEN and disability equality 1981–2014
> - clarification of SEN and disability terminology
> - the SEND Code of Practice (0–25) 2014
> - the Equality Act 2010 and its duties
> - making reasonable adjustments through risk assessment for SEND pupils
> - addressing SEN and disability stereotyping and bullying issues.

The laws and guidance on special educational needs (SEN) and disability

SENCOs will find it useful to familiarise themselves with the development of SEN and disability equality legislation and guidance, from 1981 to 2014, in order to understand the context for the most recent changes in the SEN system.

The timeline in Table 1.1 signposts SENCOs to the relevant legislation and key guidance documents. The most recent 2014 SEND legislation can be accessed at www.gov.uk/government/publications

Clarifying SEN and disability terminology

Definition of special educational needs (SEN)

A child has SEN if they have a learning difficulty that calls for special educational provision to be made for them. A learning difficulty means that the child has significantly greater difficulty in learning than most children of the same age.

Definition of disability

A child has a disability if they have a physical or mental impairment, and the impairment has a substantial and long-term adverse effect on their ability to carry out normal day-to-day activities, i.e. lasts for 12 months or more. The disability prevents or hinders the child or young person from making use of educational facilities of a kind generally provided for others of the same age.

Table 1.1   SEND timeline 1981–2014

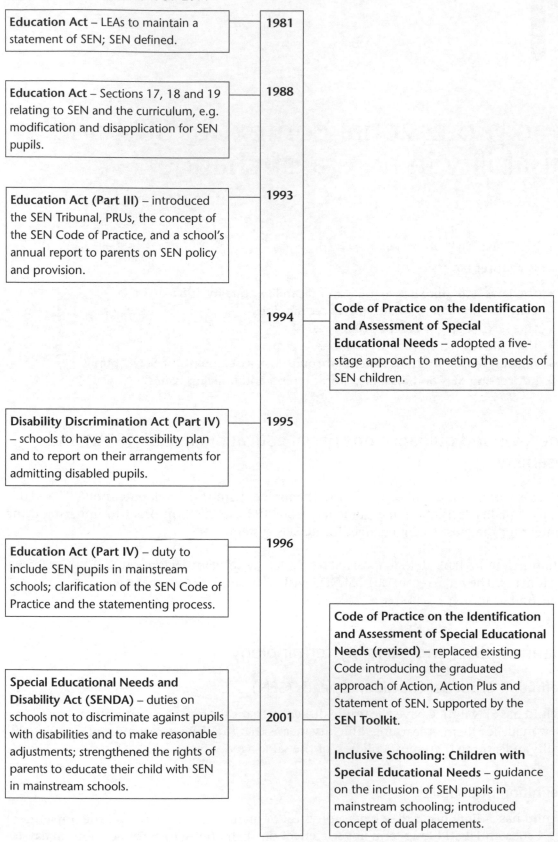

Education Act – LEAs to maintain a statement of SEN; SEN defined.	**1981**
Education Act – Sections 17, 18 and 19 relating to SEN and the curriculum, e.g. modification and disapplication for SEN pupils.	**1988**
Education Act (Part III) – introduced the SEN Tribunal, PRUs, the concept of the SEN Code of Practice, and a school's annual report to parents on SEN policy and provision.	**1993**

1994 — **Code of Practice on the Identification and Assessment of Special Educational Needs** – adopted a five-stage approach to meeting the needs of SEN children.

Disability Discrimination Act (Part IV) – schools to have an accessibility plan and to report on their arrangements for admitting disabled pupils.	**1995**
Education Act (Part IV) – duty to include SEN pupils in mainstream schools; clarification of the SEN Code of Practice and the statementing process.	**1996**

2001 — **Code of Practice on the Identification and Assessment of Special Educational Needs (revised)** – replaced existing Code introducing the graduated approach of Action, Action Plus and Statement of SEN. Supported by the **SEN Toolkit**.

Special Educational Needs and Disability Act (SENDA) – duties on schools not to discriminate against pupils with disabilities and to make reasonable adjustments; strengthened the rights of parents to educate their child with SEN in mainstream schools.

Inclusive Schooling: Children with Special Educational Needs – guidance on the inclusion of SEN pupils in mainstream schooling; introduced concept of dual placements.

Year		
2002		**Access to Education for children and young people with medical needs** – statutory guidance on the education of children unable to attend school due to medical needs. **Accessible Schools: planning to increase access to schools for disabled pupils** – guidance on increasing curriculum and physical access to schools, and access to information. **Special Educational Needs: a mainstream issue** – report of the Audit Commission on SEN children's education and provision.
2003		**The Report of the Special Schools Working Group** – acknowledged the continuing role of special schools in supporting mainstream inclusion. **Every Child Matters** (Green Paper) – outlined the government's vision and proposals for improving services for children and young people, and specified five ECM well-being outcomes for all children.
2004	**The Children Act** – provided legislative framework for ECM by improving vulnerable children's well-being outcomes, including those with SEN and disabilities; introduced ECM systems: CAF, lead professional, ContactPoint, NSF, safeguarding, integrated inspection of children's services; introduced Children's Centres, and expanded the extended school programme.	**Every Child Matters: Next Steps** – set out the timetable for implementing the Children Act 2004. **Every Child Matters: Change for Children in Schools** – outlined expected changes and introduced the ECM Outcomes Framework. **Removing Barriers to Achievement: The Government's Strategy for SEN** – set out the improvements required in SEN policy, practice and provision, focusing on four aspects: early intervention; removing barriers to learning; raising expectations and achievement; and delivering improvements in partnership.

(Continued)

Table 1.1 (Continued)

Disability Discrimination Act (DDA) – built on earlier legislation of 1995 by bringing in the Disability Equality Duty (DED) (general and specific duties), and requirement of schools to prepare and publish a disability equality scheme, and strengthened parents' rights to appeal to SENDIST if the school failed to comply with the DED.	**2005**	**Managing Medicines in Schools and Early Years Settings** – replaced previous guidance of 1996, and provided advice on developing a Policy for Medicines, the safe administration of medicines, and drawing up Health Care Plans. **Special Educational Needs: A New Look** – Mary Warnock's policy document requested a radical review of SEN, the SEN Framework and Inclusion Framework.
Education and Inspections Act – clarified the role of the SENCO, requiring them to be a qualified teacher; ensured fair access to schools for pupils, irrespective of their ability, social background, ethnicity and disability; governing bodies to promote pupils' ECM well-being.	**2006**	**House of Commons Education and Skills Committee's Report on Special Educational Needs** (July) – identified the problems existing in the government's SEN and inclusion processes and made a number of recommendations relating to improved SEN CPD for teachers, and the SENCO being a member of the senior management team in schools. **Government's Response to the Education and Skills Committee Report on Special Educational Needs** (October) – requested OFSTED to undertake a review of the SEN Framework, and proposesd an Inclusion Development Programme (IDP) focused on high-incidence SEN.
	2007	**Implementing the Disability Discrimination Act in Schools and Early Years Settings** – government guidance on putting the DDA into practice, with exemplification of including disabled children in schools and early years settings. **Aiming High for Disabled Children (AHDC): Better Support for Families** – the government's transformation programme for disabled children's services focused on three priorities: access and empowerment; responsive services and timely support; and improving quality and capacity, e.g. providing short breaks.
Special Educational Needs (Information) Act – required information about SEN children in England to be published annually in order to inform future action and improvements at LA and	**2008**	**Inclusion Development Programme (IDP)** – interactive web-based CPD SEN resource for all teachers launched, with the first materials focusing on dyslexia and speech, language and communication needs (SLCN), from early years through to primary and secondary phases of education.

school levels, in SEN pupils' ECM well-being outcomes.

The Education (Special Educational Needs Coordinators) (England) Regulations – SENCO to be a qualified teacher and the governing body to monitor the effectiveness of the SENCO. Clarified and specified the role of the SENCO.

The Education (Special Educational Needs Coordinators) (England) (Amendment) Regulations – required governing bodies to ensure the new SENCO undertakes nationally approved training to obtain the National Award for Special Educational Needs Coordination.

2009

The IDP launched: a four-year programme, to roll out between 2009 and 2011, and covered high incidence SEN: autism, BESD and MLD.

The Bercow Report: A Review of Services for Children and Young People (0 -19) with Speech, Language and Communication Needs – 40 resulting recommendations made to improve services for children and young people with SLCN; prompted government to fund research into SLC good practice, and to enhance augmentive communication.

Lamb Inquiry – Special Educational Needs and Parental Confidence – review focused on improving parental confidence in SEN assessment process, at improving information for parents of SEN children, and improving outcomes for children with SEN.

Identifying and Teaching Children and Young People with Dyslexia and Literacy Difficulties (Rose Report) – 19 recommendations related to assessing and advancing children's progress; improving school support; and strengthening intervention programmes by establishing one-to-one tuition for dyslexic pupils.

Progression Guidance 2009–10 – aimed at raising expectations about the progress of SEN pupils, based on their age and prior attainment. Provided data sets in the NC core subjects as well as P scale point-score equivalents.

Children with Special Educational Needs 2009: An Analysis – first DCSF annual SEN statistical publication in response to the SEN Information Act 2008. It focused on data relating to the types of SEN; attainment and progression; absences and exclusions; and the views of SEN pupils (from the 'TellUs' Survey).

(Continued)

Table 1.1 (Continued)

Equality Act 2010 – the Act replaced previous Acts and regulations related to race, disability and gender equality and discrimination, to provide one comprehensive law, covering all types of discrimination. The Duties in Chapter 1 of Part 6 of the Act apply to schools, and other education settings. The Act included the **Single Public Sector Equality** Duty which placed two important duties on schools: 1. **General Duty** – eliminate unlawful discrimination, harassment and victimisation; advance equality of opportunity; foster good relations. 2. **Specific Duty** – publish information to show compliance with the Equality Duty; and prepare and publish specific and measurable equality objectives, every four years.	**2010**	**Progression 2010–11 Advice on Improving Data to Raise Attainment and Maximise the Progress of Learners with Special Educational Needs** – DfE updated the previous 2009 version of this guidance, to include revised data sets. **The Special Educational Needs and Disability Review: A Statement is Not Enough (OFSTED)** – focused on three aspects: assessment and identification; access to and quality of provision; evaluation and accountability. The review evaluated how well the SEND legislative framework was serving children and young people with SEND, from early years up to the age of 19. The findings from this review helped to inform the coalition government's SEN subsequent 2014 reforms.
	2011	**Support and Aspiration: A New Approach to Special Educational Needs and Disability. A Consultation** (DfE) – the SEND Green Paper was published in March 2011. It set out the coalition government's vision for a new SEN system, which recommended the following improvements: – identification of SEN early with support put in place quickly – staff to know and understand SEN and have the skills to meet the needs of SEN children and young people – raise aspirations by an increased focus being placed on outcomes for SEND children and young people – parents better informed about what local schools, colleges, the LA and local services provide for SEND children and young people

	– parents to have more of a say over the services being used – Education, Health and Care (EHC) plan and an integrated assessment process for those children and young people aged 0–25, with more complex needs.
2011	**SEND Pathfinders** (October 2011) – DfE established 20 SEND pathfinder trials, covering 31 LAs, to test the proposals in the 2011 SEND Green Paper. Six aspects explored further by the SEND pathfinders included: introduction of a new single 0–25 coordinated assessment process and EHC planning; the Local Offer; personal budgets; joint commissioning; engagement and participation of SEND children, young people and their parents and carers; preparing for adulthood. The lessons learned from the SEND pathfinders helped to inform and support the implementation of the SEN reforms.
2012	**Support and Aspiration: A New Approach to Special Educational Needs and Disability. Progress and Next Steps** (May 2012) DfE – coalition government's plan for action set out the next stages in developing new SEN legislation. In brief: – streamlined, quicker single assessment process, involving SEN children and young people, and their families more – EHC plan to replace SEN statements, focused on outcomes, bringing services together – personal budgets for those with an EHC plan – LAs and health services joint planning and commissioning, to meet the needs of SEND children, young people and their families

(Continued)

Table 1.1   (Continued)

		– LAs to publish their local offer – mediation to resolve disputes and a trial system introduced, giving SEND children and young people the right to appeal if they are unhappy with their support and provision.
2012		**Draft Legislation on Reform of Provision for Children and Young People with Special Educational Needs** (Sept. 2012) – outlined the draft legislation required to put the DfE SEN proposals into practice. Document was in two parts: **Part 1** – clarified the legislation and duties for identifying SEN, assessing needs and making SEN provision. **Part 2** – explanatory notes prepared by the DfE to be read in conjunction with the draft legislation.
		The Framework for School Inspection (Sept. 2012) OFSTED – revised inspection schedule focused on four key areas: – achievement of pupils – quality of teaching – behaviour and safety of pupils – quality of leadership and management. Inspections also consider: – the extent to which the education provided by the school meets the needs of pupils who have a disability for the purposes of the Equality Act 2010, and who have SEN – SMSC development of pupils at the school. A revised **School Inspection Handbook** was published by OFSTED to support the inspection framework, along with **Subsidiary Guidance** – for supporting inspectors undertaking section 5 school inspections. Included guidance on: the achievement of SEN and disabled pupils; the behaviour of SEND pupils; special schools, and mainstream schools, with resourced SEND provision.

| 2013 | **Working Together to Safeguard Children (2013): A Guide to Inter-Agency Working to Safeguard and Promote the Welfare of Children** – statutory guidance came into force on 15 April 2013, replacing earlier guidance. It clarified the responsibilities of professionals safeguarding children and young people, shifting the focus away from processes onto needs; it indicated the key factors making effective safeguarding systems; it emphasised two essential principles that underpin effective safeguarding arrangements:

– safeguarding is everyone's business
– a child centred approach ensures a clear understanding of the needs and views of children and young people.

Five chapters in the revised guidance cover:

1. Assessing need and providing help
2. Organisational responsibilities
3. Local Safeguarding Children's Boards (LSCB)
4. Learning and improvement framework
5. Child death reviews.

The revised guidance improved timely information sharing and expert judgements among professionals to be used in order to safeguard children and young people promptly. |

| **Children and Families Bill 2013** – extended the SEN system to cater for those aged 0–25, taking forward the coalition government's SEN reform programme. It included measures to:

– give those in FE and training aged 16–25 the same rights as those in school
– LAs and health services to jointly commission education, health and social care services | 2013 to 2014 | **Indicative Draft: The (0–25) Special Educational Needs Code of Practice** (March 2013) DfE – this document helped parliament consider the SEN clauses in Part 3 of the Children and Families Bill, along with the related draft indicative regulations. The draft took account of feedback from consultation on the proposed SEN reforms. The indicative draft document supported the passage of the Children and Families Bill through the House of Lords during the summer of 2013. |

(Continued)

Table 1.1   (Continued)

– LAs to publish in one place a clear Local Offer of services for SEN
– promote greater cooperation between LAs and other partners
– LAs to consult SEN children and young people and their parents in reviewing SEN and social care provision
– introduce a more streamlined, integrated assessment process for those with more severe and complex needs
– replace SEN statements and Learning Difficulty Assessments with an EHC plan, focused on outcomes, and preparation for adulthood
– encourage parents and SEN young people to go for mediation to resolve disagreements about provision, before going for SEN Tribunal
– offer those with EHC plan a personal budget.

The Bill came into force on the 1 September 2014 as the Children and Families Act.

Draft Regulations (October 2013) associated with the Children and Families Bill

– SEN (Local Offer) Regulations, Clause 30
– Remaining in Special School or Post-16

Institution without an EHC Plan Regulations, Clause 34

– Education (SEN) (Assessment and Plan), Regulations, Clauses 37, 44 and 45

– It comprised of seven chapters, focused on:
– introduction to the new SEN system and SEN Code of Practice
– family centred system
– EHC integration, joint commissioning and cooperation
– Local Offer
– policy into practice for education settings
– assessments and EHC plans
– resolving disputes.

Draft Special Educational Needs (SEN) Code of Practice: For 0–25 Years. Statutory Guidance for Organisations Who Work with and Support Children and Young People with SEN (October 2013) DfE/DoH

– this draft document for consultation provided practical advice on how to carry out statutory duties to identify, assess and make provision for children and young people with SEN. The guidance in the SEN CoP refers to Part 3 of the Children and Families Bill and associated regulations.

There were nine chapters in the draft SEN Code of Practice, which covered:

– Introduction
– Summary
– Family centred system
– Working together across education, health and care
– Local Offer
– Improving outcomes for all
– Assessments and EHC plans
– Children and young people in specific circumstances
– Resolving disputes

Following consultation and amendments, the SEN Code of Practice (0–25) came into force on the 1 September 2014, along with the provisions in the Children and Families Bill and its associated regulations.

– The Approval of Independent Educational Institutions and Special Post-16 Institutions Regulations, Clause 41

– The SEN (Personal Budgets and Direct Payments) Regulations, Clause 49

– The SEN (Appeal) Regulations, Clause 51

– The SEN (Mediation) Regulations, Clause 52

– The SEN (Children's Rights to Appeal Pilot Scheme) Order, Clause 54

– **The SEN (SEN Coordinators) Regulations, Clause 63** (updated previous 2008 SENCO Regulations, and clarified extended SENCO role, to meet 2014 new SEN legislative framework)

– The SEN (Information) Regulations, Clause 65

– Policy statement on Regulations (Transitional arrangements) Clause 109

Children and Families Act 2014 Part 3 – Children and Young People in England with Special Educational Needs or Disabilities – this Act of Parliament received Royal Assent on 13 March 2014, following several amendments being made to the Bill in Part 3 by the government. These amendments related to the inclusion of disabled children and young people within the scope of the legislation, which previously only covered children and young people with SEN in Part 3. The amendments have resulted in disabled children and young people being included in a number of clauses relating to the Local Offer, and local joint commissioning arrangements. The amended clauses are: 21, 22, 23, 24, 25, 26, 27, 30, 32, 34, 68 and 73.

Supporting Pupils at School with Medical Conditions: Statutory Guidance for Governing Bodies of Maintained Schools and Proprietors of Academies in England. (February 2014) DfE – this draft guidance covered: school medical policies; content of pupil health care plans; roles and responsibilities of the governing body, head, staff, the LA and external practitioners, e.g. school nurse; training for school staff supporting pupils with medical needs and giving medication; managing medicines on school premises; record keeping; safe storage of medication; arrangements for pupils with medical needs going on day trips, residential visits, and participating in sporting activities; home to school transport arrangements.

Special Educational Needs and Disability: Research Priorities and Questions DfE (March 2014) – this paper outlined the SEND priorities the DfE wished to research in further depth. These included:

– how to measure the performance of the SEN system
– the methods used by education settings to identify pupils with SEN
– the teaching and learning approaches which have the greatest impact on the attainment of different groups of SEN pupils
– how England's approach to SEN compared with other countries
– the impact different types of support have on SEN pupil outcomes
– which are the most effective approaches to assess the achievement of SEN pupils
– how integrated working across services is impacting on children and young people with SEN

(Continued)

Table 1.1 (Continued)

2014	– how changes in teacher education are impacting on teacher competence and confidence, in identifying and supporting pupils with SEND.
	The SEN and Disability Pathfinder Programme Evaluation: Progress and Indicative Costs of the Reforms. Research report. DfE (March 2014) – the report fed back on the progress made by 31 SEND pathfinder LA areas, in preparing for, and meeting, the government's forthcoming SEND reforms.
	Overall, the majority of LA SEND pathfinders were addressing change management, but were less advanced in setting up the infrastructure for meeting the government's SEND reforms. For example, few had implemented a system for managing personal budgets for SEN; several LA pathfinders were still communicating and implementing their safeguarding information with families and providers; the development of the Local Offer remained less well developed in several LA pathfinder areas; most SEND pathfinder LAs were engaging with parents and carers and the VCO sectors, to inform service provision; however, just under half of the SEND pathfinder LAs were consulting with children and young people sufficiently to inform the Local Offer and service provision.
	Draft Special Educational Needs and Disability Code of Practice: 0–25 years. DfE (April 2014) – this third draft version added the word disability to the title of the document, and made several other improvements, following consultation: – schools' statutory and non-statutory duties were clearer – joint commissioning explained more clearly – clearer information provided on how LAs will support SEND young people aged post-16 and over 18, including transition to adulthood – school accountability for pupils on SEN support without an EHC plan was strengthened – LAs were to be more accountable for engaging service users in informing their Local Offer

Table 1.1 (Continued)

2014	– more information given on the roles and responsibilities of different service providers – more detailed information provided about where parents and carers can complain and seek redress if they are unhappy with provision. This third draft version of the SEND Code of Practice was better structured to make it easier to navigate. New chapters were added to separate out information for early years, schools and post-16 practitioners and on preparation for adulthood. Schools advised to use this version as a planning tool, until the final SEND Code of Practice was published in summer 2014.
	Implementing a New 0 to 25 Special Needs System: LAs and Partners. Further Government Advice for Local Authorities and Health Partners. DfE (April 2014) – this information pack provided further guidance for LAs and their health partners, e.g. CCGs, Health and Wellbeing Boards, on implementing the SEND reforms. It gave: – a useful timeline for implementing the new SEND system – further guidance on implementing the LA Local Offer – further information about EHC plans – further information about personal budgets – a clearer outline of the support available to LAs to help them implement the SEND reforms – further information about how to involve children, young people and their parents and carers more proactively in decisions about provision – further explanation on the role of the health service in implementing the new SEND system.

(Continued)

Table 1.1 (Continued)

2014	

Consultation on Draft Guidance for Supporting Pupils at School with Medical Conditions. Summary of Responses. DfE (April 2014) – this document reported back on the outcome from consultation on the DfE Draft Statutory Guidance, published in February 2014. Overall, feedback was positive, however the following requests were made for improvements:

– greater clarity needed about the roles and responsibilities of local health services
– greater clarity needed about the provision of staff training to support pupils with medical conditions in school
– concerns were raised about the role and capacity of the school nurse and other health care professionals, e.g. specialist nurses and children's community nurses.

Care Act 2014
This Act of Parliament was important because it had implications for young people moving from children's to adult health and social care services.

The Act addressed the following:

– improve joint working between health and social care to provide improved integrated care
– providing personal budgets for health and social care to offer greater choice of services
– removing barriers in accessing integrated care
– a named professional to oversee and coordinate integrated care provision for those with a care plan
– providing better information for health and social care staff via an electronic database, on clients' health and care needs and treatment
– improving support for those moving from one service to another, e.g. smoother transfer for young people moving from children's services to adult services, or moving from hospital to home
– enabling adult social care services to assess young people under age 18.

The Care Act 2014 was referred to in the SEND Code of Practice 0–25.

Keeping Children Safe in Education: Information for All School and College Staff. DfE (April 2014) – this eight-page document provided staff with a summary of the key statutory guidance featured in the full DfE publication, as well as signposting them to other sources of useful information. It is to be read alongside the DfE publication *Working Together to Safeguard Children,* which was issued in 2013.

Keeping Children Safe in Education: Statutory Guidance for Schools and Colleges. DfE (April 2014) – the legal duties in this document further safeguarded and promoted the welfare of children. This guidance replaced *Safeguarding Children and Safer Recruitment in Education* (2006).

The 2014 statutory guidance is to be read alongside *Working Together to Safeguard Children* (2013).

The 2014 statutory guidance is comprised of four parts:

Part 1 – Safeguarding information: types of abuse and neglect, specific safeguarding issues
Part 2 – The management of safeguarding
Part 3 – Safer recruitment
Part 4 – Allegations of abuse made against teachers and other staff.

Examples of disabilities

Disability covers a wide range of impairments. Teachers need to be aware of the diversity of pupils, who, under the Equality Act 2010, are considered to have a disability. These include:

- sensory impairments, e.g. visual impairment (VI), hearing impairment (HI) and multi-sensory impairment (MSI)
- physical impairments or illness that affect mobility, dexterity or control of movement, e.g. arthritis, multiple sclerosis, stroke
- developmental conditions, e.g. dyslexia, dyspraxia, autistic spectrum
- progressive diseases, e.g. motor neurone disease, muscular dystrophy, dementia, lupus
- illnesses with impairments with fluctuating or recurring effects, e.g. myalgic encephalitis (ME), chronic fatigue syndrome (CFS), epilepsy, diabetes
- mental health conditions and mental illnesses, e.g. depression, eating disorders, obsessive compulsive disorder (OCD), schizophrenia, bipolar affective disorders, self-harm
- HIV infection
- cancer
- facial disfigurements.

The SEND pathfinders

In October 2011, the DfE established 20 SEND pathfinder trials, covering 31 local authorities, to test the proposals in the SEND Green Paper, *Support and Aspiration: A New Approach to Special Educational Needs and Disability. A Consultation.*

The aim of the SEND pathfinders was to improve the support available to SEND children and young people, and in particular to see if there was:

- increased choice and control and improved outcomes for their families
- a clearer support system emerging, which was less confrontational and far less bureaucratic
- good value for money
- an advantage to using the voluntary sector to make the single coordinated assessment process more independent from the local authority.

Six aspects were being explored further by the SEND pathfinders:

- the introduction of a new single 0–25 coordinated assessment process and Education, Health and Care (EHC) planning
- the Local Offer
- personal budgets for SEND children, young people and their families
- joint commissioning
- engagement and participation of SEND children, young people, and their parents and carers
- preparing for adulthood.

In June 2013, the DfE launched the first in a series of six introductory SEND pathfinder information packs, one for each of the above six aspects, which brought together emerging principles, materials and case studies from the pathfinder programme. These information packs were designed to support the SEND Pathfinder Champions, appointed to support facilitation of the new SEN legislative framework in local authorities not involved in the SEND pathfinder trials. The DfE updated these six pathfinder information packs on a regular basis.

SENCOs may find it useful to read those information packs that are most relevant to their working context, as they offer some useful examples of best practice.

The evaluation and lessons learned from the SEND pathfinders have helped to inform and support the national implementation of the SEN reforms.

The SEND pathfinder information packs can be downloaded from: www.sendpathfinder. co.uk

The SEND Code of Practice (0–25) 2014

The SEN Regulations 2014, the SEND Code of Practice (0–25) 2014 and Part 3 of the Children and Families Act 2014, all effective from 1 September 2014, form the new SEND statutory framework, and represent the biggest SEN reforms for just over three decades. The revised SEND Code of Practice (0–25) replaces previous statutory guidance in the 2001 SEN Code of Practice, in Inclusive Schooling: Children with Special Educational Needs and in Section 139A of the Learning Difficulty Assessments Statutory Guidance (2013) for Local Authorities.

The 2014 SEND Code of Practice (0–25) provides practical advice on how to carry out the statutory duties in relation to identifying, assessing and making provision for children and young people with SEN and/or disabilities, from birth to age 25.

What is new and different in the 2014 SEND Code of Practice?

The main changes and differences from the previous 2001 SEN Code of Practice include:

- a wider age range, e.g. from birth to 25 years of age
- a clearer focus on the views of SEN children and young people and on their role in decision-making about SEN provision
- an increased emphasis on the joint planning and joint commissioning of services, to ensure closer cooperation between education, health and social care
- an improved coordinated single assessment process, and a new 0–25 Education, Health and Care (EHC) plan for those with more complex needs, who previously had a statement of SEN and a Learning Difficulty Assessment
- new guidance on the support SEN children and young people should receive in education and training settings
- a greater focus on support that enables those with SEN to succeed in their education and make a successful transition to adulthood
- a change in terminology from behavioural, emotional and social difficulties (BESD) to social, emotional and mental health difficulties
- Action and Action Plus replaced by a single school-based category of 'SEN Support'
- individual education plans (IEPs) replaced by a personalised planning approach focused on outcomes.

Table 1.2 provides an overview of Chapter 6 'Improving outcomes for all' from the SEND Code of Practice (0–25). Other major topics from the 2014 SEND Code of Practice, i.e. EHC plans, the one page profile, the person centred approach, the structured conversation, personal budgets, the Local Offer, joint planning and delivery, are all covered in greater depth in Chapter 5 of this book.

Table 1.2 SEND Code of Practice 2014 – Improving outcomes for all

	SEN Support	EHC plan
Which children and young people / **Triggers for intervention**	Single category of SEN, school-based, replacing Action and Action Plus, for those whose needs can be met in the mainstream. Where a pupil falls behind their peers, or continues to make less than expected progress, given their age and starting point, and despite high quality personalised teaching targeted at their area of weakness, and differentiated approaches being utilised.	Education, Health and Care (EHC) plan for all those aged 0–25 who previously had a SEN statement or a Learning Difficulty Assessment. Needs more complex and severe, where a pupil, despite the additional and different SEN Support being put in place in the education setting, continues to make little or no progress, and the SEN provision is no longer able to meet the pupil's needs.
Whose responsibility	The class/subject teacher with the SENCO, both undertaking further assessment to identify whether the pupil has a significant learning difficulty. Parents of the child are informed and consulted on SEN support required. The class/subject teacher takes lead responsibility for planning and reviewing the pupil's SEN Support.	The local authority (LA) conducts an integrated statutory EHC needs assessment, and prepares and issues an EHC plan (20-week timescale), when there is robust evidence from the education setting, multi-agency professionals, the parents and the SEN pupil, that such a plan is required. Where the LA does not issue an EHC plan it gives reasons why to relevant parties (16-week timescale), and the pupil remains on SEN Support. Parents and the young person can request that the LA prepare a personal budget to deliver all or some of the provision, set out in the EHC plan. This provision is likely to cater for the holistic needs of the pupil, and can include: • Weekend or holiday respite care, or short break • Personal assistant support during school holidays • Participation in sports activities or day trip with additional transport needs • Specialist equipment or learning aids, i.e. electronic communication tools and supportive software • Social worker support • Extra therapy services • Home modifications – ramp for wheelchair access • Transport to attend special school play scheme or to undertake work placement. The EHC plan is reviewed annually and any changes to provision made.
Nature of additional or different provision	Graduated approach – Assess, plan, do and review. • Personalised plan with stretching relevant academic/developmental targets; expected outcomes specified, and nature of provision • Evidence-based interventions • Additional support from within the school • Adaptations to the support provided made • Involvement of specialist staff or support service as appropriate • Termly review of pupil progress towards meeting targets set and achieving expected outcomes, involving parents and the SEN pupil, where appropriate.	

The Equality Act 2010 and its duties

The Equality Act 2010 replaced and unified all existing equality legislation, i.e. the Race Relations Act, the Disability Discrimination Act and the Sex Discrimination Act. The Equality Act came into force in education settings in October 2010. Chapter 1, Part 6 of the Equality Act 2010 sets out the duties that apply to early years providers, schools, academies, post-16 institutions and local authorities.

Duties for educational settings

Education settings must not discriminate against a child or young person or a prospective child/young person because of their disability, race, sex, gender reassignment, religion or belief, sexual orientation or because they are pregnant.

In addition, an education setting must not discriminate against a child or young person in relation to the following activities:

- admission to the education setting
- the provision of education
- access to any benefit, facility or service
- exclusion from the education setting
- subjection to any other detriment.

The Equality Act 2010, includes two duties:

1. General Public Sector Equality Duty (PSED)

This requires education settings to have 'due regard' to the need to:

- eliminate unlawful discrimination, harassment and victimisation
- advance equality of opportunity
- foster good relations.

2. Specific Duties

These aim to help education settings to meet the PSED. They are:

- to publish information to show how they are complying with the PSED (which must be updated annually)
- to prepare and publish at least one specific and measurable equality objective, at least every four years.

Some examples of measurable SEN and disability equality objectives are:

- to improve the attendance rates of SEND pupils in Year 7 in order to meet a target of at least 92% or more attendance, by the end of the academic year 2014–15
- to further increase the participation of pupils who are wheelchair users by 50% in the school's youth club activities
- to enable 100% of staff to feel confident in responding effectively to any bullying issues among SEND pupils.

Making reasonable adjustments through risk assessment for SEND pupils

The Equality Act 2010 and its related duties are closely linked with health and safety legislation, which requires the governing body and the headteacher to consider whether they have taken 'reasonable steps' by amending their health and safety policies, procedures and practices to ensure pupils with SEND are not placed at a substantial disadvantage compared with their peers.

Reasonable adjustments are to be made in relation to:

- changing provisions, criteria or practices
- providing auxiliary aids and services.

Schools will be expected to provide an auxiliary aid or service for a disabled pupil when it would be reasonable to do so, and if such an aid would alleviate any substantial disadvantage.

The duty to make reasonable adjustments is also anticipatory, i.e. adjustments must be planned and put in place in advance, to prevent any disadvantage occurring prior to a disabled child's or young person's admittance to the education setting.

The SENCO will need to consider the following factors when assessing the reasonableness of an adjustment for a disabled pupil:

- the financial and human resources required for the adjustment
- the effectiveness of the reasonable adjustment for the pupil
- the effect the reasonable adjustment will have on other pupils
- health and safety requirements
- whether the auxiliary aid can be made available through the SEN route or the pupil premium route.

The Draft SEND Code of Practice (DfE, 2014e: 6: xviii) states:

> Schools **must** publish accessibility plans (and local authorities, accessibility strategies) setting out how they plan to increase access for disabled pupils, to the curriculum, the physical environment and to information.

OFSTED inspections may include a school's accessibility plan as part of their review. OFSTED looks at how schools meet diverse needs and advance equality through their focus on securing and maintaining excellent teaching, learning and assessment for all pupils; narrowing the gaps in achievement between different groups; ensuring pupils are free from bullying in all its manifestations; dealing with unacceptable behaviour and disruptions to learning; and building cohesive school communities, where all pupils can thrive.

SENCOs will find OFSTED's document *Inspecting Equalities: Briefing for Section 5 Inspection* (2014d) a very useful publication, available at www.ofsted.gov.uk, and DfE (2013a) *Equality Act 2010: Departmental Advice for School Leaders, School Staff and Governing Bodies of Maintained Schools and Academies*. Chapter 4 in this DfE guidance document focuses on disability, and on the special rules that apply to fluctuating conditions.

The Equality and Human Rights Commission (EHRC) resources include: *New Equality Act Guidance*, and *Education Providers: Schools' Guidance*, available at: www.equalityhumanrights. com/advice-and-guidance/new-equality-act-guidance/

Risk assessment and pupils with SEND

Advances in medical science have brought more pupils with physical disabilities and medical needs into mainstream schools who may require specialist handling, special aids and facilities, specialist therapies, minor medical treatment on school premises, or the administration of medication during the school day. The SENCO needs to work in partnership with a range of health professionals, such as the school nurse, physiotherapists and occupational therapists, as well as with the parents/carers of the SEND pupil, in order to ensure that they have up-to-date information and knowledge on what is reasonable to expect and deal with on the school premises, and outside school on any residential, educational or sporting trips or events. This information needs to be shared with teachers and teaching assistants, to enable them to undertake a robust risk assessment as part of making reasonable adjustments.

A risk assessment is simply a careful examination of what could cause harm to a pupil or staff, to enable the person in charge, in this case the SENCO, to weigh up whether they have taken sufficient precautions, and if they need to do more to prevent potential harm occurring. It is a dynamic, ongoing, sustainable process that is a legal requirement in terms of recording and regular review.

The purpose of a risk assessment is to balance health and safety considerations with the prevention of unreasonable restrictions on a pupil with SEND's right to equality of opportunity, dignity and privacy. A risk is defined as the chance, high or low, of someone being harmed, together with an indication of how serious the harm could be.

Risk assessments are undertaken at the early planning stage of any educational within-school or out-of-school activity or event, and also in advance of a pupil with SEND being admitted to a nursery, school, academy, college or work placement, which may pose potential health and safety risks. An alternative activity (Plan B) must always be prepared and risk assessed, in the event of the SEND pupil not being able to participate in the main activity with their peers on the day. Table 1.3 offers a template for a risk assessment.

SENCOs will be familiar with the five steps to undertaking a risk assessment:

1. Identify the hazards (a hazard is anything that may cause harm).
2. Decide who might be harmed and how.
3. Evaluate the risks and decide on precautions.
4. Record the findings and implement them.
5. Review the assessment and update if necessary.

The SENCO must ensure that the risk assessment shows that:

- a proper check has been made
- they have consulted with those who might be affected
- they have dealt with all the significant hazards, taking into account the number of staff/pupils/people who could be involved
- the precautions are reasonable and the remaining risk is low
- relevant staff, the pupil and the child's parents or carers have been involved in the process.

The SENCO will allocate in-class support to those pupils with physical or sensory impairments, or more complex medical needs, in practical subjects such as science, and ask the class or subject teacher to check that these SEND pupils wear protective clothing, and work at benches of an appropriate height if they are a wheelchair user.

SENCOs need to ensure that they, and their team of teaching assistants/learning support assistants, are familiar with the relevant health and safety regulations relating to: manual handling; use of display screen equipment; exposure to hazardous substances; infection control; and the administration of medicines, for which there should be a school medicines policy in place.

Some SEND pupils with medical needs may take medication before or during the school day, which can produce resulting side effects that cause barriers to their learning, e.g. tiredness, poor concentration or weak memory recall.

Table 1.3 Template for a risk assessment

School name:		Date of risk assessment:	
Activity venue:		Date of activity:	
Brief description of the nature of the activity:			

List of actual hazards	Who is affected	Risk rating (Low, Moderate or High)

Key areas where potential hazards may occur	Control measures (action being taken)
Group/pupils involved:	
Staffing details:	
Equipment:	
Venue/environment:	
Travel arrangements:	
Emergency procedures:	

RISK ASSESSMENT REVIEW

Date of risk assessment review:
Any significant changes affecting the risk assessment:
Nature of the revision required to the risk assessment:

While there is no legal duty on staff to administer medicines, under the Equality Act 2010 duties reasonable adjustments should be made in these instances, to ensure the SEND pupil is not excluded from participating in learning and the life of the school. Where staff are administering medication to SEND pupils onsite or offsite, this should be indicated in their job descriptions. These staff must have been appropriately guided and trained by health professionals. SENCOs will find clear guidance on the administration of medication to pupils in the DfE document *Supporting Pupils at School with Medical Conditions: Statutory Guidance for Governing Bodies of Maintained Schools and Proprietors of Academies in England* (2014b), and in the OFSTED publication *Pupils with Medical Needs: Briefing for Section 5 Inspection* (2014e).

Addressing SEN and disability stereotyping and bullying issues

Bullying creates a barrier to children's learning and prevents them from leading a fulfilled and happy life. Research shows that pupils with special educational needs and/or disability (SEND) are significantly more likely to be bullied or victimised than those who do not have any SEND. The reasons for SEND pupils being a target for bullying and experiencing personal distress are due to their:

- being perceived by some other peers as being 'different', and therefore an easy target for bullying
- not realising they were actually being bullied and therefore incidents going unreported
- having limited communication skills and thus finding it difficult to tell an adult that they were being bullied
- being more isolated as a result of having fewer friends than other peers
- forgetting to report a bullying incident immediately because of their poor memory skills
- being a dual placement pupil spending time in a mainstream school for some part of the week, and therefore being more exposed to bullying from some of their mainstream peers.

Definition of bullying

Bullying is defined as behaviour by an individual or a group which is repeated over time, and which intentionally hurts another individual or group, either physically or emotionally.

The Anti-Bullying Alliance's pupil-friendly definition of bullying is:

> People doing nasty or unkind things to you on purpose more than once, which it is difficult to stop.

Cyber-bullying is the act of using the internet and other digital (mobile) technologies to upset or humiliate another.

Pupils with SEND have the same rights and entitlements to be safe and free from bullying as all other children and young people, under the Equality Act 2010.

SEN and disabilities: developing effective anti-bullying practice

Since 2013 the Anti-Bullying Alliance (ABA) has been working in partnership with Achievement for All 3As, Contact a Family, Mencap and the Council for Disabled Children (CDC) on a new project, funded by the DfE, which is aimed at reducing the incidence and impact of bullying on SEND children and young people. The project is:

- improving practice in schools (led by Achievement for All 3As)
- targeting early intervention through providing information, advice and support for parents and carers (led by Contact a Family)

- disseminating information training to the wider sector (led by the ABA)
- ensuring that all training and resources are influenced and informed by children and young people with SEND themselves (led by the CDC).

During the course of the project ABA will have targeted thousands of schools, parents and carers and other professionals to reduce the incidence and impact of bullying of children and young people with SEND. ABA has created an information hub of downloadable resources and information. This can be found at: www.anti-bullyingalliance.org.uk/1198

SENCO role in tackling bullying issues

The SENCO plays a crucial role in securing the good emotional and mental health of pupils with SEND. They do this by:

- acting as a champion of inclusion
- raising staff awareness through training about disability equality
- making valuable contributions to the development and review of the education setting's anti-bullying and behaviour policies
- promoting the participation of pupils with SEND in any consultations on behaviour and bullying in school
- ensuring any less tolerant and understanding peers learn about respect and to view 'difference' and diversity positively
- ensuring SEND pupils who are the victims of bullying receive the necessary support and interventions to help them deal with it, and giving them coping strategies to tackle bullying in the future
- monitoring the impact of anti-bullying interventions for individual pupils with SEND.

Teaching assistants and mid-day welfare assistants also play an important role in preventing pupils with SEND being bullied, particularly outside the classroom, at break and lunchtimes, and when these pupils are undertaking extra-curricular activities.

Table 1.4 offers some recommended strategies at a whole school level and also at a class-room level to prevent stereotyping and bullying of SEND pupils from occurring.

Cyber-bullying and SEND pupils

Research has shown that SEND pupils tend to be the victims of cyber-bullying owing to peer rejection, social isolation and social skills deficits. The internet and digital technology are a popular medium for SEND pupils to use for social engagement, because it does not have to reveal their disability to others.

Unfortunately, cyber-bullying can occur 24 hours a day, seven days a week, and much of it outside school hours.

Cyber-bullying ranges from threatening messages being sent via email, text or instant messaging (IM), to having an email account hacked into, or having an online identity stolen. Some proficient cyber-bullies can also create a social media webpage to bully a victim. There is a gender difference in the type of cyber-bullying undertaken. For example, boys usually resort to 'sexting' or sending messages that threaten physical harm. Girls, on the other hand, prefer to spread lies and rumours and expose their victim's secrets online, or to exclude the victim from emails. Figure 1.1 illustrates the ways in which cyber-bullies can hurt SEND pupils.

Table 1.4 Strategies to address stereotyping and bullying of SEND pupils

Whole school strategies	Classroom strategies
• Displays of positive images of successful disabled people	• The SEAL bullying related materials are utilised
• School drama productions include SEND pupils, and have a theme on disability, in some productions	• Alternative methods of recording are available to enable SEND pupils to report bullying and their feelings in a range of ways
• School assembly on inclusion has a focus on disability	• SEND pupils views are listened to by staff
• Pupils with SEND have an opportunity to meet with the governors to present their views	• Staff know which agencies to seek further information from about anti-bullying and SEND pupils
• Parents of disabled pupils contribute their knowledge and expertise on disability at staff INSET	• The Equality Act 2010 duties are displayed in a pupil-friendly format, within the classroom
• A consistent system for recording bullying incidents is in place which is followed by all staff	• Staff work in partnership with special school staff to further develop their inclusive practice and knowledge about the needs of SEND pupils
• Robust whole school behaviour and anti-bullying policies are in place, which engage SEND pupils in their regular review and updates	• Positive images of disability are promoted across the curriculum
• A good range of extra-curricular activities are fully accessible to SEND pupils, including wheelchair users	• Each class has a nominated pupil anti-bullying representative
• An anti-bullying week takes place annually	• Class teachers use three positive statements for every one negative statement when feeding back to SEND pupils on their effort and achievements
• A Quiet Zone exists in school, for SEND pupils who need a safe haven	• Teachers analyse SEND pupil-level attendance data to look for any correlation between absences of these pupils from school and bullying incidents, and follow any issues up promptly
• There is a system of peer supporters and playground buddies operating	• Circle time provides a forum for discussing bullying
• Anti-bullying interventions are evaluated for effectiveness	
• Visible staff are around school and out at break times and lunchtimes	
• Counselling provision is available in school, and an email forum exists for SEND pupils to access and report bullying issues in confidence	

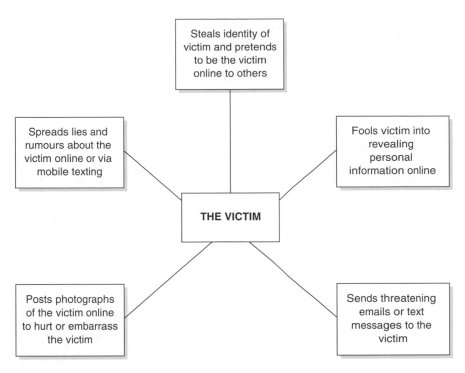

Figure 1.1 How cyber-bullies hurt victims

Cyber-bullying can have many negative effects on victims, which include: low self-esteem, feeling hurt, angry, helpless, isolated, depressed or even suicidal. Unfortunately cyber-bullying can be done anonymously, which results in the pupil with SEND not being sure who is targeting and taunting them.

SENCOs may find it useful to read the McAfee research report entitled *Digital Deception: The Online Behaviour of Teens*, published in January 2014, which gave some alarming facts and figures about children and young people's access to, and use of, online and digital (mobile) technology. Some of the highlights are:

- 53% of children and young people go online without parental supervision
- 66% of children and young people use a smart phone for internet access
- 26% of children and young people spend between four and six hours or more online, every day
- 22% of children and young people have witnessed the cyber-bullying of a friend or classmate
- 16% of children and young people have been victims of cyber-bullying
- 10% of teenagers have been approached online by an adult they do not know
- only 19% of parents have installed parental controls on computers and other mobile devices which their child accesses
- 31–35% of children and young people have posted their email address online, or have posted a photograph of themselves online, or have given an online description of what they look like.

How to spot if a SEND pupil is experiencing cyber-bullying

The SENCO, teachers and teaching assistants, as well as parents, should look for the following signs of the effects of cyber-bullying on a SEND pupil:

- becomes sad, angry, distressed during or after using the internet or mobile phone
- appears anxious when receiving an email, text, instant message or email

- avoids discussion and is secretive about their computer or mobile phone activities
- withdraws from family, friends, and activities that they previously enjoyed
- school work declines in output and completion
- begins to not want to go to school
- shows changes in mood, behaviour, disturbed sleep patterns, loss of appetite, anxious, depressed or suicidal.

Top tips for internet and digital technology safety

The following top tips are useful for SENCOs to use and share with other staff, including parents and carers of SEND pupils:

- Don't allow the child or young person to respond to any text messages, emails or other online posts which are negative or hurtful about them
- Keep all the evidence of cyber-bullying incidents, and report any inappropriate sexual images they have received to the headteacher, who must then refer this on to the police, as it is a child protection issue.
- Invite the local police community support officer into school to give an input in assembly on the legalities of cyber-bullying and the consequences for perpetrators, and how to be cyber savvy, including some real stories.
- Keep reinforcing online/digital safety with the SEND pupils – posters with rules and reminders about never sharing their password or posting any personal details online, or meeting unknown people from online.
- Ensure staff and parents attend sessions on e-safety, which should cover online etiquette and online safety: how to block an email address or mobile phone number, how to report cyber-activity to an internet service provider, or to a mobile phone company, how to delete personal details from a social media contact list, how to change the email address and put pin locks on a mobile phone, how to avoid online identity fraud and email hacking.
- For those parents and staff who have been unable to attend e-safety sessions, provide them with a CD/DVD on e-safety that they can view at home.
- Encourage parents to have the home computer the child accesses in a busy downstairs family area, to enable them to keep a check on activity.
- Ensure parental controls are installed on smart phones and tablets as well as the home computer, to filter any inappropriate web content.
- Set limits and boundaries for internet and smart phone use and show an interest in the social networking and websites the child or young person has been using.
- Teach SEND pupils how to create safe and strong passwords for log-ins.

SENCOs will find the following websites helpful on cyber-bullying and for sign-posting SEND pupils and their parents to these sites for further information:

> www.kidscape.org.uk/cyberbulling
> www.childline.org.uk
> www.antibullyingalliance.org.uk
> www.thinkuknow.co.uk, which is a Child Exploitation and Online Protection (CEOP) programme providing a range of free resources.

Additionally, the ABA and Contact a Family (2012) produced *Cyberbullying and Children and Young People with SEN and Disabilities: Guidance for Teachers and Other Professionals. SEN and Disability: Developing Effective Anti-bullying Practice,* which can be downloaded for free from: www.anti-bullyingalliance.org.uk or from www.cafamily.org.uk/

SENCOs can find further information and resources relating to bullying and SEN and disability on the DfE website: www.gov.uk. Of particular interest will be: DfE (2013d) *Preventing and Tackling Bullying: Advice for Headteachers, Staff and Governing Bodies.*

Two excellent video resources which can be used with pupils are *Make Them Go Away* (which features bullying involving young children with disabilities: www.youtube.com/watch?v=Cw0VrC5ODKA) and *Let's Fight it Together* (which focuses on cyber-bullying: www.childnet.com/resources/lets-fight-it-together).

Finally, McLaughlin et al.'s (2012) *Perspectives on Bullying and Difference: Supporting Young People with Special Educational Needs and/or Disabilities in Schools* can be purchased from the National Children's Bureau (NCB) website (www.ncb.org.uk). It gives evidence-based practice on effective approaches to use with bullies and victims.

Points to remember

- There is a greater focus in the 2014 SEND Code of Practice (0–25) on support that enables SEND pupils to succeed in their education.
- Not all pupils with disabilities have SEN.
- SEND is everyone's responsibility in the education setting.
- Reasonable adjustments must be made to ensure that no SEND pupils are placed at a substantial disadvantage compared to their peers.
- A risk assessment balances health and safety considerations with equality of opportunity.
- Cyber-bullying can occur 24/7 and much of it outside school hours.

Further activities

The following questions, focused on aspects covered in this chapter, meet the requirements of the National Award for Special Educational Needs Coordination, and support reflection and the professional development of experienced and newly appointed SENCOs.

1. In light of the 2014 SEND statutory framework, which aspects of SEN and disability present the greatest challenges to you as a SENCO, and how will you overcome these?
2. In response to the Equality Act 2010 specific duties, which two SEND measurable equality objectives will you include in the education setting's published SEN information?
3. After reading the latest version of the SEND pathfinders information packs, briefly outline one new piece of learning you can apply and use to support the implementation of the latest SEN reforms, in your education setting.
4. A newly qualified teacher has planned an educational day visit for their class, and is anxious about ensuring reasonable adjustments are in place to ensure access for a SEND pupil with a visual impairment. What advice and guidance would you give to the NQT in preparing a risk assessment, prior to the visit?
5. A parent of a SEND pupil informs you that their child has revealed that they are being bullied by another pupil in their form group. Describe the steps you would take as SENCO to address the issue.

 Online materials

To access electronic versions of the material in this chapter visit: www.sagepub.co.uk/cheminais2e

Figure 1.1 How cyber-bullies hurt victims
Table 1.2 SEND Code of Practice 2014 – Improving outcomes for all
Table 1.3 Template for a risk assessment

2

Leading improvement for SEN

> **This chapter covers:**
>
> - the role of the SENCO in an era of significant SEN change
> - opportunities and challenges for the SENCO
> - the concept, principles and approaches of strategic leadership
> - the characteristics and skills of a strategic leader of SEN
> - the SENCO as an emotionally resilient leader managing time effectively
> - delegation and distributed leadership
> - the role of the SEN governor
> - SEN information and reporting on SEN policy
> - getting to grips with funding for SEN pupils
> - exploring provision mapping as a strategic management tool.

The role of the SENCO in an era of significant SEN change

The SEND Code of Practice (0–25) 2014 clarifies the role of the SENCO to include the following responsibilities:

- ensure that the Equality Act 2010 duties are met, with regard to making 'reasonable adjustments' and access arrangements
- promote the inclusion of SEN pupils in the school community and access to the curriculum, facilities and extra-curricular activities
- provide professional guidance to colleagues
- work closely with staff, parents and carers, and other agencies, to secure relevant services for the pupil with SEN
- be aware of the provision in the Local Offer
- identify pupils with special educational needs
- inform parents and carers that their child has been identified as having SEN
- oversee the daily operation of the school's SEN policy
- coordinate provision for pupils with SEN, including those who have an EHC plan
- liaise with the relevant designated teacher where a looked after pupil has SEN
- advise on a graduated approach to providing SEN Support
- advise teachers about differentiated teaching methods appropriate for individual pupils with SEN
- advise on the deployment of the delegated budget and other resources to meet the needs of pupils with SEN
- liaise with early years providers, other schools, educational psychologists, health and social care professionals and independent or voluntary bodies

- be a key point of contact with external agencies, especially with the local authority (LA) and their support services
- liaise with potential next providers of education to ensure a smooth transition is planned, and that the parents and the pupil are informed about options
- ensure all relevant information about the pupil's SEN and their SEN provision is passed on, when they transfer to another school or education setting
- ensure that SEN pupil records are maintained and kept up-to-date
- monitor the effectiveness of SEN provision
- liaise with, and provide information to, parents of SEN pupils, on a regular basis, regarding their child's SEN and the additional provision being made for them
- select, supervise and train learning support assistants
- contribute to in-service training for teachers at the school
- prepare and review the information required to be published on SEN provision and the SEN policy.

Figure 2.1 summarises the core role of the SENCO.

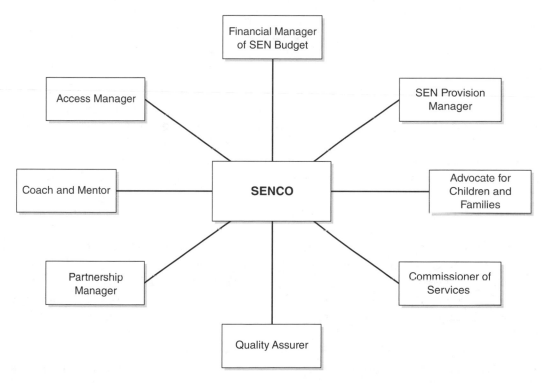

Figure 2.1   Core roles of the SENCO

SENCO professional portfolio of evidence checklist

It is good practice for the SENCO to build a professional portfolio of evidence which records and documents the significant developments and achievements in their career in undertaking the strategic leadership of SEN policy and provision. The following checklist exemplifies what to include in the portfolio:

- job description
- curriculum vitae
- qualification and CRB certificates
- performance management evidence
- certificates of attendance, record of courses attended with evaluations of their impact

- cameos of examples of significant successful SENCO achievements
- relevant extracts from the most recent OFSTED inspection report or other testimonials from the LA, external professionals, parents and carers, and from SEN pupils
- multi-media evidence of SENCO effectiveness, e.g. video clips, blogs, photographs, school website, which shows SENCO team teaching, modelling best practice in SEN, coaching
- examples of involvement in successful projects, initiatives and action research on SEN
- evidence of external achievements in SEN, e.g. publications, conference presentations, inputs to local SENCO networks, impact as an SLE in SEN.

Opportunities and challenges for the SENCO

The implementation of a new SEND statutory framework provides the SENCO with a springboard for action, in ensuring that SEN and disability remains a top priority for the senior leadership team and the governing body. The revised SEND framework with its accompanying legislation, outlined in Part 3 of the Children and Families Act 2014, brings several opportunities and challenges for the SENCO in the twenty-first century, as illustrated in Table 2.1.

Table 2.1 Opportunities and challenges for SENCOs in an era of SEN change

Opportunities	Challenges
- Strengthening of SENCO's strategic leadership role - Greater focus on SEN pupil outcomes in new SEN system - Working more closely with the governors, to keep them informed about the impact of SEN policy and provision - Marketing the education setting's SEN provision, through the local offer - Further development of productive partnership working with new and different agencies, e.g. voluntary community sector - Utilising coaching and mentoring approaches with staff to change or improve their practice in meeting the needs of SEN pupils - Networking with SENCOs from other schools and SLEs in SEN to share best practice and ideas in working within a new SEN system	- Coordinating the smooth transition from the 2001 SEN system over to the 2014 improved SEN system - Getting every teacher to accept that SEN is their responsibility - Keeping abreast of SEN funding and other funding sources to secure additional SEN provision that is effective - Guiding parents/carers through the local authority 'Local Offer' to find the right good quality services to spend the personal budget on - Getting to grips with commissioning and joint planning, to ensure coordinated provision for SEN pupils is in place - Supporting teachers and teaching assistants to understand and cope with working within a new SEN framework - Maintaining a healthy work–life balance throughout the implementation period of a new SEN system, and allowing time for reflection

The concept, principles and approaches of strategic leadership

The Draft SEND Code of Practice (0–25) states:

> The SENCO has an important role to play with the headteacher and governing body, in determining the strategic development of SEN policy and provision in the school. (DfE, 2014e: 6.82)

In view of this statement, it is important that the SENCO has a clear understanding about what strategic leadership entails.

The concept of strategic leadership

Strategic leadership entails anticipating change or events, envisioning possibilities, maintaining flexibility and empowering others to create strategic change as necessary. It is a process of looking forward to a new way of operating the revised SEN system, and developing the best means of planning the journey, for its implementation.

Strategy is a delivery method which translates values into action. The key aim of strategic leadership for the SENCO is knowing what they want to achieve in relation to SEN policy

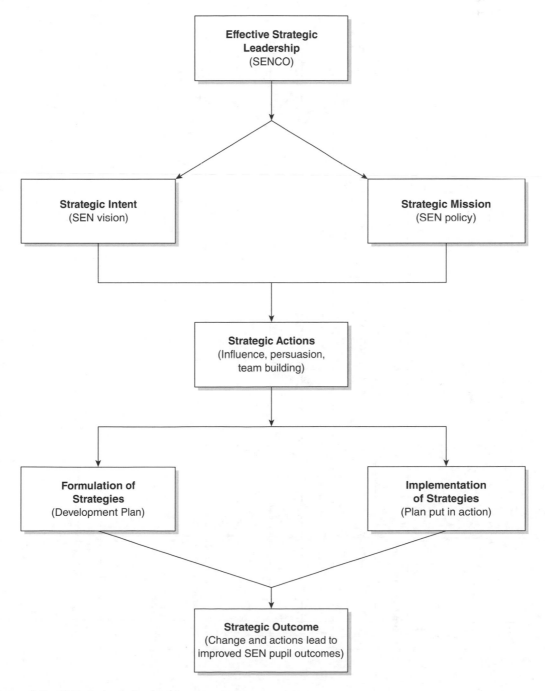

Figure 2.2 SEN strategic leadership process

Priority 1:

Success criteria:

(i)

(ii)

(iii)

Overall lead person:

Activity	Lead person(s)	Timescale (Start and end date)	Resources (Cost in time and £)	Monitoring (Who, when and how)
1a				
1b				
1c				
1d				

Total resources required: | | Time: Cost (£): | |

Evaluation | | | | |

Figure 2.3 SEN development plan template

Table 2.2 SENCO leadership survey

Strategic leadership competence	Skill level *(Indicate 1, 2 or 3)
Leadership – works with others to create the right environment for high performance	
Influencing – influences others to make things happen	
Decision-making – makes well-reasoned and thought-through decisions	
Interpersonal skills – uses a range of skills and approaches to interact effectively with others	
People development – encourages others to develop to their full potential	
Leading change – adopts a proactive approach to change	
Results focus – delivers results which achieve objectives	
Strategic thinker – develops a long-term plan to enable strategies to be met	
Manages resources – uses resources effectively to ensure objectives and goals are met	
Forward planner – defines priorities and plans all resources to achieve strategic objectives	

Operational leadership competence	Skill level *(Indicate 1, 2 or 3)
Leadership – creates a working environment where other colleagues are highly motivated and developed	
Influencing – has the ability to affect other colleagues' attitudes, beliefs and behaviours without using force or formal authority	
People management – works with other colleagues to get the best from them	
People development – encourages other colleagues' development by investing own time and effort	
Self-management – shows awareness of the skills and processes necessary for effective self-management	
Interpersonal skills – uses a range of skills and approaches to interact effectively with others	
Change agent – demonstrates an open mind and copes well with uncertainty and ambiguity	
Decision-making – gathers data in order to evaluate the situation and make effective decisions	
Financial management – shows an understanding of resource management and best value principles	

*(Scoring key: 1 = emergent; 2 = developing; 3 = skilled)

SENCOs are likely to feature attributes of both strategic and operational leadership

Rita Cheminais' Handbook for SENCOs Second Edition, SAGE Publications Ltd © Rita Cheminais, 2015

and provision across the school, justifying the direction of travel taken, and finding the best ways to get there, in order to reach their ultimate goal. This approach influences SEN policy; it informs the SEN strategy, the priorities of the SEN development plan, as well as the SEN priorities of the whole school improvement plan. Figure 2.2 exemplifies this strategic process.

Figure 2.3 provides a model template for a SEN development plan, which can be customised and tailored to suit the context of the education setting.

The SENCO will need to keep a balance between their operational and strategic leadership roles during the implementation of a new SEND system. The SENCO may find it useful to undertake a leadership self-review in order to help them identify which three strategic leadership skills they need to develop further. A template leadership survey is provided in Table 2.2.

The increased emphasis on the strategic role of the SENCO in the twenty-first century school relies on the expectation that they will be a respected member of the senior leadership team, thereby demonstrating the importance attached to SEN by the headteacher and the governing body.

The principles of strategic leadership

The SENCO will find it helpful to follow the seven principles of effective strategic leadership:

- Futures oriented and have a futures strategy for SEN.
- Focused leadership actions and decisions based on evidence, backed up by research.
- Get things done as a professional of action and achievement, because as SENCO, they reliably deliver outcomes.
- Open new horizons by being innovative and receptive to change.
- 'Fit to lead' because they are resilient in times of stress and rapid change.
- Good collaborative partnership worker, and perceived by others to be so.
- Values driven, with a credibility of leading effectively, because they do the next right thing.

Strategic leadership approaches

The SENCO, who is leading the development and improvement of SEN whole school, is likely to utilise at least two or more strategic approaches, in order to effect change, and implement a new SEND statutory framework. Four popular strategic approaches are summarised in Figure 2.4.

Effective strategic leadership components

There are five key components to effective strategic leadership. These are:

- determining the school's strategic direction for SEN – what SEN will look like in the school in three, five and ten years' time
- effectively managing the school's SEN resources (financial and human) – utilising best value principles, which demonstrate good value added progress in relation to SEN pupils outcomes
- sustaining an effective inclusive school culture that welcomes SEN pupils and their parents/carers, because SEN is a collective responsibility, and therefore every teacher's responsibility
- emphasising ethical practice – the moral purpose, i.e. 'every child with SEN and/or disabilities matters', as underpinned by the coalition government's 2014 SEND legislation: the Children and Families Act 2014, the SEND Code of Practice (0–25) 2014 and the Equality Act 2010
- establishing balanced organisational controls, i.e. striking a healthy balance between creative management within the parameters of the SEN funding available.

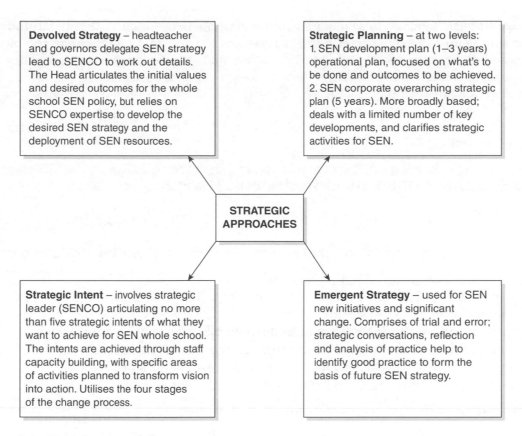

Figure 2.4   Strategic approaches

SENCOs, as effective strategic leaders, challenge complacency and relentlessly pursue the continual drive for further improvement in outcomes for SEN pupils.

The four stages of change

The process of change is developmental, and its purpose is to improve practice and introduce new policies and functions, in addition to altering the 'status quo'.

Table 2.3   The four stages of change in transforming strategic intent into action

Stage	Action
1. Articulate	The strategic intent is articulated via the moral purpose, i.e. SEN values and vision shared with stakeholders, i.e. that the new SEN system is going to make a positive difference for SEN pupil outcomes.
2. Build	Building capacity among other colleagues in the education setting for SEN helps them to understand the reason for the change, and to feel better equipped to cope with the change to a new SEN system.
3. Create	Creating a learning culture, whereby SEN knowledge is shared across the education setting. Skills and strategies are developed for effecting positive change in implementing a new SEN system. Talents among staff are fostered and encouraged, in relation to best practice in SEN.
4. Define	The strategic perspective for SEN is defined through clear plans. There is coherence in the way forward to bring about the new SEN system change, which avoids staff/SENCO 'burnout' and overload, and allows for creativity in implementation.

Change brings challenge in working in new ways, especially in changing the attitudes of other colleagues to be more accepting of a revised SEND system. Change entails the process of reassessing existing assumptions, beliefs, values and theories relating to SEN policy and provision. Successful change is dependent on keeping a clear focus on the ultimate goal of improved outcomes for pupils with SEN.

Table 2.3 summarises the four stages of change, which help to transform SEN strategic intent into action.

Characteristics of an effective strategic leader

There are five key characteristics which SENCOs, as strategic leaders, display:

- They challenge and question – they are dissatisfied and restless with the status quo:

  o school improvers for SEN, and not maintainers
  o constantly look for the next SEN development or initiative
  o see the future for SEN offering better opportunities for SEN pupils
  o view change in the SEN system as being desirable
  o solution focused seeing challenges rather than problems
  o keep up-to-date with SEN developments locally and nationally
  o network with other SENCOs to draw on ideas and best practice.

- They prioritise their own strategic thinking and learning:

  o see the big picture for SEN, and learn from this broader perspective
  o make time for reflection in order to understand new SEN ideas and information
  o understand the leadership context
  o spend time on their own professional development.

- They display strategic wisdom based on a clear values system:

  o able to balance the effects of change for SEN in relation to themselves, others and the school, in the short and long term
  o do the right thing in the right way at the right time
  o clarify values and make decisions in the context of those values, which in turn convince others of the credibility of their ideas for introducing a new SEN system.

- They have powerful personal and professional networks:

  o place a high importance on SENCO networks and networking in general, to benchmark their own school's SEN policy and provision
  o seek new ways of thinking and working to build their own solutions.

- They have high quality personal and interpersonal skills:

  o confidence and resilience to drive through SEN change
  o listen to others' views, concerns and anxieties about SEN change
  o have the courage to admit when they have made a mistake in taking a particular course of action
  o are flexible and adaptable
  o emotionally intelligent, respecting others' feelings
  o highly motivated in the pursuit of SEN excellence
  o keep their promises to deliver what they agreed to
  o have integrity in that they mean what they say
  o are honest and are trusted by others, who can rely on what they say
  o are effective communicators, earning the respect of other colleagues
  o are able to resolve conflict by finding creative solutions.

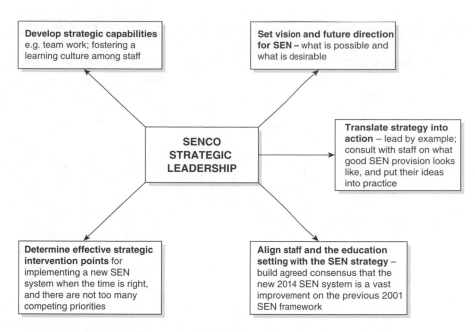

Figure 2.5   Five key activities of a strategic leader of SEN

What SENCOs do as a strategic leader of SEN

There are five key activities that the SENCO, as a successful strategic leader of SEN, does. These are illustrated in Figure 2.5.

The SENCO as an emotionally resilient leader managing time effectively

The strategic leadership of a new SEN system requires the SENCO to develop a good level of emotional resilience, i.e. being able to cope with and recover from any setbacks in leading the transition and change from the 2001 SEN system over to the 2014 SEND statutory framework.

Frequently the SENCO is so overwhelmed and focused on making a difference to SEN pupils that their own well-being suffers, particularly in relation to experiencing burnout, from trying to accomplish too many tasks in a limited time.

The following six top tips will help the busy SENCO to become more emotionally resilient, and enjoy an improved work–life balance:

1. Share with another SENCO you trust, your stresses and anxieties about SEN leadership and managing change, to help keep SEN developments in perspective.
2. If things become too much for you at work, go and visit a lunchtime club or drop into a lesson, where you know you will be welcomed, and witness SEN pupils enjoying learning and social time with their peers.
3. Think positively about why you do the job of SENCO, e.g. to make a real difference to the lives of SEN pupils. Just remind yourself about the recent successes you have had in leading and coordinating SEN policy and provision.
4. Remind yourself and other colleagues that you are not a 'superman' or 'wonder woman'. Learn to say 'No' when extra tasks are added to your workload which could easily be

Answer the following questions yourself and then ask your line manager and another colleague who knows you to answer the same questions.

Compare your answers and then identify which aspects of emotional resilience you wish to improve.

QUESTIONS			
1. How self-aware are you as SENCO?			
2. How well do you express and deal with your emotions at work?			
3. How well do you handle yourself in difficult or challenging work situations?			
4. How good are you in relating to other people?			
5. How well do you get along with other people in the work context?			
6. How effective are you in influencing others?			
7. How much do you operate from a principle of interdependency?			

Figure 2.6 Emotional resilience survey
© *The Coaching Manual*, third edition. Julie Starr, Pearson Education Limited.

Place a tick √ in the relevant column which best represents your time management style

Questions	Rarely	Sometimes	Often
1. Are the tasks you work on during the day the ones with the highest priority?			
2. Do you find yourself completing tasks at the last minute, or asking for time extensions?			
3. Do you set aside time for planning?			
4. Do you know how much time you are spending on the various tasks you do?			
5. How often do you find yourself dealing with interruptions?			
6. Do you use goal setting to decide what tasks and activities you should work on?			
7. Do you leave contingency time in your work plan to deal with 'the unexpected'?			
8. Do you know whether the tasks you are working on are high, medium or low value?			
9. When you are given a new task, do you analyse it for importance and prioritise it accordingly?			
10. Do you get stressed about deadlines and work commitments?			
11. Do distractions often keep you from working on critical and urgent tasks?			
12. Do you find you have to take work home, in order to get it done?			
13. Do you prioritise your 'To Do List'?			
14. Do you regularly confirm your priorities with your line manager/headteacher?			
15. Before you take on a task, do you check that the results will be worth the time put in?			
TOTAL =			

- Total up each column's response.
- Analyse and reflect on the outcomes from this exercise.
- Identify the first three aspects of time management you will target for improvement.

Figure 2.7 Time management self-review audit

Rita Cheminais' Handbook for SENCOs Second Edition, SAGE Publications Ltd © Rita Cheminais, 2015

done by someone else, or ask what you will be giving up in your role if the colleague insists you are to do the extra task.

5. If you feel really stressed at work, then slow down, delegate one or two operational administrative tasks, and remember that you cannot be expected to implement a new SEN system on your own.

6. Accept that perfection takes time, therefore do two or three tasks really well rather than never completing anything in a working day.

To find out how emotionally resilient you are, undertake the survey in Figure 2.6. You will need to ask two other colleagues, one of whom should be your line manager, to answer the same questions about you. Then get together and compare your answers. This will enable you to identify aspects of emotional resilience you need to develop further.

Effective time management

Every SENCO, irrespective of the length of time in post, can identify ways in which they could better organise their time in the workplace. Undertake the time management self-review audit in Figure 2.7, and complete the follow-up activity.

- For those activities ticked in the 'Rarely' column, select the top three that you wish to improve.
- Identify the actions and strategies you will adopt to address and improve each one.

Keep your time management under regular review, identifying how much time you spend on key aspects of your role. With your line manager, agree on how you can work 'smarter' and not 'harder', and whether there is any further opportunity to delegate one or two activities.

You may also find the following top tips for effective time management a useful point of reference. They are easy to put into practice, and they are effective.

Top tips for effective time management

- Make a list of all the time-wasting, trivial activities you encounter in your daily work. For each one, identify what you could change or do differently, to stop or reduce the time-wasting activities. Keep this list with solutions as an aide memoire.
- Set a deadline, which has a realistic timescale, for the completion of key tasks.
- Keep your workspace clear. An untidy desk conveys a message of being disorganised, or of not coping, to others. To achieve this, use RAFT:

   R – refer on to someone else, e.g. catalogues with subject specific SEN resources, pass on to the relevant subject leader.
   A – action and prioritise those important tasks which must be done, e.g. ring a parent and an external professional to confirm additional support for the child.
   F – file reports which have arrived through the post or by email for attention later on in the week.
   T – trash/throw away the junk mail and other unimportant bits of paper that have been sitting in your in-tray for a long time.

- Tackle procrastination by working from home to complete an intensive piece of work, e.g. work offsite to write up the SEN report for governors, or to draft the SEN development plan.
- Minimise interruptions at work by finding a quiet place to work, put the phone on silent, and limit responding to emails to half an hour at the end of the working day. To address staff interruptions, run a weekly drop-in session for staff, or operate an appointment system.

Delegation and distributed leadership

The art to effective strategic leadership is managing through others. The SENCO cannot be expected to lead the implementation of a new SEN system alone. Therefore, delegation and distributed leadership offer a way forward for a busy SENCO, to keep on top of the change process.

Delegation is the process of entrusting somebody else with the appropriate responsibility for the accomplishment of a particular activity. Effective delegation means choosing the right tasks to delegate, identifying the right colleagues to delegate to, and delegating in the right and proper way.

Delegation of some operational tasks to other staff will enable the SENCO to spend more time on their strategic leadership role. Prior to delegating a task, the SENCO will need to answer the following questions:

- Is this a task that someone else can do?
- Does the delegated task provide a real opportunity for that team member to develop professionally?
- Is the task likely to reoccur again?
- Will I as SENCO have the time to advise, support and check the progress of the person undertaking the delegated task?
- Have I identified the right person to undertake the task?

The SENCO should keep a log of the tasks they have delegated to others, in order to ensure a fair distribution of work occurs. This information can contribute evidence to an annual appraisal or performance management review.

Distributed leadership as a shared activity refers to the distribution of aspects of leadership across different staff at all levels, in order to divide up tasks and responsibilities more equitably. Distributed leadership is a group activity that works through and within relationships rather than individual action, and is dependent on who has the relevant expertise or creativity, irrespective of where they appear in the school staffing structure.

There are particular factors that promote distributed leadership in a school. These are as follows:

- trust
- confidence
- a supportive, emotionally intelligent atmosphere
- a no-blame culture for risk taking where mistakes are viewed as a learning opportunity.
- high level communication
- openness and a willingness to change and to challenge
- a willingness to share and pursue common goals.

Examples of distributed leadership are where the SENCO deploys teaching assistants to take on subject specialisms, by assigning them to a specific subject department or curriculum area, as opposed to them being 'jack of all trades', solely performing a generic in-class support role. Another example is where teaching assistants with particular skills, strengths and talents are assigned to run a lunchtime or after-school club, or to deliver a specific targeted intervention.

The role of the SEN governor

Most school governing bodies appoint a SEN governor, who has specific oversight of the school's arrangements and provision for monitoring special educational needs. The SEN governor acts as a 'critical friend' and a champion for SEN pupils, and their parents, working in partnership with the headteacher and the governing body to decide the school's or the academy's general policy and approach to meeting the needs of pupils on SEN Support, and those with an Education, Health and Care (EHC) plan.

The Education (Special Educational Needs Coordinators) (England) Regulations 2014 state:

> The governing body must determine the leadership and management role and the key responsibilities of the SENCO, and monitor the SENCO's effectiveness in undertaking those responsibilities.

The *Governors' Handbook* (DfE, 2014a: 40) outlines the responsibilities of the SEN governor as being:

- to use their best endeavours in exercising their functions to ensure that the necessary special education provision is made for any pupil who has SEN
- to ensure that parents are notified by the school when special education provision is being made for their child because it is considered that he or she has SEN
- to make sure that the responsible person makes all staff who are likely to teach the pupil aware of that pupil's special educational needs
- to make sure that the teachers in the school are aware of the importance of identifying pupils who have SEN and of providing appropriate teaching
- to designate a member of staff at the school (to be known as the 'special educational needs coordinator') as having responsibility for coordinating the provision for pupils with SEN
- to consult the local authority and the governing bodies of other schools when it seems necessary to coordinate special educational teaching in the area
- to ensure that pupils with SEN join in the everyday activities of the school together with children without SEN, as far as is compatible with them receiving the necessary special educational provision, the provision of efficient education for all other pupils and the efficient use of resources
- to publish information on the school's SEN policy on its website, and reflect any changes to the policy as soon as is practicable, and complete an annual update
- to take account of the SEND Code of Practice when carrying out their duties towards all pupils with SEN
- to admit a child to the school where a local authority or First-Tier Tribunal (SEND) names the school on an EHC plan as the one the child will attend (the local authority must have consulted the governing body of the school before naming the school on the EHC plan)
- to make 'reasonable adjustments' under the Equality Act 2010 duties to avoid substantial disadvantages being experienced by disabled pupils, and to provide, where reasonable, auxiliary aids and services as part of the 'reasonable adjustments' duty.

In practice, the SEN governor should:

- be clear about the role of the SENCO
- keep up-to-date with SEN legislation and developments
- attend any relevant SEN governor training locally and nationally
- meet with the SENCO at least once every term formally, to discuss SEN issues, policy, provision and ongoing developments
- know how many pupils are on the school's SEN register at SEN Support and EHC plan stages, and the nature of special educational needs within the school
- meet with the team of teaching assistants at least once a term, to gain insight about their work first hand, and to view facilities and resources in use
- listen to the views of SEN pupils about their additional provision

- know the views of parents/carers of SEN pupils, in relation to SEN policy and provision within the school
- know the strengths and weaknesses of SEN in the school
- monitor the use of the school's SEN funding, to ensure value for money
- have oversight of the school's SEN provision map
- be kept informed about the progress of SEN pupils
- be kept informed of the views of the local authority on the school's SEN provision
- be clear about the school's contribution to the local authority's 'Local Offer'
- seek opportunities to be involved in any local authority SEN working groups or forums
- be involved in the appointment of the next SENCO.

Telling questions for the SEN governor to ask the SENCO

1. What is the attendance of SEN pupils like, are any of them persistent absentees, and how is this impacting on their progress?
2. What impact are the additional interventions delivered by external services having on SEN pupils' outcomes?
3. How does the progress made by our school's SEN pupils compare with that of similar schools?
4. How many parental complaints about SEN provision, or appeals to the First-Tier Tribunal (SEND), have been made?
5. How many SEN pupils have moved off the graduated approach of SEN Support, or off an EHC plan?
6. What has been the impact of any SEN training or INSET attended by staff and governors?
7. How are any gaps identified in the school's SEN provision being addressed?

Table 2.4 offers further questions for governors on SEN.

A valuable joint activity for the SENCO to undertake with the SEN governor is to work through the OFSTED criteria for judging the effectiveness of governance, from the perspective of the leadership and governance of SEN, whole school.

Similarly, a paired SENCO/SEN governor 'learning walk' across school enables the SEN governor to see SEN policy and provision in practice.

Reporting on the effectiveness of SEN policy and provision to governors

Figure 2.8 provides a framework for SENCOs to utilise when they are reporting to the governing body and to the headteacher on SEN policy and provision.

SEN information and reporting on SEN policy

SEN policy in the twenty-first century is grounded in improvement and effectiveness. The SEND Code of Practice (0–25) 2014 and the Children and Families Act 2014 clearly stipulate the SEN information which maintained schools, maintained nursery schools and academies must publish on their websites, in respect of the implementation of their SEN policy, which informs the local authority's 'Local Offer'. This key SEN information covers:

1. The areas of special educational needs for which special educational provision is made at the education setting.
2. How pupils' special educational needs are identified and assessed.

Table 2.4 Challenging questions for governors on SEN

SEN leadership

- What is the governing body's view on the quality of SEN leadership in the school?
- How have the governors supported and challenged the school on its SEN strategy?
- Is there sufficient non-contact time for the SENCO to oversee the daily operation of the school's SEN policy?

SEN pupil outcomes

- How do the school's systems enable the governing body to have a clear view about the progress and attainment of SEN pupils in all year groups, across the school?
- How does the governing body know if SEN pupils are achieving better in certain subjects and aspects of a subject?
- How does the governing body know if pupils with a particular type of SEN are doing better than other SEN pupils?
- Has the governing body identified a cohort/critical group of SEN pupils who are underachieving? If so, who are they, and what is being done to address the issue?

SEN development plan

- How does the governing body monitor and evaluate the effectiveness of the SEN development plan?
- How does the governing body know that the priorities on the SEN development plan are appropriate?

SEN provision

- What contribution does the governing body consider it has made to improving SEN provision in the school?
- Which additional interventions have had the greatest impact on improving SEN pupil progress?

SEN policy

- How does the governing body know that the school's SEN policy is effective?
- How does the governing body know if the SEN policy in school is reflecting and meeting the needs of SEN pupils?

SEN and disability equality

- How is the governing body ensuring equality of opportunity for pupils with SEN and/or disability?
- How does the school's SEN development plan reflect elements of its accessibility plan?

SEN funding

- How does the governing body know if the notional SEN budget (Element 2) is being used effectively to meet the needs of SEN pupils?
- How does the governing body know how the school's SEN funding is spent?
- What improvements has the SEN funding allocation brought about?
- How is the effectiveness of the SEN funding measured and reported to governors and parents/carers?

Communication with parents

- How are parents and carers informed that their child has SEN?
- Can the governors give a couple of examples of when the views of parents and carers of SEN pupils have been sought and acted upon?

SEN training

- What SEN training have governors accessed during the year, and what has been the impact of this training?
- How are the SEND training needs of governors identified and addressed?
- What difference has the SEN staff training made to SEN pupils' outcomes?

SEN pupil voice

- How does the governing body know the views of SEND pupils in relation to how they feel about their SEN provision and the progress they have made?

REPORT TO THE GOVERNING BODY ON SEN POLICY AND PROVISION

SENCO: _____   Date: _____

1. SEN Register update

Key Stage	SEN Report	EHC Plan	Total
EYFS			
Key Stage 1			
Key Stage 2			
		Grand Total=	

Number of pupils moving down a threshold on the SEN register _____
Number of pupils moving up from SEN Support to EHC plan _____
Number of pupils coming off the SEN register _____
Number of pupils awaiting an EHC assessment _____

Comments:

2. Effectiveness and impact of additional SEN provision on pupils' outcomes

KS2 Test	Outcomes for SEN pupils by %
Reading	% reached expected standard
	% not reached expected standard
Grammar, punctuation & spelling	% reached expected standard
	% not reached expected standard
Maths	% reached expected standard
	% not reached expected standard

KS1 Phonics Screening Test
% SEN pupils reaching expected standard
% SEN pupils not reaching expected standard

Comments:

3. Attendance, exclusions and mental well-being of SEN pupils

Percentage of persistent absentees _____ Percentage with 100% attendance _____
Percentage of fixed term exclusions _____ Percentage of permanent exclusions _____
Percentage of mental health referrals to CAMHS team _____

Comments:

4. The effectiveness and impact of multi-agency interventions and support

Comments:

5. The effectiveness of partnership working with SEN pupils' parents/carers

Percentage of parental complaints relating to SEN _____
Percentage of parents accessing Tier 1 (SEND) Tribunal _____
Percentage of parents satisfied with SEN _____
Percentage of parents attending _____ not attending _____ their child's EHC plan review

Comments:

6. Impact of staff training for SEN on improving SEN pupils' outcomes

Comments:

7. Income and expenditure on SEN
(Please refer to the attached SEN funding breakdown and SEN provision map)

Comments:

8. Impact of SEN Support and EHC plan levels
(Please refer to the attached SEN provision map)

Comments:

9. SEN governor comments on the strengths and weaknesses of SEN policy and SEN provision existing within the school

Comments:

Figure 2.8 Template for reporting on SEN to the governing body

Rita Cheminais' Handbook for SENCOs Second Edition, SAGE Publications Ltd © Rita Cheminais, 2015

3. The education setting's policies for making additional and different provision for pupils at SEN Support, and for those with an EHC plan, including:

   o how the effectiveness of SEN provision is evaluated
   o how SEN pupils' progress is assessed and reviewed
   o the approach taken to teaching SEN pupils
   o how the curriculum and the learning environment are adapted for SEN pupils
   o the additional support for learning available to SEN pupils
   o the additional extra-curricular activities available for SEN pupils
   o the support available for improving the emotional and social development of SEN pupils.

4. The name and contact details of the SENCO.
5. The expertise and training of staff in relation to meeting the needs of SEN pupils, and how specialist expertise will be secured.
6. How equipment and facilities to support SEN pupils will be secured.
7. How parents and carers of SEN pupils will be consulted about and involved in the education of their child.
8. How pupils with SEN are consulted about and involved in their education.
9. The complaints procedures and arrangements for parents and carers of SEN pupils concerning SEN provision.
10. How health, social care, local authority support services and voluntary organisations are involved in meeting the needs of SEN pupils and their families.
11. The contact details of support services for parents and carers of pupils with SEN; the education setting's arrangements for supporting SEN pupils' transfer between phases of education, and/or in preparing for adulthood and independent living.
12. The information on where the local authority's 'Local Offer' is published.

Figure 2.9 provides a model parent-friendly leaflet on a school's SEN policy and provision in light of the 2014 new SEND system, which can be customised to suit the context of the education setting.

It is important that the SEN information provided on an education setting's website, or in any leaflets or documents, must be written in parent-friendly language, be jargon-free and avoid using too many acronyms. It should also be made available in different multi-media formats and different languages. SEN information must be updated annually, and also amended accordingly, throughout the year, as changes occur in relation to SEN policy and provision.

For example, the outcomes of SEN pupils collectively will need to be publicised, in order to demonstrate the effectiveness of SEN policy, and the additional and different SEN provision.

Getting to grips with funding for SEN pupils

The SEN funding a maintained mainstream school receives is intended to:

- support the raising of standards and achievement of SEN pupils
- support early intervention
- support equal opportunities and reasonable adjustments for SEND pupils
- safeguard the rights and entitlements of SEN pupils with an EHC plan, as well as those on SEN Support, to ensure appropriate additional provision is made available
- demonstrate good value for money, following the best value principles.

The School SEN Policy

At Leafy Lane School we aim to:
Meet the needs of the whole child
Remove barriers to learning
Raise pupil self-esteem
Build pupil confidence
Develop pupil independence
Provide access to a relevant tailored curriculum

A Parent's Guide to Special Educational Needs at Leafy Lane School

The school SEN policy is reviewed every year and revised in discussion with parents, SEN pupils, staff and governors. You can get a copy of the school SEN Policy from the school office or from the school website: www.leafylane.sch.uk

The Local Authority SEN Policy
You can get a copy of the local authority SEN policy off their website: www.anywherecc.gov.uk
or ask the SENCO for a copy.

For further information contact the:
SENCO: Rita Gold
SEN Governor: Stan Long
at:
Leafy Lane School
Phone: 09627 118634
Email: rgold@leafylane.sch.uk

All about special educational needs

Approximately one in five children will have special educational needs (SEN) at some time during their school career.
This means they may have difficulty with:

- Reading, writing, mathematics
- Understanding information and others, and expressing themselves
- Organising themselves
- Sensory perception or physical mobility
- Managing their behaviour
- Making friends or relating to adults

These difficulties cause barriers to the child's learning. The school will assess your child to identify their strengths, needs and the extra help they require.
They may be at one of two stages on the SEN Code of Practice SEN thresholds:

SEN Support: Extra help in-class from a teaching assistant, small group support, ICT access and advice or support from outside specialists, e.g. specialist teacher, speech and language therapist, health professional.

Education, Health and Care plan : when needs are complex and severe

What is offered to your child
The school offers the following according to your child's special educational needs, in addition to high quality teaching

- A curriculum to match needs
- Enhanced access to ICT or specialist equipment and aids
- In-class support from teaching assistants
- Additional programmes in literacy and numeracy delivered in a small group or on a one-to-one basis
- One-to-one or small group work with a learning mentor
- Homework support
- Pupil counselling
- Access to a 'key worker'
- Test and exam concessions
- Extra help from other services

Other sources of information and help:
Parent' Partnership Service
Offers free impartial advice in confidence.
Phone: 09627 333555
email: pps.anywhere.org.uk
Publications
Special Educational Needs and Disability Code of Practice (0–25) 2014
You can view a copy online at:
www.gov.uk

Outcomes for pupils

The extra help the school offers will enable your child to:

- Reach their full potential
- Achieve their personal best
- Make progress
- Feel valued and included
- Enjoy school

Partnership with parents
The school works in partnership with parents to meet the child's needs. This means:

- We listen to the views of parents
- Parents are equal partners in decisions about their child's education
- Parents are kept informed about their child's needs and progress

What parents want to know

- What the school thinks your child's special needs are
- What the school is doing to meet your child's needs
- Whether what the school is doing is working
- How your child feels about what the school is doing to help them
- How parents can be involved.

What to do if you have any concerns
- Speak to the teacher and SENCO
- Speak to the SEN governor and the headteacher
- Get advice from the local Parent Partnership Service

And if your concern is not resolved:

- Follow the school's complaints procedure

Figure 2.9 Model parent SEN leaflet

Best value principles to inform SEN financial planning

The best value principles comprise of the four 'Cs':

Challenge – why, how and by whom an additional SEN intervention is being provided.
Compare – performance outcomes of SEN pupils in relation to the extra provision put in place with that of other similar schools.
Consult – with key stakeholders, e.g. service users, parents/carers, to seek their views about the additional provision they have received, and to identify and inform future provision.
Compete – fairly, to secure efficient and effective services/additional provision for SEN pupils.

SENCOs are advised to have regard for the four best value principles when they are planning, provision mapping and procuring SEN resources to meet the needs of pupils with SEN.

The SENCO must ensure that:

- the school actively monitors and reviews the impact of all additional and different SEN provision on individual pupils' experience, progress and outcomes
- the school draws routinely on evidence-based research to guide its decision-making about which interventions have the greatest impact, and therefore to include in its provision for SEN
- all SEN provision made by the school is evaluated and reviewed systematically, as part of the overall school self-evaluation process.

The SENCO's responsibilities in relation to SEN funding are as follows:

- resources are allocated with maximum efficiency, against explicit criteria, published in the school's SEN policy and the school development plan, and against an audit of SEN pupils' needs
- there are well-established systems for monitoring and evaluating the impact of additional resources/provision on SEN pupils' progress
- the governors, headteacher, senior leadership team and the SENCO collaborate over the budget-setting process, and the management of resources for SEN
- the data relating to the needs of individual and groups of SEN pupils inform the SEN budget-setting process
- the appropriate governors and senior managers are able to identify value for money in SEN provision, by linking budget headings to data, relating to SEN pupil progress and outcomes, e.g. via a provision map
- parents/carers with personal budgets for SEN have been identified and well advised in relation to using this funding wisely, in order to secure effective additional provision.

The SENCO should ask the school's business or financial manager for a financial breakdown of the SEN budget at the beginning and end of each financial year.

Table 2.5 provides a useful template for the SENCO to keep a record of SEN income and expenditure over a financial year.

How SEN funding is allocated

The coalition government's new SEN funding arrangements for schools and academies took effect on 1 April 2013. The new funding arrangements are far more transparent and simplified. LAs fund maintained schools and the Education Funding Agency (EFA) funds free schools and academies for SEN.

There are three elements to SEN funding allocation:

Element 1: Core pupil funding, known as the Basic Per Pupil Entitlement (BPPE), allocates an amount of money, for every pupil in the school, irrespective of ability or individual needs.

The amount of money per pupil may vary, from one local authority to another, and between the primary and secondary phases of education. For example, primary schools may be allocated £2,000 per pupil, and secondary schools may be allocated £3,000 per pupil. The recommended core budget per pupil for Element 1 is £4,000 per pupil, irrespective of the phase of education or the individual needs of the pupils. Element 1 funding is used to make a general provision for all pupils.

Element 2: The notional SEN budget, Additional Pupil Funding (APF), is an additional amount of money per SEN pupil. The EFA made the allocation of £6,000 per SEN pupil a mandatory threshold requirement, through the finance regulations, for the financial year 2014–15. Element 2 funding is triggered on the basis of a pupil's prior attainment. The triggers and formula for allocating this additional funding are:

- primary school phase – pupils who have scored below 73 on the Early Years Foundation Stage Profile

- secondary school phase – pupils who have scored at or below Level 3 in English and mathematics.

The Element 2 funding follows the SEN pupil throughout their primary school career to the end of Year 6, and to the end of Key Stage 4 in a SEN pupil's secondary school career. It is to pay for up to £6,000 worth of special educational provision to meet low cost high incidence SEN.

The coalition government expects maintained schools, for example, to be spending up to £10,000 per SEN pupil (core and notional SEN budget funding combined). The sum of £10,000 could, for example, fund 20 hours of SEN support per week, over an academic year, if that is how a school chooses to use the funding.

Element 3: Top-up funding, High Needs Pupil Block, is available from the local authority where a school can show that a pupil with SEN needs more than £6,000 worth of special educational provision. For example, this would be for those SEN pupils with more complex and severe needs, who have an EHC plan. Element 3 funding allocation is based on individually assessed need, and the local authority in partnership with the education setting has the commissioning responsibility regarding the level of additional support required from the LA. The education setting has to provide robust evidence to the LA which indicates why the pupil with SEN requires the top-up Element 3 funding, i.e. pupil-level attainment and progress data. The amount of money allocated will vary according to the complexity and severity of the pupil's SEN.

Early years settings, schools and academies must keep and maintain records to show how Element 1, Element 2 and Element 3 funding has been used, along with evidence to demonstrate the impact the additional funding has had on SEN pupils' outcomes. SENCOs need to ensure that this information is to hand, e.g. the relevant provision map, when the school is inspected by OFSTED or local authority officers.

The following government publications provide further information about SEN funding allocation, and each can be downloaded at: www.gov.uk/publications

DfE (June 2013) *School Funding Reform: Findings from the Review of 2013–2014*

Table 2.5 SEN budget summary template

SEN INCOME – Financial year April 20_____ to April 20_____		
Income source	**Amount (£)**	**Comments**
Element 1: Core budget @ £4,000 per pupil	£	
Element 2: Notional SEN budget @ £6,000 per pupil	£	
Element 3: Top-up funding High Needs Block	£	
Other funding sources:		
Pupil Premium/Plus	£	
Year 7 catch-up literacy	£	
TOTAL SEN Income	£	
SEN EXPENDITURE – Financial year April 20____ to April 20 ___		
Provision	**Amount (£)**	**Comments**
Staffing expenditure (SENCO release time)	£	
Dedicated SEN teaching time (from SEN teachers and SENCO)	£	
Mainstream staff taking smaller lower ability sets	£´	
Support for SEN from teaching assistants (in-class support and programme delivery)	£	
Administration for SEN Code of Practice, SEN Support, EHC plans, TAF	£	
Other: (please specify): transport for work placement	£	
External services e.g. outreach; specialist support, counselling services, VCS services, art/play therapy	£	
Specialist equipment and specialist aids	£	
Curriculum materials and SEN resources, e.g. new Intervention programmes	£	
Computer SEN software programs and hardware	£	
SEN INSET expenditure: (supply cover, course fees, travel, trainers' fees)	£	
Other: e.g. lunchtime and after-school clubs, additional mid-day supervision	£	
TOTAL SEN Expenditure	£	

Rita Cheminais' Handbook for SENCOs Second Edition, SAGE Publications Ltd © Rita Cheminais, 2015

Arrangements and changes for 2014–15:

> EFA (July 2013) *2014–2015 Revenue Funding Arrangements: Operational Information for Local Authorities*

> EFA (July 2013) *Implementing High Needs Place Funding Arrangements for 5–25 Year Olds. 2014–2015*

Other funding sources available

The SENCO will need to be mindful that some SEN pupils, i.e. those on free school meals (FSMs), those who are a looked after child, or a child from an armed services family, will also be eligible for pupil premium funding.

For example, in the financial year 2014–15:

- a primary school-aged SEN pupil on free school meals will be eligible for pupil premium funding of £1,300
- a secondary school-aged SEN pupil on free school meals will be eligible for a pupil premium of £935
- a looked after child (LAC) will be eligible for pupil premium plus of £1,900
- a SEN child from an armed services family will be eligible for a pupil premium of £300.
- some SEN pupils in Year 7, particularly those who are operating at Level 3 or below in English and mathematics, are also eligible for an additional literacy and numeracy catch-up premium, of £500 per pupil.

The SENCO will need to ensure that the provision map captures how these other sources of additional funding are being used with eligible SEN pupils for extra interventions.

Exploring provision mapping as a strategic management tool

The Draft SEND Code of Practice (0–25) 2014 comments on provision mapping as follows:

> Provision maps are an efficient way of showing all the provision that the school makes which is additional to and different from that which is offered through the school's curriculum. The use of provision maps can help SENCOs to maintain an overview of the programmes and interventions used with different groups of pupils and provides a basis for monitoring the levels of intervention. (DfE, 2014e: 6.71)

Provision mapping, previously referred to as provision management, is a strategic management tool which provides a comprehensive 'at-a-glance' overview of how the SEN funding, including any other funding sources relevant to SEN pupils, has been utilised on additional specific interventions. It also summarises who is delivering the additional interventions, how frequently, over what timescale, at what cost and from which funding source.

The process of provision mapping enhances a school's ability to manage different funding streams more coherently, in order to target particular areas of additional needs for individual or cohorts of SEN pupils, as well as to plan for the deployment of SEN staffing, and build the capacity of the school staff to meet the needs of SEN pupils.

Provision maps provide evidence-based information, to support measuring the impact of additional interventions, on SEN pupils' progress and achievements. Where a provision map also includes entry and exit data for those accessing additional interventions, this helps the SENCO to gain an initial impression of which interventions have the greatest impact and give good value for money in relation to improving SEN pupils' progress and outcomes. This will be important to show where parents have their own SEN budgets for their child. An individual SEN pupil provision map, underpinned by attainment data depicted visually, via bar charts for example, will help parents and carers as well as the SEN pupil to see instantly which additional SEN provision has helped them the most.

Using a provision map in this way will also enable the SENCO to demonstrate to the governing body, the headteacher, staff, OFSTED and the local authority how the SEN funding is being used effectively.

Organisation of the provision map

Provision maps can be organised to fit any of the following formats:

- by a particular class or form group
- year group, key stage
- by whole school additional needs – the full ability range, including gifted and talented pupils, English as an additional language (EAL), looked after children (LAC)
- by the graduated approach: of the single category SEN Support and EHC plan
- by the four broad areas of SEN, as specified in the 2014 SEND Code of Practice (0–25).

Developing a provision map

Eight strategic stages are identified in developing a provision map, as illustrated in Figure 2.10.

Provision mapping supports the SENCO in:

- knowing how well SEN pupils are doing, compared with their peers and against national standards
- knowing what works to prevent underachievement
- knowing what else could be done, currently, and in the near future, to prevent any further potential underachievement
- identifying potential barriers to learning for individual or groups of SEN pupils.

Reviewing provision maps

The provision map needs to be kept under review each term, as SEN pupils move onto or off SEN Support, or move onto or off an EHC plan. It also needs to be reviewed annually, in consultation with the headteacher, SEN governor, school business manager, parents and carers, SEN pupils and relevant multi-agency professionals. Some schools hold a provision map day in the summer term to undertake this review, with the stakeholders and partners mentioned above. Figure 2.11 illustrates the six interlinked aspects for reviewing a provision map.

Tables 2.6, 2.7 and 2.8 provide model templates for provision maps which can be customised to suit the context of the education setting.

The SENCO will find it useful to combine the provision mapping process with SEN financial planning. The process of provision mapping enables the governing body, the headteacher and the SENCO to evaluate and analyse the cost-effectiveness and added value of the additional and different provision on improving outcomes for SEN pupils.

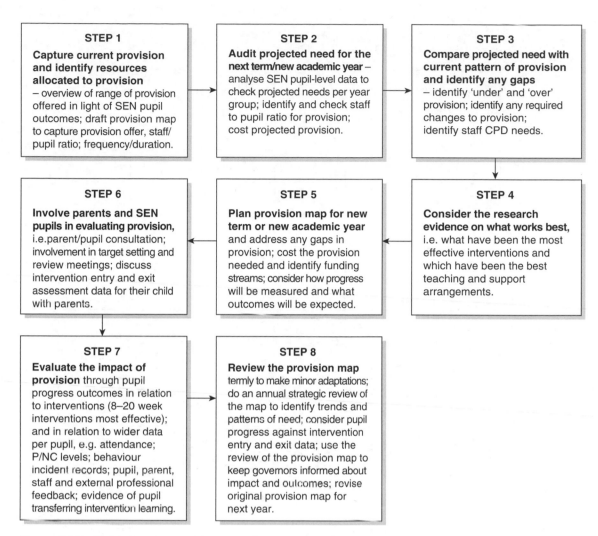

STEP 1

Capture current provision and identify resources allocated to provision – overview of range of provision offered in light of SEN pupil outcomes; draft provision map to capture provision offer, staff/pupil ratio; frequency/duration.

STEP 2

Audit projected need for the next term/new academic year – analyse SEN pupil-level data to check projected needs per year group; identify and check staff to pupil ratio for provision; cost projected provision.

STEP 3

Compare projected need with current pattern of provision and identify any gaps – identify 'under' and 'over' provision; identify any required changes to provision; identify staff CPD needs.

STEP 6

Involve parents and SEN pupils in evaluating provision, i.e. parent/pupil consultation; involvement in target setting and review meetings; discuss intervention entry and exit assessment data for their child with parents.

STEP 5

Plan provision map for new term or new academic year and address any gaps in provision; cost the provision needed and identify funding streams; consider how progress will be measured and what outcomes will be expected.

STEP 4

Consider the research evidence on what works best, i.e. what have been the most effective interventions and which have been the best teaching and support arrangements.

STEP 7

Evaluate the impact of provision through pupil progress outcomes in relation to interventions (8–20 week interventions most effective); and in relation to wider data per pupil, e.g. attendance; P/NC levels; behaviour incident records; pupil, parent, staff and external professional feedback; evidence of pupil transferring intervention learning.

STEP 8

Review the provision map termly to make minor adaptations; do an annual strategic review of the map to identify trends and patterns of need; consider pupil progress against intervention entry and exit data; use the review of the provision map to keep governors informed about impact and outcomes; revise original provision map for next year.

Figure 2.10 Eight steps to provision mapping

Knowing the needs of all SEN pupils

Assessing and tracking SEN pupil progress

Developing the workforce

Provision Mapping Informed choices, Maximising impact

Monitoring and evaluating impact and analysing data

Developing the quality of SEN provision

Identifying the right provision for all SEN pupils

Figure 2.11 Six interlinked aspects for reviewing a provision map

Table 2.6 Example of an individual pupil's provision map for SEN Support

Pupil name: _____ Class: _____ D.O.B. _____

SEN Support Cognition & learning	Entry levels/Point scores			Additional provision	Delivery method & by whom	Frequency and duration of entire intervention	Cost & funding source	Exit levels/ Point scores			Comments on impact
	Reading	Grammar, Punctuation & Spelling	Maths								
Literacy skills	11/50	12/70		Read Write Inc. Fresh Start Programme	1:6 small group SEN teacher	20 minutes per day for 20 weeks	£				
Poor numeracy skills			15/100	Numicon Intervention Programme	1:5 small group Teaching assistant	20 minutes x 3 sessions per week for 18 weeks	£				
Attendance issues	80 absences out of 380 sessions, tend to be absences on a Monday or Friday			Incentive scheme	Extra certificates + Family Support Worker		£				
Low self-esteem	Scoring 40/100 on QOL test			Self-esteem programme	1:1 Learning Mentor	1 x 25 min per week for 10 weeks	£				
Low level behaviour needs	The Boxall Profile low score on Developmental strands and high scores on Diagnostic Profile			Behaviour for learning programme	1:1 Behaviour support teacher	1 x 25 min per week for 10 weeks	£				

Rita Cheminais' Handbook for SENCOs Second Edition, SAGE Publications Ltd © Rita Cheminais, 2015

Table 2.7 SEN provision map template for a year group

School name:							
			Term and Year:				
Year 7 SEN threshold	SEN area of need	Evidence-based intervention and extra support being delivered	Frequency and duration of intervention	Staff/ pupil ratio (Who is delivering and to how many pupils)	Weekly cost in time (hours)	Cost per term (£) and funding source	Impact and outcomes Comments
SEN Support	Communication and interaction						
EHC plan							
SEN Support	Cognition and learning						
EHC plan							
SEN Support	Social, mental and emotional health						
EHC plan							
SEN Support	Sensory and/or physical impairment						
EHC plan							

Rita Cheminais' Handbook for SENCOs Second Edition, SAGE Publications Ltd © Rita Cheminais, 2015

Table 2.8 SEN/Pupil premium provision map for a year group and area of SEN

Year Group: _____ Start date: _____ End date: _____

Pupil Premium category and SEN threshold	Area of SEN being covered	Additional interventions/ programmes being delivered	Frequency and duration of intervention programme	Staff/pupil ratio (Who is delivering and to how many pupils)	Termly cost (£) & budget source	Comments: Impact and outcomes (in relation to pupil progress)
FSM **SEN Support** **Pupil Premium**						
No. of pupils						
FSM EHC plan **Pupil Premium**						
No. of pupils						
LAC **SEN Support Pupil Premium Plus** No. of pupils						
LAC EHC plan Pupil Pr. Plus No. of pupils						
Armed Service **SEN Support Pupil Premium** No. of pupils						
Armed Service EHC plan **Pupil Premium** No. of pupils						

Rita Cheminais' Handbook for SENCOs Second Edition, SAGE Publications Ltd © Rita Cheminais, 2015

Points to remember

- The key to successful strategic leadership is managing through others.
- The SENCO has a key role to play in determining the strategic development of SEN policy and provision.
- Delegation and distributed leadership provide excellent development opportunities for other colleagues.
- Use the RAFT strategy for prioritising tasks and managing time effectively.
- The governing body of the school has a statutory responsibility for SEND.
- SEN information must be kept up to date annually and be in parent-friendly language.
- Additional SEN funding must be shown to improve outcomes for SEN pupils.
- A provision map is a useful strategic management tool.

Further activities

The following questions, focused on aspects covered in this chapter, meet the requirements of the National Award for Special Educational Needs Coordination, and support reflection and the professional development of experienced and newly appointed SENCOs.

1. What would be your whole school vision and strategic intent for SEN in relation to introducing and implementing a new SEN system?
2. As SENCO, how will you balance the operational and strategic aspects of your leadership role for SEN?
3. The SEN governor is new to the role in school. As SENCO, what aspects of their role will you develop first and why?
4. What evidence would you present to the chair of governors to justify the decision to fund additional administrative time for the SENCO?
5. An aspect of SEN provision requires changing, but some staff are reluctant to make the change. As SENCO, explain how you will successfully manage this situation.
6. Prior to producing the SEN provision map, and in order to ensure best value for money, identify what key information you will require from the school business manager or finance officer.

 ## Online materials

To access electronic versions of the material in this chapter visit: www.sagepub.co.uk/cheminais2e

Figure 2.3 SEN development plan template
Figure 2.6 Emotional resilience survey
Figure 2.7 Time management self-review audit
Figure 2.8 Template for reporting on SEN to the governing body
Figure 2.9 Model parent SEN leaflet
Table 2.2 SENCO leadership survey
Table 2.4 Challenging questions for governors on SEN
Table 2.5 SEN budget summary template
Table 2.6 Example of an individual pupil's provision map for SEN Support
Table 2.7 SEN provision map template for a year group
Table 2.8 SEN/Pupil premium provision map for a year group and area of SEN

3

Coordinating and implementing an effective SEN system

> **This chapter covers:**
>
> - **identifying pupils with high incidence SEN**
> - **meeting the needs of those with high incidence SEN: a graduated approach**
> - **addressing underachievement among SEN pupils to close the gap**
> - **assessment for learning and SEN pupils**
> - **using and analysing SEN pupil-level attainment data to evaluate progress**
> - **high quality teaching**
> - **making best use of the pupil premium**
> - **the transfer of children and young people with SEN.**

Coordinating and implementing an effective SEN system

Figure 3.1 illustrates four key components relating to the coordination and implementation of the new SEN system, across an education setting. This chapter traces the journey a SENCO takes putting each piece of the jigsaw into practice.

Identifying pupils with high incidence SEN

It is important that all teachers and teaching assistants are alert to any emerging difficulties in learning that a pupil may experience, and respond early. A pupil has a learning difficulty if they have significantly greater difficulty in learning than the majority of their peers of the same age. Identifying that a pupil has SEN must equate to the respective broad area of SEN, as defined in the Draft SEND Code of Practice (0–25) 2014. The four broad areas of SEN are:

- communication and interaction
- cognition and learning
- social, emotional and mental health difficulties
- sensory and/or physical needs.

The Draft SEND Code of Practice goes on to comment:

> The four broad areas give an overview of the range of needs that should be planned for. The purpose of identification is to work out what action the school needs to

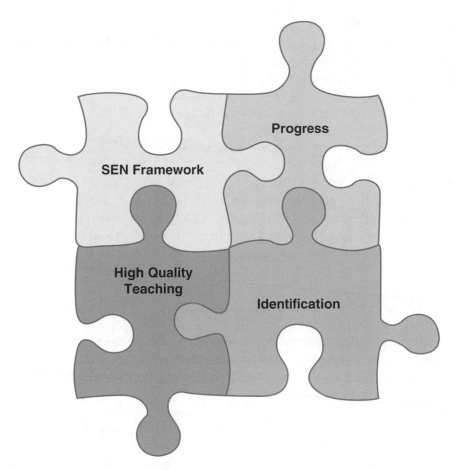

Figure 3.1 The SEN system

take, not to fit a pupil into a category. In practice, individual children or young people often have needs that cut across all these areas and their needs may change over time. ... A detailed assessment of need should ensure that the full range of an individual's needs is identified, not simply the primary need. The support provided to an individual should always be based on a full understanding of their particular strengths and needs and seek to address them all using well-evidenced interventions targeted at their areas of difficulty and where necessary specialist equipment or software. (DfE, 2014e: 6:24)

It is important that staff do not identify pupils as having SEN as a result of poor quality whole class teaching. OFSTED recommended, as an outcome of their review of SEN and disability (2010), that:

When a child or young person is underachieving, the school or setting should begin by analysing the effectiveness of its generic teaching and systems for support before deciding that she or he has special educational needs. (OFSTED, 2010: 13)

The identification of pupils who may have a special educational need requires the use of a range of methods to gather the necessary evidence that the child is functioning at a level below that of peers of the same age.

The SENCO will liaise closely with the class teacher to collect evidence of the pupil's learning difficulties through:

- observation of the child in lessons
- discussion with teachers, parents/carers of the pupil, and with the child (where appropriate), to gather qualitative information
- completion of relevant checklists
- samples of the pupil's work from across the curriculum
- attainment and progress data (teacher assessment and test)
- attendance data and behaviour records
- results from any screening or diagnostic assessments.

Assessment (diagnosis) of a pupil's special educational needs assists the SENCO and class teacher in identifying the particular areas of learning difficulty; it provides a measure and record of the child's attainment and progress, which inform the planning of additional interventions and provision. The use of such evidence supports any external professional observations and assessments, for example those undertaken by the educational psychologist.

Screening a pupil on entry to school to establish a baseline of their strengths and needs provides an objective means of confirming a teacher's or SENCO's own observations in identifying children who require more extensive assessment and examination. Examples of standardised screening tests include: the Group Reading Tests, Cognitive Abilities Test (CAT) and Suffolk Reading Scale. Standardised tests are uniformly developed, administered and scored.

Diagnostic assessment follows on from initial screening in order to provide more in-depth evidence on the particular aspects and severity of learning or behaviour in which the pupil is experiencing difficulties. Examples of diagnostic tests include: the Neale Analysis of Reading Ability, the Connors ADHD Rating Scale, the Aston Index and the British Picture Vocabulary Scale (BPVS).

The SENCO will need to build up a bank of basic screening and diagnostic assessment tools. They can seek advice on which to use by networking with other SENCOs locally, or asking the educational psychologist. The main companies who publish these tests are GL Assessment, Hodder Education and Pearson Education. Visit their websites for further details:

www.gl-assessment.co.uk
www.hoddertests.co.uk
www.pearson-uk.com

Meeting the needs of those with high incidence SEN: a graduated approach

High quality teaching, differentiated for individual pupils, is the first step in responding to pupils who have been identified as having SEN. The Draft SEND Code of Practice (0–25) comments:

> Early years providers, schools and colleges should know precisely where children and young people with SEN are in their learning and development. They should:

- ensure decisions are informed by the insights of parents and those of children and young people themselves

- have high ambitions and to set stretching targets for them

- track their progress towards these goals

- keep under review the additional or different provision that is made for them

- promote positive outcomes in the wider areas of personal and social development and

- ensure that the approaches used are based on the best possible evidence and are having the required impact on progress. (DfE, 2014e: 1.25)

OFSTED in their SEN and disability review (2010) identified that

> The best learning occurred in all types of provision when teachers or other lead adults had a thorough and detailed knowledge of the children and young people; a thorough knowledge and understanding of teaching and learning strategies and techniques, as well as the subject areas of learning being taught; and a sound understanding of child development and how different learning difficulties and disabilities influence this. (OFSTED, 2010: 11)

SENCOs may find Table 3.1 a useful aide memoire for teachers and teaching assistants to refer to in relation to knowing how to meet the needs of SEN pupils who fall into the four broad areas of special educational needs.

The Draft SEND Code of Practice (0–25) recommends a graduated approach to meeting the needs of SEN pupils with high incidence needs (DfE, 2014e: 6.40):

> Where a pupil is identified as having SEN, schools should take action to remove barriers to learning and put effective special educational provision in place. This SEN support should take the form of a four-part cycle through which earlier decisions and actions are revisited, refined and revised with a growing understanding of the pupil's needs and of what supports the pupil in making good progress and securing good outcomes. This is known as the graduated approach. It draws on more detailed approaches, more frequent review and more specialist expertise in successive cycles in order to match interventions to the SEN of children and young people.

The graduated approach comprises of four stages: assess, plan, do and review.

The graduated approach should be undertaken regardless of whether the pupil is entitled to an EHC plan or not. Figure 3.2 provides an overview of what the four stages comprise of.

Addressing underachievement among SEN pupils to close the gap

Underachievement refers to a mismatch between current levels of attainment and potential, which results in a pupil not achieving the national expectation at the end of a key stage. Pupils are considered to be underachieving when standards in attainment, pupil progress or

Table 3.1 Meeting the needs of pupils with high incidence SEN

Communication and interaction	Cognition and learning
Which children: Speech, language and communication needs (SLCN), Specific learning difficulties (SpLD), Autistic spectrum disorders (ASD), hearing impaired (HI)	**Which children:** Moderate learning difficulties (MLD), Severe learning difficulties (SLD), Profound and multiple learning difficulties (PMLD), Specific learning difficulties (SpLD)
Barriers to learning:	**Barriers to learning:**
• Difficulty with communication because they don't understand what others have said, or they can't form sounds, words or sentences (SLCN) (HI)	• Difficulties with reading, writing, spelling and number; poor coordination; poor concentration and lack of spatial awareness; mismatch between achievement and ability; poor behaviour as a result of being a frustrated learner (SpLD)
• Difficulty recognising words, difficulty with fine motor skills (writing) and coordination (SpLD)	• Learn at a slower pace; difficulty acquiring basic skills in literacy and numeracy; difficulty understanding concepts; low self-esteem; some language delay; poor concentration; underdeveloped social skills; (MLD, SLD)
• Difficulty with comprehending/understanding some communication and instructions (masked by learned phrases or echoing what a teacher says) (ASD)	• Poor self-help skills; poor coordination and perception; severe and multiple learning difficulties with physical or sensory impairment (PMLD)
• Difficulty with social interaction and imagination (ASD)	**Strategies to meet needs:**
• Easily distracted, cannot cope with any change in routine, and gets upset by certain stimuli, e.g. loud noise (ASD)	• Give extra time where needed, allowing pupil to work at own pace
Strategies to meet needs:	• Break learning and tasks down into smaller steps
• Use shorter sentences	• Give step-by-step instructions and write down homework for them
• Speak clearly and avoid speaking too quickly	• Model what you want the pupil to do (demonstration)
• Pair the pupil up with another peer who is a good language role model, and with a supportive group of friends	• Provide breaks between learning tasks
• Give the pupil simple messages to take to other peers or staff (verbal and written)	• Support written tasks with mind maps, writing frames, prompt cards, word lists, visual prompts, symbols
• Use open questioning, giving pupils time to respond	• Check pupil's understanding by asking them to repeat back what you have said and asked them to do, and to say what they have learned in the lesson
• Read aloud and use commentary to improve pupils' listening skills	• Allow pupils to present their work/responses in a range of ways to writing, e.g. using multi-media, ICT
• Use discussion and visual cues (symbols, pictures, photographs) to support written communication	• Utilise a range of multi-sensory teaching and learning approaches (VAK)
• Use props to encourage pupils to talk more, e.g. telephone, audio recorders, digital camera, digital video camera, iPad	
• Engage the pupil in sequencing and matching activities to develop language	

Communication and interaction	Cognition and learning

Communication and interaction

- Teach language skills through games, e.g. 20 questions, role play, guessing games using verbal cues, hot seating
- Provide a quiet area for talking and listening activities in the classroom
- Provide key vocabulary and word lists
- Pre-tutor a pupil before a lesson to familiarise them with new vocabulary

Cognition and learning

- Give immediate positive praise and feedback to reward effort/outcomes
- Provide opportunities for over-learning to consolidate, use peer-to-peer tutoring
- Give pupils sufficient thinking time to process information
- Enable pupils to work in pairs, in a small group, independently, and whole class

Social, emotional and mental health difficulties

<u>Which children:</u> Attention deficit disorder (ADD), Attention deficit hyperactivity disorder (ADHD), Obsessive compulsive disorder (OCD),

- Oppositional defiance disorder (ODD), Autistic spectrum disorders (ASD), including Asperger's syndrome and autism, bipolar disorder, anxiety disorder

<u>Barriers to learning:</u>

- Immature social skills, difficulty in making friends, withdrawn, socially isolated
- Challenging, disruptive or disturbing behaviour; aggressive behaviour
- Depression, mood swings
- Self-harming, eating disorders, substance misuse

<u>Strategies to meet needs:</u>

- Consistently apply classroom/school rules for behaviour
- Model good behaviour for learning, and pair the pupil up with a positive peer role model
- Incorporate turn taking cooperative learning activities in lessons
- Give one instruction and one task at a time, don't overwhelm the pupil
- Catch the pupil being good, use positive praise, focus on the pupil's strengths, talents and interests
- Defuse confrontation with humour, change the subject, send the pupil on a message, give them a classroom responsibility
- Provide time-out in a quiet calm distraction-free area of the classroom

Sensory and/or physical needs

<u>Which children:</u> Visually impaired (VI), Hearing impaired (HI), Multi-sensory impaired (MSI), Physical disability (PD)

<u>Barriers to learning:</u>

- Limited mobility, physical tiredness due to side effects of medication or medical condition, poor concentration (PD)
- Unable to distinguish or hear sounds and speech (HI)
- Unable to see fully or partially (VI)
- Unable to see, hear or speak (MSI)

<u>Strategies to meet needs:</u>

- Ensure pupils can see the interactive whiteboard, TV, PC monitor who don't have a VI
- Use a visualiser, enlarged text, or put text onto an audio player for those with VI
- Dim bright light to reduce glare, use window blinds, or re-seat pupil (VI)
- Provide a reader, where appropriate (VI)
- Produce written text in a range of alternative multi-media formats
- Provide extra time for completing tasks and tests
- Face HI pupils when speaking so they can lip read
- Use a hearing loop/lapel microphone for HI pupils

(Continued)

Table 3.1 (Continued)

Communication and interaction	Cognition and learning
• Provide them with anger management strategies, e.g. count to 10, deep breathing, use a stress ball, sit on hands • Seat pupil at the front of the classroom away from busy areas and distractions, e.g. away from windows or doors • Use non-verbal cues to deal with minor behaviour, e.g. raised eyebrows, being silent, making eye contact, using symbols, e.g. thumbs up, thumbs down; traffic light colours for mood, understanding • Incorporate social stories in lessons, where appropriate, to help them understand feelings, develop empathy • Use role play, hot seating, drama activities • Develop their resilience, it is OK to make mistakes, adopt a fresh start and 'can-do' approach • Use visual timetables, symbols, pictorial instructions • Prepare pupils in advance for any change in routines • Make teacher expectations clear • Provide access to multi-media technology for task completion	• Use subtitles on TV, video clips, and provide written transcripts (HI) • Make use of visual or talking timetables and pre-tutoring (HI, VI) • Ensure any misunderstandings, mistakes or misconceptions are dealt with sensitively and positively in the classroom • Give breaks between learning activities • Ensure safe movement around the classroom for wheelchair users (PD) • Ensure learning resources for pupil use are accessible and clearly labelled (PD, VI) • Seat pupils at the front of the class, away from busy areas (doors, windows) to avoid distractions, background noise • Pair pupils up with other peers, enable them to work in a supportive group of peers (VI, HI, MSI, PD)

attendance fall below the national averages. High levels of school exclusions, pupil absences, truancy, poor behaviour or high rates of pupil mobility are other indicators of underachievement. Recent government statistics on SEN found that these pupils were one of the vulnerable underachieving groups of children and young people.

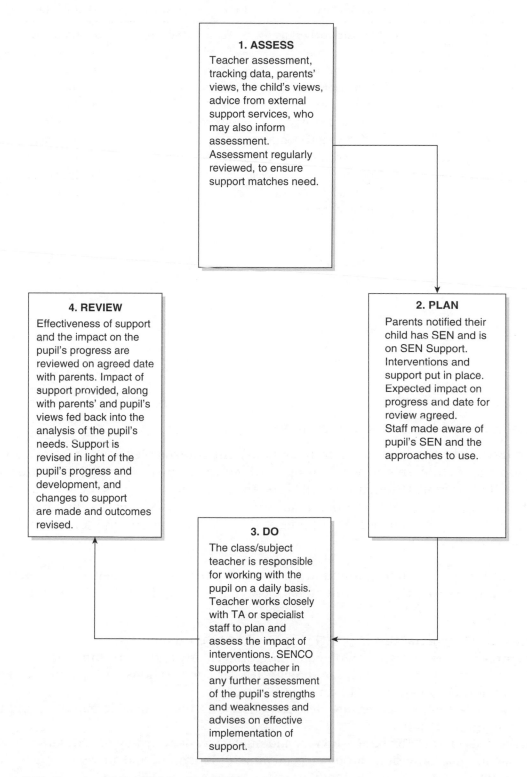

1. ASSESS
Teacher assessment, tracking data, parents' views, the child's views, advice from external support services, who may also inform assessment. Assessment regularly reviewed, to ensure support matches need.

4. REVIEW
Effectiveness of support and the impact on the pupil's progress are reviewed on agreed date with parents. Impact of support provided, along with parents' and pupil's views fed back into the analysis of the pupil's needs. Support is revised in light of the pupil's progress and development, and changes to support are made and outcomes revised.

2. PLAN
Parents notified their child has SEN and is on SEN Support. Interventions and support put in place. Expected impact on progress and date for review agreed. Staff made aware of pupil's SEN and the approaches to use.

3. DO
The class/subject teacher is responsible for working with the pupil on a daily basis. Teacher works closely with TA or specialist staff to plan and assess the impact of interventions. SENCO supports teacher in any further assessment of the pupil's strengths and weaknesses and advises on effective implementation of support.

Figure 3.2 Overview of the SEN graduated approach's four stages

The causes of underachievement

The main causes of underachievement are summarised in Table 3.2.

Table 3.2 Causes of underachievement

School factors	Classroom factors	Family circumstances	Within-child factors
• Inappropriate curriculum • Ineffective rewards system • Lack of flexibility in timetabling • Inconsistently applied behaviour policy	• Mismatch between delivery of the curriculum and pupil's preferred learning style • Lessons too long • Poor differentiation • Lack of challenge • Unclear instructions and explanations • Poorly paced and structured lessons • Passive learning environment • Inappropriate groupings and seating arrangements	• Family break-up • Family illness • Family bereavement • Neglect • Abuse	• Tiredness • Low self-esteem • Lack of self-confidence • Poor social skills • Sensory or physical impairment • Specific learning difficulty

Strategies to address underachievement

The government has invested heavily in addressing underachievement among vulnerable groups of children and young people, which includes those with SEN and/or disabilities, for example through free child care, the pupil premium, literacy and numeracy catch-up programmes for Year 7 pupils operating at or below NC Level 3, summer school activities to support transfer from primary to secondary school and an anti-bullying programme.

The coalition government also found the following strategies to be effective in helping to close and narrow the attainment gap between SEN pupils and their more affluent peers:

• having high expectations that SEN pupils will make good progress
• assessment for learning, tracking pupil progress regularly and intervening early
• engaging positively with parents through regular conversations with parents, to keep them informed about their child's progress
• strong leadership, which ensures teachers know who the vulnerable pupils are and the provision they require
• targeted support in the basics (literacy and numeracy) delivered by skilled staff
• extra-curricular provision through a good range of lunchtime and after-school activities, including educational and residential trips.

How the SENCO can check if pupils with SEN are underachieving

Undertaking work scrutiny and sampling of SEND pupils' work across the curriculum is a valuable way of identifying potential underachievement. When doing this activity the SENCO should look for:

- variations in the presentation of written work – legibility, untidiness
- unfinished pieces of work and homework
- poor written expression and work lacking clarity or sense
- inaccurate work with misunderstandings and irrelevance
- poor quality diagrams
- patchy or no evidence of transference of learning from additional literacy or numeracy interventions across the curriculum
- erratic performance from subject to subject, and/or over time.

The SENCO needs to seek the pupils' views about the variation, and cross-check these with subject teachers or class teacher's perceptions and comments.

Work scrutiny needs to be supported by other contextual evidence relating to pupil attendance, ability, dual placement, behaviour, emotional and social well-being, the nature of the SEN and disability. The entire process will help to identify SEN pupil underperformance, the reasons for it and the strategies to address issues.

Some pupils with disabilities may underachieve as a result of not having had reasonable adjustments made to remove barriers to learning, i.e. the appropriate resources to access the curriculum, or because teachers don't allow them extra time in which to complete tasks. Therefore, it cannot be assumed that all pupils with disabilities necessarily have inherent special educational needs.

The SENCO needs to ensure that teachers and learning support staff are aware of these barriers, are able to identify them within the classroom and know what approaches to utilise in order to remove or minimise them.

There is an excellent table in the archived Primary National Strategy resource entitled *Learning and Teaching for Children with Special Educational Needs in the Primary Years* (DfES, 2004e: 39–42), which provides practical strategies for removing barriers to learning. The archived Key Stage 3 booklet Part 1: *Using Data – Target Setting and Target Getting* in the resource *Maximising Progress: Ensuring the Attainment of Pupils with SEN* (DCSF, 2005: 8) also provides a comprehensive list of practical approaches the SENCO can advise class and subject teachers to adopt in order to ensure pupils with SEN and disabilities reach their optimum potential.

An update on the changes to assessment policy and procedures in schools

The National Association of Headteachers (NAHT) Commission explored 'Assessment without Levels' with the DfE, OFSTED, academics and other organisations, during 2013. On 13 February 2014 the NAHT findings were published in a report, which featured a set of underpinning principles for good assessment, an evaluation assessment design checklist for schools and examples of assessment best practice currently existing in schools. The NAHT principles will help to inform schools' own assessment systems, in light of the development of new national curriculum assessment criteria from September 2014. The *Report of the NAHT*

Commission on Assessment, which includes the underpinning principles for assessment on page 8, can be downloaded at: www.naht.org.uk

The then Education Secretary Michael Gove commented:

> The NAHT's report gives practical, helpful ideas to schools preparing for the removal of levels.

Lord Sutherland, who chaired the NAHT Commission, remarked:

> It is essential that everyone involved in education – not least, pupils and their families – has confidence in the methods used to assess pupil performance.

Concept and purpose of assessment

The NAHT Commission's report on assessment reminds the reader about the concept and purpose of assessment. The term assessment denotes a range of measurement functions for formative, diagnostic and summative uses. Assessment is part of every teaching activity as it is embedded in the classroom. It is integral to high quality teaching and learning, as it ensures teaching is appropriate and that learners make the expected progress.

The main purpose of assessment is to help teachers, parents and pupils to plan the next steps in learning. Teachers assess pupils' progress on an ongoing basis in the classroom, to determine what is being learned, what pupils know, understand and can do, and what they need to do next to progress.

Assessment:

- informs teaching and learning
- informs pupils and their parents about the performance of the individual
- holds schools to account for the attainment and progress of all pupils
- enables benchmarking between schools to occur
- supports the award of accreditation and external qualifications.

NAHT recommendations

The NAHT made a series of key recommendations in their report. Some of the most important included:

- schools should review their assessment practice against the NAHT underpinning principles for assessment and the assessment design checklist
- assessment should be driven from the curriculum, with assessment criteria derived from the new national curriculum
- pupils should be assessed against objective and agreed criteria rather than ranked against each other
- pupil progress and achievement should be communicated in terms of descriptive profiles
- schools should work collaboratively in clusters, to ensure a consistent approach to assessment
- external moderation of teacher assessment that is reliable and comparable over time is essential
- initial teacher training (ITT), newly qualified teachers' (NQTs) induction and the continuing professional development (CPD) of qualified teachers need to include training in assessment methodology and practice to support teaching and learning, including those with SEN

- schools are required to publish their principles of assessment from September 2014, with a view to having a detailed school assessment framework in place and published by September 2016
- the NAHT to develop and promote a set of model assessment criteria based on the new national curriculum
- the DfE should make clear what assessment data schools will be required to submit, and what their expectations are in relation to teacher assessment and moderation
- the DfE should identify and publicise where excellent practice in assessment already exists
- OFSTED need to make clear to schools what they expect of the school's assessment processes.

The SENCO is likely to be asked by the assessment coordinator in school to contribute a statement of principle relating to assessment and SEN pupils, for inclusion in the school's revised assessment principles and framework.

It is interesting to note that the NAHT's assessment design checklist mentions the structured conversation:

> The information from assessment is communicated to parents and pupils on a termly basis through a structured conversation. Parents and pupils receive rich qualitative profiles of what has been achieved and indications of what they need to do next. (NAHT, 2014: 9)

Pupils, including SEN pupils, will be assessed and judged against new curriculum assessment criteria, which include using the revised P scales, where appropriate, as to whether they are:

- working towards (emerging, developing)
- meeting (mastered, confident, secure, expected)
- exceeding.

These recorded judgements can be translated into numbers (a scaled score), and teachers and the SENCO can still monitor SEN pupils' progress through the use of the 'traffic light' (RAG) system on attainment data tracking grids.

The NAHT comments on their assessment design checklist:

> Children may be working above or below their school year and we must ensure we value the progress of children with special needs as much as any other group. The use of P scales here is important to ensure appropriate challenge and progression for pupils with SEN. (NAHT, 2014: 10)

The NAHT Commission conclude that:

> ... there is a need for a logical, mutually compatible assessment process that covers the whole of a child's education through whatever educational setting he/she attends. (NAHT, 2014: 19)

Assessment for learning and SEN pupils

The Draft SEND Code of Practice (0–25) comments:

> Class and subject teachers, supported by the senior leadership team, should make regular assessments of progress for all pupils. These should seek to identify pupils making less than expected progress given their age and individual circumstances. (DfE, 2014e: 6.14)

Assessment for learning (AfL) is defined as the process of seeking and interpreting evidence for use by pupils and their teachers to decide where the pupils are in their learning, where they need to go next and how best to get there. AfL is essential because it helps to guide classroom practice for all pupils, including those with SEN and/or disabilities.

The SENCO will need to ensure that class/subject teachers are engaging these pupils in assessing their own learning and progress, wherever possible. Class/subject teachers should track the progress of pupils every term, and engage in pupil progress meetings, where any underachieving pupils are identified, and appropriate strategies are put in place to address the issue early.

The SENCO will check if regular ongoing assessment is enabling class/subject teachers to identify:

- what is helping or hindering pupils with SEN to access and participate in the curriculum and learning
- the impact of teaching and learning support on SEN pupils' learning
- the strengths and talents SEN pupils have
- any gaps, misconceptions or misunderstandings in SEN pupils' learning
- the appropriate level of challenge to set in relation to SEN pupils' targets
- what the views of SEN pupils are in relation to their learning and progress.

The SENCO will find the table on page 15 in *Part 2: Approaches to Learning and Teaching in the Mainstream Classroom*, which is in the archived Key Stage 3 National Strategy series *Maximising Progress: Ensuring the Attainment of Pupils with SEN* (DCSF, 2005), very useful to share with teaching and learning support staff, as it offers a range of strategies to support assessment for learning.

The progress of SEN pupils

Every teacher is responsible and accountable for the progress and development of the SEN pupils in their class, even where they access support from teaching assistants or specialist staff, within or outside the mainstream classroom.

SENCOs should refer teachers to the Draft SEND Code of Practice (0–25), which describes what less than expected progress constitutes. This states:

> Class and subject teachers ... should seek to identify pupils making less than expected progress given their age and individual circumstances. This can be characterised by progress which:
>
> - is significantly slower than that of their peers starting from the same baseline
>
> - fails to match or better the child's previous rate of progress
>
> - fails to close the attainment gap between the child and their peers
>
> - widens the attainment gap. (DfE, 2014e: 6.14)
>
> Where progress continues to be less than expected the class or subject teacher, working with the SENCO, should assess whether the child has SEN (DfE, 2014e: 6.16).

There is no single definition of what 'good progress' looks like for SEN pupils. However, the DfE, in its updated *Progression 2010–11* guidance, clarified three key principles which lead to SEN pupils making good progress. These are:

- High expectations are key to securing good progress.
- Accurate assessment is essential to securing and measuring pupil progress.
- Age and prior attainment are the starting points for developing expectations of pupil progress.

OFSTED, in relation to pupils whose cognitive ability means they are unlikely to ever rise above 'low', judge their achievement based on pupils' learning and progress relative to their starting points at particular ages. Progress measured on the basis of age and starting point enables more objective comparisons and judgements to be made as to what constitutes good progress for pupils with SEN. This information also helps to inform the setting of more stretching targets for SEN pupils.

In the latest version of their *Subsidiary Guidance* (January 2014) OFSTED offer useful information about judging SEN pupil progress. They comment in relation to the achievement of pupils with SEN and/or disability with less complex needs:

> The starting point for evaluation is that expected progress is the median level for pupils' age and starting point. (OFSTED, 2014c: 17:54)

OFSTED expect SEN pupils who are receiving additional interventions to be demonstrating accelerated or sustained progress, i.e. ideally they should make double the rate of progress, in relation to their starting point, on an intervention programme supporting literacy improvement.

OFSTED will expect SENCOs as well as headteachers to be using the RAISEonline Transition Matrices, as well as the DfE *Progression 2010–11* data sets 2–3, as a guide to judging SEN pupils' progress in the education setting.

Both data sources offer a national picture of pupils' progress, which includes those starting from a low baseline, on P levels. However, these data sets should be used with caution, as they use assessment data based on the old national curriculum assessment criteria.

The OFSTED *Subsidiary Guidance* (January 2014 version) can be downloaded from the following website: www.ofsted.gov.uk

The SENCO needs to consider the rates of progress of all SEN pupils in their education setting, year-on-year, but, in particular, carefully track critical groups of SEN pupils, e.g. those who are summer births, those on pupil premium, who are also an LAC or on FSMs.

P levels

Where there are pupils working below National Curriculum Level 1, the use of the differentiated performance criteria (P levels) has been encouraged to enable schools to measure smaller stepped progress, set targets and evaluate the impact of their provision for these SEN pupils, aged 5–16. An average point score conversion was developed for each P scale, which enabled P level data to be incorporated into the RAISEonline data sets (Transition Matrices).

P levels were originally developed in every national curriculum subject, including religious education (RE) and personal, social and health education (PSHE).

P1 to P3 related to the early levels of general attainment

P4 to P8 related to subject attainment.

The P levels were designed to support summative assessment at the end of an academic year or key stage. They helped to track and identify linear and lateral pupil progress. They provided a best-fit judgement on SEN pupil performance, as a pupil may not demonstrate every element of a P level descriptor.

In light of the new revised national curriculum introduced in maintained schools in September 2014, the P level descriptors are being updated to align with the new curriculum. Until the revised P scales are published, moderated 'in-house' teacher assessment, using modified levels or other appropriate smaller stepped summative assessment tools, will need to be adopted, in the interim period, as a temporary measure.

Using and analysing SEN pupil-level attainment data to evaluate progress

The effective use of data helps to improve teaching and learning and support the development of a strategic approach to the management of SEN. Data collection and analysis are essential elements in developing a more 'forensic' approach to removing barriers to learning, raising expectations and supporting the setting of realistic and stretching targets for SEN pupils.

The analysis of SEN pupil-level data can provide a deeper understanding of the performance of individual and groups of SEN pupils over time. It helps to inform which additional interventions are required to ensure SEN pupils make the expected progress. SEN data analysis also offers the SENCO a better understanding of the impact of the additional and different types of interventions and provision on SEN pupils' progress. Effective strategic analysis and interpretation of robust SEN data help to inform teaching and learning at the classroom level.

The SENCO needs to reflect on the following aspects, which are essential to using and analysing SEN pupil-level data:

- the criteria being used to determine whether SEN pupils are underachieving
- the strategies and approaches being used to address any SEN pupil underachievement and to narrow the attainment gap
- the key national indicators and SEN data sets essential to monitoring SEN pupil progress
- the systems and approaches being used across the school to assess, target set and evaluate SEN pupils' rates of progress
- what constitutes good progress for SEN pupils within the school, which takes account of linear and lateral progress
- the effectiveness of the SENCO working with subject leaders and key stage coordinators in the school to jointly analyse and interpret SEN pupil-level data, in order to identify strengths and gaps in subject coverage or aspects of a subject that require further development and improvement.

Why analyse SEN data?

The SENCO, in partnership with the assessment coordinator in the school, will need to interrogate SEN pupil-level data in RAISEonline and Fischer Family Trust (FFT) in addition to the information in their own internal data sets in order to:

- contribute evidence to the whole school self-evaluation process, in judging how well pupils with SEN and/or disabilities are progressing
- evaluate the impact of additional intervention programmes and in-house provision on SEN pupils' outcomes, and in relation to providing good value for money
- evaluate the progress towards meeting the targets set for SEN pupils
- make informed decisions about the deployment of SEN resources
- evaluate the support and interventions provided by external agencies, including the impact of any extended school activities SEN pupils have accessed
- identify trends over three years
- compare the school's SEN pupil performance with that of similar schools, locally and nationally
- identify any gaps existing in SEN provision
- identify any SEN pupils who may be underachieving.

What data should the SENCO be using and analysing?

The SENCO needs to gather qualitative as well as quantitative evidence to gain a secure view about the progress of SEN pupils. The following questions provide some useful prompts:

1. What does SEN pupil data tracking tell me about their progress?
2. What are the SEN pupils' views about their progress?
3. What are the views of staff and external professionals about SEN pupils' progress?
4. What do observations from lessons indicate about pupils' progress?
5. What does the scrutiny of SEN pupils' work across the curriculum indicate about their progress, and the effectiveness of interventions?

The SENCO will need to give careful consideration to the type of SEN data that will be most useful to collect and analyse, and how and when the SEN data should be used. The following list suggests the types of data the SENCO could analyse:

- value added data which compare each SEN pupils' result with the median result for all pupils nationally with the same average point score at an earlier key stage, i.e. the difference between a pupil's actual result and the expected result at the end of a key stage
- attendance data, particularly persistent absenteeism data, unauthorised absence data, e.g. where SEN pupils are taken on holidays in term time
- exclusions data (fixed term and permanent exclusions)
- rewards and sanctions data including behaviour data
- well-being data, e.g. Health Related Behaviour Questionnaire (HRBQ), Pupil Attitude to Self and School (PASS).

Analysis of the SEN pupil-level data should help to demonstrate the impact additional provision is making, identify any gaps in provision, and whether particular groups of SEN pupils are making better progress than others.

Understanding RAISEonline and Fischer Family Trust data

RAISEonline and Fischer Family Trust are two data packages used by schools, local authorities and OFSTED inspectors. Both resources use data gathered from the school census to compare attainment and progress linked to levels of interventions for pupils at SEN Support and on EHC plans.

SENCOs are expected to be able to use and analyse SEN pupil-level data in both of the data packages, as well as interpret and compare their school-level SEN data with the national data sets for SEN. The SENCO would be advised to book a session with the school's assessment coordinator and/or the headteacher to take them through the operational aspects of accessing different data sets within each package, if they are new to this aspect of their role. In addition, the local authority data team or school improvement team often provide resources on the use of these data packages. Another option is for the SENCO to spend half a day with another local skilled SENCO who is conversant with both data packages. These strategies will become more important in light of the forthcoming changes to national curriculum assessment.

SENCOs will find two archived resources useful for giving further background information about using and analysing data. The first is *Leading on Inclusion* (Section 2: *Using and Understanding Data*), and the second is Part 1: *Using Data – Target Setting and Target Getting*, in *Maximising Progress: Ensuring the Attainment of Pupils with SEN* (DCSF, 2005).

SENCOs may wish to build up a toolkit of practical resources on data analysis. The RAISEonline document library is worth browsing to keep up-to-date with any changes to the Transition Matrices or Summary Reports:

RAISEonline 2013 Summary Report Key Stage 1 Key Stage 2 (24 October 2013)

> *RAISEonline 2013 Summary Report Key Stage 4* (28 November 2013) at: www.raiseonline. org/documentlibrary/
> *Progression 2010–11* with accompanying data sets can be downloaded from: www.gov.uk/ government/uploads/system/uploads/attachment_data/file/180840/Dfe-00557-2010.pdf

The National Governors' Association website offers the following downloadable resources which may also be of interest to those SENCOs who value a more user-friendly guide to understanding and interpreting data:

> *Knowing Your School: RAISEonline for Governors of Primary Schools*, 2nd edn (January 2014)
> *Knowing Your School: RAISEonline for Governors of Secondary Schools*, 2nd edn (January 2014)
> *Knowing Your School: The FFT Governor Dashboard for Primary School Governors* (May 2013)
> *Knowing Your School: The FFT Governor Dashboard for Secondary School Governors* (May 2013)

All the above resources are available from: www.nga.org.uk

Online guidance on how to navigate and interpret Fischer Family Trust data can be accessed at: www.fischertrust.org

The SENCO needs to look out for information regarding future changes to RAISEonline and Fischer Family Trust, in light of the new national curriculum revised assessment system, as previous data sets will not be valid for comparison, being based on the previous national curriculum assessment criteria. Assessment without curriculum levels based on scaled scores and a best-fit subject descriptor will need to be taken on board by SENCOs.

High quality teaching

High quality teaching is that which is differentiated and targeted at the child or young person's areas of weakness. Previously referred to as quality first teaching, it is part of the daily repertoire of teaching strategies for all pupils that ensures SEN pupils' progression in learning. The Draft SEND Code of Practice (0–25) 2014 comments:

Schools should regularly and carefully review the quality of teaching for all pupils, including those at risk of underachievement. This includes reviewing, and where necessary improving, teachers' understanding of strategies to identify and support vulnerable pupils and their knowledge of the SEN frequently encountered. (DfE, 2014e: 6.34)

SENCOs, in coordinating and monitoring provision for pupils with SEND across the school, in partnership with the senior leadership team, should see the following aspects of high quality teaching in practice:

- lessons differentiated and personalised to match learners' needs, and in particular, use of curriculum resources matched to SEN pupils' reading age (OFSTED will track this across the curriculum for SEN pupils)
- pupils as active participants and cooperative learners in the learning process
- teachers and teaching assistants model good learning, explanation, the use of open questioning, thinking aloud and mind mapping
- pupils talk about their learning, and think aloud (tell other pupils how they found an answer or solved the problem)
- meta-cognition is evident: pupils know how to learn, they think about thinking, they problem solve, they question, and they do this together with other peers, as collaborative learners
- learning builds on prior knowledge and understanding
- links made to and transfer of learning across the curriculum
- teachers using a range of teaching approaches (VAK)
- pupil voice is encouraged, with assessment for learning embedded
- pupils accept responsibility for their own learning, and are given the opportunity to work independently
- pupils given the opportunity in the lesson to review their learning, e.g. '*Three new things I have learned in today's lesson are ...*'
- pupils develop confidence and persistence in learning, e.g. pupil mistakes are turned into positive learning opportunities (peer coaching is utilised)
- ICT is used and applied to enhance curriculum access, extend learning and demonstrate understanding
- regular use of encouragement and authentic praise to engage and motivate SEN pupils is adopted by teachers and teaching assistants.

An understanding of SEN pupils' needs as learners is central to high quality teaching, as it informs the range of strategies that teachers consider using; it also informs the nature of the provision and the nature of reasonable adjustments to be made.

Making best use of the pupil premium

Concept of the pupil premium

The pupil premium was introduced by the coalition government in April 2011. This additional funding targets extra support for looked after children (LAC) who have been looked after continuously for more than six months, those on free school meals (FSM) from low income families, including those who have been eligible for FSMs at any point in the past six years, and children with a parent in the armed forces, from Reception to Year 11. The extra funding is designed to enable schools to narrow the attainment gap between pupils from disadvantaged and more affluent backgrounds, some of whom may have SEN. In 2015–16, the Early Years Pupil Premium will be introduced to enable the most disadvantaged early years children to get more support.

Reporting on the use of the pupil premium

It is up to schools to decide how they spend the pupil premium. They are accountable for their use of the funding and they have to publish online information about their annual pupil premium allocation and how they spent it, year-on-year. Schools must also indicate what impact the extra funding has had on the learning, progress and attainment of pupil premium children. During school inspections OFSTED will want to know why the school decided to spend the pupil premium in the way it has. Inspectors evaluate the performance of pupil premium children in English and mathematics, by considering average points scores in national assessments at the end of the Key Stage 2, and at GCSE at the end of Key Stage 4. Where a gap is identified between the performance of pupils supported through the pupil premium and all others in the school, this is reported on as to whether it is narrowing.

How schools are using the pupil premium

From April 2011, when the pupil premium was first introduced, schools had little if any guidance from the DfE on how best to use this additional funding. Therefore schools went for a fairly narrow menu of support and interventions. These included:

- creating smaller classes, but this does little to boost achievement when the targeted pupils are not being taught by good or outstanding teachers
- one-to-one tuition, which is expensive and will only have an impact if a good quality professional is delivering the intervention
- ability grouping, but this may bring stigma to the most disadvantaged underachieving pupils in the bottom group
- recruiting extra teaching assistants, but they will only have an impact if they are confident in modelling and using meta-cognitive strategies in their learning support work
- extending the school day to fit in after-school activities, but this will not benefit those vulnerable or disadvantaged pupils who are tagged and on curfews, and who have to be home by 4 p.m.

OFSTED undertook their first review on how schools were using the pupil premium to raise the achievement of disadvantaged pupils in 2012. The most common use for the pupil premium at that time was to pay for teaching assistants to deliver in-class support or small group time-limited interventions in literacy and/or numeracy, or for existing or new well-qualified or specialist teachers to deliver focused support in English and/or mathematics, or for help to reduce class sizes, or deliver out-of-hours learning. Other schools have used the pupil premium money to fund support workers, learning mentors, parent support workers, behaviour support workers and counsellors, to address pupil well-being.

Schools had also used the additional money to fund extra-curricular activities, educational trips and residential visits for disadvantaged pupils, to pay for school uniform, and to supply basic equipment to support pupils' learning. Some secondary schools funded summer schools from the pupil premium money.

OFSTED undertook a follow-up review on the pupil premium in 2013, which once again focused on how schools were using the pupil premium to maximise achievement. This report was more sharply focused, as it offered several case studies as evidence of good practice, on what was working well. In summary, schools that had successfully spent the pupil premium to improve achievement shared the following characteristics:

- ring-fenced the pupil premium funding to target the right disadvantaged pupils to achieve the highest levels

- used data to thoroughly analyse which eligible pupils were underachieving in English and mathematics, and why
- drew on research evidence undertaken by the Sutton Trust/Education Endowment Foundation to allocate funding to activities that would have the best impact
- ensured high quality teaching across the school was at least consistently good or better
- tracked pupil premium children's progress regularly each term to check whether additional support and interventions were working, and made any necessary adjustments
- ensured that teaching assistants were highly trained and understood their role in helping pupils to achieve
- systematically gave pupil premium children useful diagnostic feedback on their work, indicating ways that they could improve it
- ensured that a designated senior leader had a clear overview of how the pupil premium funding was being allocated and the difference it was making to the outcomes for pupils
- ensured that class and subject teachers knew which pupils were eligible for pupil premium funding and therefore understood their responsibility for accelerating their progress as part of high quality teaching
- provided well-targeted support to improve the attendance and behaviour of eligible pupil premium children, including supporting the families of these children
- had discussions about the performance of pupil premium children as part of the staff performance management system
- had a clear policy on spending the pupil premium, agreed by governors, which was published on the school website
- thoroughly involved governors in the pupil premium decision-making and evaluation process
- were able, through careful monitoring and evaluation, to demonstrate the impact of each aspect of their spending on the outcomes for pupils.

In January 2013, OFSTED published *The Pupil Premium: Analysis and Challenge Tools for Schools*, which accompanied their 2013 report on *The Pupil Premium: How schools were spending the funding successfully to maximise achievement*.

This OFSTED toolkit enables schools to analyse where there are gaps in achievement between pupils who are eligible for the pupil premium and those who are not, and to plan the subsequent action they need to take. It aligns with and supports a school's self-evaluation and school improvement processes.

SENCOs will find this OFSTED toolkit helpful, especially when they are analysing provision maps, and evaluating the impact of additional interventions for SEN pupils who are also eligible for pupil premium funding. The self-review questions on pages 13–15 in the OFSTED pupil premium analysis and challenge tools document are useful. The toolkit and the pupil premium reports by OFSTED can be downloaded at: www.ofsted.gov.uk

What works best in raising the achievement of those on pupil premium

SENCOs will find Table 3.3 of interest, as this identifies in terms of value for money and impact which additional interventions and support from pupil premium funding are the most effective, and give the quickest 'wins'. This was based on research undertaken by the Education Endowment Foundation (EEF) and Durham University, on behalf of the Sutton Trust. The interactive *Teaching and Learning Toolkit* (2014) can be viewed on and the report downloaded from: www.educationendowmentfoundation.org.uk/toolkit/

SENCOs will discover from reading the EEF research and looking at Table 3.3 that the most effective provision, i.e. what works best and gives quick wins in relation to making best use of the pupil premium funding, is as follows:

Table 3.3   Pupil premium approaches and their effectiveness

Approach	Potential gain	Cost	Impact
After-school programmes	2 months	££££	Low impact for a high cost
Arts participation	2 months	££	Low impact for a low cost
Aspiration interventions	0 months	£££	Very low or no impact for a moderate cost
Behaviour interventions	4 months	£££	Moderate impact for a very high cost
Block scheduling	0 months	£	Very low or no impact for a very low or no cost
Collaborative learning	5 months	£	Moderate impact for a very low cost
Digital technology	4 months	££££	Moderate impact for a high cost
Early years intervention	6 months	£££££	High impact for a very high cost
Extended school time	2 months	£££	Low impact for a moderate cost
Feedback	8 months	££	High impact for a low cost
Homework (Primary)	1 month	£	Low impact for low or no cost
Homework (Secondary)	5 months	£	Moderate impact for a very low or no cost
Individualised instruction	2 months	£	Low impact for a low cost
Learning styles	2 months	£	Low impact for a very low cost
Mastery learning	5 months	££	Moderate impact for a low cost
Mentoring	1 month	£££	Low impact for a moderate cost
Meta-cognition and self-regulation	8 months	££	High impact for a low cost
One-to-one tuition	5 months	££££	Moderate impact for a high cost
Oral language interventions	5 months	££	Moderate impact for a low cost
Outdoor adventure learning	3 months	£££	Moderate impact for a moderate cost
Parental involvement	3 months	£££	Moderate impact for a moderate cost
Peer tutoring	6 months	££	High impact for a low cost
Performance pay	0 months	££	Very low or no impact for a low cost
Phonics	4 months	£	Moderate impact for a very low cost
Physical environment	0 months	££	Very low or no impact for a low cost
Reducing class size	3 months	£££££	Low impact for a very high cost
Repeating a year	−4 months	£££££	Negative impact for a very high cost
School uniform	0 months	£	Very low or no impact for a very low cost
Setting or streaming	−1 month	£	Negative impact for a very low or no cost
Small group tuition	4 months	£££	Moderate impact for a moderate cost
Social and emotional learning	4 months	£	Moderate impact for a very low cost
Sports participation	2 months	£££	Moderate impact for a moderate cost
Summer schools	3 months	£££	Moderate impact for a moderate cost
Teaching assistants	1 months	££££	Low impact for a high cost

Source: The Education Endowment Foundation, *Teaching and Learning Toolkit*, 2014: 2.

- pupils being given regular constructive feedback on their learning
- meta-cognition and self-regulation as part of everyday high quality teaching and learning
- peer tutoring
- collaborative learning opportunities for pupils
- phonics interventions for those who require catch-up.

The transfer of children and young people with SEN

Transfer and transition are two terms often used interchangeably to refer to a child or young person's move from one education phase to another (transfer), or a move within the same education setting between different year groups (transition).

Transfer at any phase of education, whether it is from pre-school to primary school, or from primary to secondary school, or post-16/post-18 to college or HE, can be a particularly stressful period in a SEN child or young person's life, causing them to become anxious, worried and uncertain about moving on.

Children and young people with SEN worry about a number of issues prior to attending a much larger organisation. For example, whether they will make friends easily; how they will cope with being taught by many different teachers or tutors; whether they will be able to do the work; how much learning support they will receive; if they will be bullied by older pupils or students; how they will find their way around a much larger school, college or university; and how they will travel to school, college or university.

The range of practices used to make transfer a seamless move

A range of practices are utilised by nurseries, schools and post-16 organisations in order to support the smooth transfer of children and young people with SEN from one phase of education to another. Those with an EHC plan will have their provision for the next phase of education clearly specified. For those children and young people on SEN Support, without an EHC plan, their pre-planning for provision in the next phase of education will be variable, as they are likely to be moving on from many different nurseries, schools or colleges.

However, good practice evidence-based research on transfer indicates the following approaches work well with SEN children and young people:

- providing one-to-one mentoring and support from a learning mentor or key adult, focused on reassuring the SEN child or young person about their transfer
- providing extra taster days or half days in the summer term, prior to the transfer
- commencing preparation for transfer a year earlier, giving taster sessions and opportunities for parents/carers to meet earlier, to share information
- offering a peer-to-peer buddy system, whereby the child or young person with SEN can keep in touch 'virtually' or face-to-face, pre- and post-transfer
- getting the child or young person to produce a one-page profile or a pupil/student passport, which strengthens their 'voice' in the information sharing process
- moving a teaching assistant or a learning support assistant with the child or young person to the next phase of education, to enable them to spend the first term, or first year, supporting their learning and emotional well-being in the new education setting
- in addition to the usual parents' evening/open day, offering parents and children and young people with SEN smaller group sessions with other parents and SEN children and young people with similar needs, perhaps via a coffee morning or afternoon tea, to make it less formal

Name: _____

D.O.B. _____

Age: _____

My best friends at school are:

_____

_____

_____

The things I am good at: _____

_____

Hobbies/interests: _____

_____

Favourite school subjects: _____

_____

Things I find difficult: _____

_____

The things I like doing best: _____

_____

The things I don't like doing:

_____

_____

The subjects at school I don't enjoy:

_____

_____

[photo]

Favourite foods: _____

_____

Favourite TV programmes: _____

_____

Who/What helps me when I am upset:

_____

_____

Who is in my family: _____

_____

_____

How I feel about going to my next school/
college: _____

_____

What I'm not sure about at the next school/college:

_____

_____

Extra help I need at the next school/college:

_____

_____

_____

What my new teachers/tutors must do to help
me learn: _____

_____

_____

_____

What else my next school/college should know
about me:

_____

_____

_____

Figure 3.3   Model SEN pupil/student transfer passport

- providing information about the transfer and what goes on in the new education setting in more parent-friendly and more child-friendly formats, e.g. multi-media resources, as well as written information, making use of symbols for children, where appropriate (some settings produce YouTube or video clips focused on a 'Day in the life' of a pupil or student with SEN at the school, college or university)
- offering joint team building and fun activities prior to transfer, perhaps on a short-term summer school basis
- providing the SENCOs or learning support managers with sufficient quality non-contact time to meet together, to jointly plan and share more detailed information about the pupil's or student's attainment, and the additional interventions and provision which have been most effective.

Children's and young people's views about transfer

Children and young people generally identify five aspects which lead to a successful transfer to the next phase of education. These are:

- making new friends who help to make them feel more confident and better about themselves
- having parents, teachers and tutors who explain, encourage and reassure them about coping in the next education setting
- studying new subjects, which are interesting, taught by subject specialists
- being supported in finding their way around the new school or college and becoming familiar with the rules and routines of the organisation
- not repeating work or topics previously covered in the last school.

Figure 3.3 provides the SENCO with a model pupil/student passport, to help support the transfer of SEN pupils and students to the next phase of education. It can be tailored to suit the context of the education setting.

Points to remember

- Qualitative and quantitative approaches should be utilised to identify SEN.
- Underachievement is the mismatch between current levels of attainment and potential attainment.
- Assessment for learning strengthens pupil voice in relation to having more of a say about their learning and progress.
- The effective use and analysis of pupil-level attainment data help to improve teaching and learning for SEN pupils.
- SEN pupils on additional intervention programmes in literacy should make double the rate of progress, in relation to their starting point.
- High quality teaching is part of the daily repertoire of teaching strategies that ensure SEN pupils' progression in learning.
- Effective use of the pupil premium helps to narrow the attainment gap between those from disadvantaged and more affluent backgrounds.
- Earlier preparation for the transfer of SEN pupils to the next phase of education is good practice.

Further activities

The following questions, focused on aspects covered in this chapter, meet the requirements of the National Award for Special Educational Needs Coordination, and support reflection and the professional development of experienced and newly appointed SENCOs:

1. Which two barriers to learning and participation for a cohort of pupils with SEND present the greatest challenge in your school or setting? Describe how you would minimise and remove these barriers.
2. After analysing the summative SEN pupil-level attainment data, you notice there is a cohort of SEN pupils who have underachieved. Describe the action you would take to address the issue.
3. As SENCO, what evidence would you collect to demonstrate the impact an additional intervention is having on improving SEN pupils' learning and progress?
4. The headteacher has asked you to report on the progress made by SEN pupils on free school meals, who are in receipt of pupil premium funding. Prepare an outline for this report.
5. Identify one issue relating to SEN pupil or student transfer which requires improvement. Describe the actions you would take, working in partnership with other colleagues, to address the issue.

 Online materials

To access electronic versions of the material in this chapter visit: www.sagepub.co.uk/cheminais2e

Figure 3.2 Overview of SEN graduated approach's four stages
Figure 3.3 Model SEN pupil/student transfer passport
Table 3.1 Meeting the needs of pupils with high-incidence SEN
Table 3.3 Pupil premium approaches and their effectiveness

4

Building capacity among colleagues to respond to SEN

This chapter covers:

- identifying the SEN professional development needs of staff
- the SENCO role in building staff capacity to meet the needs of SEN pupils
- top tips for planning and delivering a SEND INSET for staff
- how to make best use of the DfE SEN training resources
- coaching and mentoring to build staff capacity for SEN
- the effective development and deployment of teaching assistants
- managing conflict and staff resistance to SEN changes
- research and development to inform evidence-based practice
- the SENCO building teacher capacity for SEN in other education settings, as an SLE.

Identifying the SEN professional development needs of staff

Prior to building capacity for SEN among staff, it is useful for the SENCO to audit the current level of SEN skills and knowledge existing across the entire staff. An analysis of feedback from the staff SEN training audit will help the SENCO to plan a programme of ongoing SEN professional development activities, to support the implementation of a new SEN system. A model SEN training audit is offered in Figure 4.1, which can be modified as necessary.

SENCO role in building staff capacity to meet the needs of SEN pupils

A SENCO will very often be viewed by other colleagues in the education setting as being the 'expert' in SEN. However, under the revised 2014 SEND Code of Practice, it is clearly every teacher's responsibility to meet the needs of SEN pupils in their class or form group. One of the key SENCO roles is clearly to build capacity for SEN among the entire teaching staff in the education setting, in order to stop 'learned helplessness' and a dependency culture existing.

In order to lead the building of SEN capacity effectively across a school, the SENCO will need to:

- deliver an initial whole school INSET session on the SEND changes
- model effective classroom practice in teaching pupils with SEN

SEN Staff Training Audit

Name: _____ Date: _____

_____

From the list of topics below, please choose three and number in order of priority

- **Identifying special educational needs**
- **Meeting pupils' social, emotional and mental health needs**
- **Meeting pupils' communication and interaction needs**
- **Meeting pupils' cognition and learning needs**
- **Making reasonable adjustments to meet the needs of pupils with physical/sensory impairments**
- **Differentiating the curriculum**
- **Assessment for learning: using the Progression Guidance and Data sets to judge progress**
- **Target setting for pupils with SEN**
- **Working productively with parents and carers of SEN pupils (structured conversation)**
- **Making best use of ICT to enhance SEN pupils' access to learning**
- **Effective deployment of teaching assistants to support and promote SEN pupils' learning**
- **Meeting the OFSTED inspection requirements for SEN and disability**
- **Person centred planning and supporting SEN pupils reviewing their own progress and provision**
- **Any other SEN topic** (Please specify)

_____

_____

Please indicate your preferred method for accessing the training topics identified:

External course	☐	**Online multi-media resources**	☐
SENCO drop-in	☐	**Workshops in-house**	☐
Printed information	☐	**Teaching school CPD sessions**	☐
School INSET	☐	**1:1 coaching/mentoring**	☐

Figure 4.1   SEN training audit for staff

- support teachers in identifying barriers to learning and participation
- advise on the best teaching and learning approaches to meet the four main high incidence areas of SEN
- advise on and support teachers' lesson planning to ensure curriculum access
- provide guidance via TAs, on curriculum differentiation to match SEN pupils' reading age (OFSTED track this across the curriculum)
- advise on appropriate ICT software and other multi-media technology to support SEN pupils' learning
- provide guidance on target setting for SEN pupils across the curriculum
- advise on engaging SEN pupils in reviewing their own progress
- advise on the use of smaller stepped assessment, e.g. P levels
- advise on what constitutes good classroom practice for SEN pupils
- advise on reasonable adjustments for SEND pupils
- provide guidance on deploying TAs effectively
- encourage class and subject teachers to become more reflective practitioners, participating in professional dialogue about what works best in relation to SEN pupils' learning
- signpost staff to utilise further SEN professional development resources.

The SENCO cannot hope to successfully implement a new SEN system alone

SENCOs will value the support of the headteacher, the senior leadership team, the SEN governor and members of the SEN team, i.e. SEN teachers, HLTAs, TAs and learning mentors, in building SEN capacity among staff, across the school.

Teamwork, as a cooperative and collaborative process, empowers others to develop professionally, with each person bringing a range of knowledge, skills and expertise. The SENCO will maximise on the strengths of the senior leadership team, in relation to their providing back-up support for the SENCO when working with those teachers who require further professional support with SEN, beyond that of a 'one-off' whole school SEN INSET session, e.g. NQTs, supply teachers or teachers who require improvement in the classroom context, and who may benefit from mentoring or coaching.

Other external professionals may also provide advice to help build capacity among staff, in enabling them to remove barriers to learning and participation in relation to enhancing SEND pupils' access and inclusion. These may include: a specialist leader of education for SEN, commissioned from a teaching school; the local authority strategic lead for SEN; an independent freelance SEN consultant or national expert; the school nurse, physiotherapist, occupational therapist, speech and language therapist, behaviour support teacher, or an educational psychologist.

The SEND Code of Practice (0–25) 2014 identifies the need to ensure SEND professional development secures the expertise of staff at different levels:

- awareness (to give a basic awareness of a particular type of SEN, appropriate for all staff who will come into contact with a child or young person with that type of SEN)

- enhanced (how to adapt teaching and learning to meet a particular type of SEN, for early years practitioners, class and subject teachers/lecturers and teaching assistants working directly with the child or young person on a regular basis), and

- specialist (in-depth training about a particular type of SEN, for staff who will be advising and supporting those with enhanced-level skills and knowledge) (DfE, 2014e: 4.32).

Schools' continuing professional development (CPD) budgets are not extensive and therefore the most cost-effective training option is likely to be the SENCO delivering an initial INSET session in-house. Delivering INSET to colleagues within their own school can either be a daunting or 'comfortable' and non-threatening experience for the SENCO, depending on their own confidence level.

Once the SENCO knows they will be leading the training session on SEN they will need to begin to prepare for the INSET, usually one or two weeks before the event. The session should comprise of a direct input, and one or two sharply focused SEN short, practical group activities, designed to get colleagues to reflect on their classroom practice with others. A follow-up task could be set which enables staff to make use of the DfE SEN training resources.

Top tips for planning and delivering a SEN INSET for staff

- Define the scope and content of the INSET session. Plan the session using a concept map/mind map to record ideas, concepts, key content, and number each aspect on the mind map in order of priority. Identify where the practical tasks will fit in.
- Consider the specific needs of the audience – what do they already know about the topic? Content must be relevant, practical and enable the staff to benefit from acquiring new knowledge, and strategies that they can apply and try out in the classroom.
- Organise the direct presentation to have the following structure:

  o a five-minute opener, e.g. a story/anecdote, real scenario, facts, a quiz
  o three chunks of seven minutes each, focused on three different key aspects of the SEN topic, using some variety to deliver the message, e.g. pictures, cartoons, sound, animation
  o a 'closer' of four minutes to allow time for questions, distribute handouts and end with a memorable 'big' finish with a call for action.

- Produce the PowerPoint slides transferring the ideas and information from the mind map. Don't have too many slides (one slide per minute).

Use a font size of between 20 and 30 point and Arial for the font type. Keep the slides simple – use three or four short sentences or bullet points per slide. Check spelling and grammar, and overuse of jargon and acronyms. Utilise subtle backgrounds to slides. Use humour selectively in the presentation.

- Practise the presentation to check the time it takes to deliver. Check that the version your presentation is in will be compatible with the computer you will be using at the session, if not using your own laptop computer.
- On the day of the INSET open the presentation by informing the audience of how long you intend to speak for, and what the programme for the session will comprise of. Don't read out each slide word for word. Make eye contact with the audience. Seek audience participation. Split up the presentation into segments, with practical tasks followed by reflection on a PowerPoint slide.
- Limit the number of questions you take after the presentation from the audience to two or three, and ask colleagues to leave any further questions on 'post-it' notes for you to respond to later on in the week.

Figure 4.2 provides an example of a SENCO's PowerPoint presentation for an INSET on the new SEND statutory framework, suitable for use with staff and governors.

AN OVERVIEW OF THE NEW SEND SYSTEM

Presented by the SENCO

SYNOPSIS OF SESSION

- SEN & Disability legislation
- What is different in the new SEND system
- Clarifying SEND terminology, areas of SEN and identification
- SEN provision under the new SEND framework for SEN Support; and Education, Health & Care plans
- Implications of the SEND changes for Every Teacher and Teaching Assistant
- SENCO role
- Signposting to useful SEN resources

SEN & DISABILITY LEGISLATION

- Children and Families Act 2014

- Special Educational Needs & Disability Code of Practice (0–25) 2014

- The Equality Act 2010

WHAT IS DIFFERENT IN THE NEW SEN SYSTEM

- SEN covers 0–25 age range

- SEN pupils & their parents to inform SEN provision

- SEN support (replacing Action and Action Plus)
- IEPs replaced by an individual plan, outlining targets, expected outcomes, SEN provision made & its impact

- Education, Health & Care plans replace SEN statement
- Education, Health & Care services working closer together to provide additional SEN provision

DEFINITION OF SEN

- A child has SEN if they have a learning difficulty or disability which calls for special educational provision to be made for them

- A school age child has a learning difficulty or disability if they have **significantly** greater difficulty in learning than their same age peers

DEFINITION OF DISABILITY

- A child has a disability if they have a physical or mental impairment, and the impairment has a **substantial and long-term** adverse effect on their ability to carry out normal day-to-day activities.

- The disability prevents or hinders the child from making use of educational facilities of a kind generally provided for others of the same age.

IDENTIFICATION – FOUR AREAS OF SEN

The SEND Code of Practice (0–25) 2014 identifies four areas of SEN (high incidence SEN):

1. **Communication & interaction,** e.g. Autistic spectrum, SLCN, SpLD, sensory, physical needs

2. **Cognition & learning,** e.g. MLD, SLD, SpLD, PMLD

3. **Social, emotional & mental health,** e.g. ADD, ADHD, Austistic spectrum, bipolar disorder, self harm, eating disorders, substance abuse, depression

4. **Sensory and/or physical,** e.g. HI, VI, MSI, PD

SEN PUPILS – LESS THAN EXPECTED PROGRESS

With the right SEN provision, SEN pupils should make **expected progress.**

Less than expected progress is characterised by progress which:
- is systematically slower than that of their peers starting from the same baseline
- Fails to match or better the pupil's previous rate of progress
- Fails to close the attainment gap between the pupil and their peers
- Widens the attainment gap

HIGH QUALITY TEACHING FOR ALL

High quality teaching for all features:
- builds on SEN pupils' prior learning
- SEN pupils are active learners & extend learning
- uses multi-sensory learning approaches (VAK)
- teachers/TA model good learning & how to learn
- good use is made of open questioning, thinking aloud, explanation, & thinking time is given
- pupils talk about their learning, & work in pairs, groups, whole class, & independently
- curriculum materials match pupils' reading age
- learning broken down into small steps

DEFINITION OF SEN PROVISION

- SEN provision is that which is something **additional to** or **different from** that which is provided for the majority of pupils

- It goes beyond the differentiated approaches and learning arrangements normally provided as part of high quality teaching.

- It includes **reasonable adjustments** being made for disabled pupils, to ensure access to the curriculum, extra-curricular activities, facilities and information.

SEN IS EVERY TEACHER'S RESPONSIBILITY

The SEN Code of Practice (0–25) 2014 states:

- *Every teacher is responsible and accountable for the progress and development of all pupils in their class, wherever or whoever the pupils are working with, which includes SEND pupils, who may be working with a specialist teacher, external professional or a teaching assistant, on an additional intervention.*

- *Every teacher is expected to have an understanding of the strategies to identify & support vulnerable pupils, and knowledge of the special educational needs most frequently encountered.*

SEN PROVISION: SEN SUPPORT

- SEN Support for those who don't have an EHC plan
- Graduated approach – four types of action: **Assess, Plan, Do, Review**
- **Assess** – range of information gathered to establish SEN pupil's needs (learning & well-being)
- **Plan** – parents informed about pupil's need for SEN Support; class teacher, SENCO, parent & pupil agree upon additional provision and expected progress
- **Do** – Class teacher responsible for SEN pupil's assessment for learning, progress, curriculum planning
- **Review** – class teacher reviews impact of SEN support termly, with parent/pupil & revises SEN Support

SEN PROVISION: EDUCATION, HEALTH AND CARE (EHC) PLAN

EHC plans are:
o for those with more complex needs
o reviewed formally annually – using person centred planning & the structured conversation
o outcomes focused
o clear about how services will work together to support the outcomes & meet the pupil's needs
o SEN pupil & parent focused, putting them at the centre of decision-making about SEN provision
o including information about how the parents personal budget for SEN is to be used

IMPLICATIONS OF THE SEN CHANGES FOR EVERY TEACHER & TA

All teachers and TAs must:
o know where SEN pupils are in their learning & development
o listen to the views and insights of parents & the SEN pupil to inform planning for provision
o have high expectations & ambitions for SEN pupils
o set stretching targets
o track SEN pupil progress towards meeting target set every term
o make regular assessments of SEN pupil progress.

IMPLICATIONS OF THE SEN CHANGES FOR EVERY TEACHER & TA

All teachers and TAs must:
o keep the additional/different provision under review
o ensure intervention approaches used are evidence-based & are having a positive impact on SEN pupil progress
o plan & review SEN support, in partnership with parents/carers, the SEN pupil & SENCO
o request more specialist assessments where a SEN pupil appears to be making inadequate progress, & falling considerably behind their peers.

THE ROLE OF THE SENCO

o **Strategic leader** – of SEN policy & provision
o **Adviser** – providing professional advice & guidance to staff, on the graduated approach to SEN Support
o **Capacity builder** – contributing to the professional development of teachers & TAs in meeting the four areas of SEN
o **Collaborator** – commissioning support from external agencies
o **Quality assurer** – evaluating the impact of SEN Support & EHC plan provision, across the school
o **Advocate** – for SEN pupils & their parents/carers

SIGNPOSTING TO FURTHER SEN RESOURCES

o Advanced training materials for autism; dyslexia; speech, language and communication; emotional, social and behavioural difficulties; & moderate learning difficulties
o (www.advanced-training.org.uk)
o Training materials for complex needs (www.complexneeds.org.uk)
o Inclusion Development Programme (IDP) (www.idponline.org.uk)
o Nasen resources: A Whole School Approach to Improving Access, Participation and Achievement (www.nasentraining.org.uk/training-pack)

REFLECTION & NEXT STEPS

o Any questions?

o What will be your first priority for action following this presentation?

Figure 4.2 Model SENCO PowerPoint presentation for SEND INSET

How to make best use of the DfE SEN training resources

The SENCO will need to support teachers and teaching assistants in how to get maximum value out of accessing the Inclusion Development Programme (IDP) resources, and the online DfE multi-media advanced training materials for autism, dyslexia, speech, language and communication, emotional, social and behavioural difficulties and moderate learning difficulties. There are also online DfE multi-media training resources available on complex needs, which may be of value where there are pupils with severe learning difficulties (SLD) being taught in the mainstream classroom.

The SENCO could find it useful to show snapshot video clips from some of these resources when they deliver their initial whole school INSET on the new SEND statutory framework. They could also offer a weekly or fortnightly staff drop-in session, where colleagues can be guided through accessing these training resources online, with the support of the SENCO.

These training resources are available to download or access online at:

> www.idponline.org.uk
> www.advanced-training.org.uk and www.complexneeds.org.uk
> www.education.gov.uk

The NASEN website also offers phase specific training toolkits for SEN, entitled *A Whole School Approach to Improving Access, Participation and Achievement*. These can be accessed at: www.nasentraining.org.uk/primary-training/ and www.nasentraining.org.uk/training-pack/ (for the secondary phase toolkit).

An overview of the SEN training resources for staff

The Inclusion Development Programme (IDP)

This bank of online resources was produced by the previous Labour government to support their SEN strategy *Removing Barriers to Achievement* (DfES, 2004c). It comprises download-able materials and video clips and is designed to enable teachers to improve outcomes for pupils with SEN. The resources are organised by phase: early years, primary and secondary, and they cover the following SEN aspects: social, mental and emotional health; autism spectrum; speech, language and communication needs (SLCN); and dyslexia. The SENCO may wish to download some of the documentary materials, which can support further activities for professional development with teachers and teaching assistants new to their role.

A whole school approach to improving access, participation and achievement

Each primary and secondary phase toolkit has four training modules, which the SENCO can use to develop future tailored training sessions with groups of staff.

The four modules cover:

- inclusive teaching and learning
- tracking progress
- working with others
- communication with pupils.

Each module comprises a series of activity and information sheets, which the SENCO may wish to use to support the other online SEN training resources.

The advanced training materials for autism; dyslexia; speech, language and communication; emotional, social and behavioural difficulties; and moderate learning difficulties

These phase specific SEN resources, comprising of five modules, one for each area of SEN, and feature reading-based materials and practical training tasks, with a range of audio/ video clips to support study. They are designed to improve teachers' knowledge, skills and understanding about each area of SEN, as well help school staff to raise the achievement of these SEN pupils.

Training materials for teachers of learners with severe, profound and complex learning difficulties

These training resources may be useful for those working or training in a special school setting. However, children with severe learning difficulties (SLD), such as those with Down's syndrome, may be accessing learning in a mainstream setting, either full-time, or part-time as a dual placement pupil. The SENCO will need to be familiar with the online resource, and select which of the 16 modules would be appropriate to use with mainstream staff teaching and supporting pupils with SLD. The modules cover four broad subject areas:

- the context of specialist teaching
- specialist teaching strategies
- specialist teaching procedure
- collaboration and leadership.

This is another excellent SEN training resource, like the advanced training materials, which includes video clips to illustrate best practice in the classroom.

Subject areas 2 and 3 would be the most useful, as these focus on: planning, curriculum access, assessment for learning and communication.

The National Scholarship Fund for teachers and SEN support staff

Teachers and SEN support staff who wish to deepen and extend their knowledge relating to SEN, including specific impairments and disabilities, may be interested in applying online, via the National College for Teaching and Leadership, for the National Scholarship Fund (this should be done by April, before they begin their course of study in September). Over the last two years, scholarship funding of up to a maximum of £2000 has been available to support higher level study in SEN. There is an expectation that the teacher, HLTA or TA undertaking SEN study will share their learning, knowledge and expertise across the school system.

Coaching and mentoring to build staff capacity for SEN

The SENCO may take on either a coaching or mentoring role within or beyond their own education setting, and where they do so, they must have sufficient, quality time to commit to the role. Where a SENCO is new to coaching or mentoring, it is advisable that they shadow an experienced coach or mentor, prior to commencing a coaching or mentoring assignment.

Coaching is a structured sustained process for enabling the development of a specific aspect of a professional learner's (coachee) practice. It doesn't tell the coachee what to do, but helps them to find their own solutions to workplace challenges. It involves helping the coachee to identify new ways of improving their performance. Coaching encourages the coachee to reflect on their practice, and to see the bigger picture.

Mentoring is a process for supporting teachers, as professional learners, through significant career transitions.

Ten principles of effective coaching and mentoring

- structured professional dialogue which is evidence-based from practice
- establishing the ground rules and boundaries of the coaching/mentoring relationship
- coachee/mentee takes increasing responsibility for their own professional development throughout the process
- understanding the theory and how it works in practice in various contexts
- trying out new approaches in practice in a learning environment that supports risk taking and innovation
- building up trust, mutual respect and sensitivity between the coach/mentor and the coachee/mentee
- procuring specialist expertise to extend the skills and knowledge of the coachee/mentee, and to model good practice
- identifying and setting coachee/mentee agreed personal goals
- recognising the benefits of the experience for coaches and mentors
- sustaining regular professional learning, action and reflection on behalf of the coachee/mentee.

Types and styles of coaching

- **Informal coaching conversations** – a school leader or leading teacher utilises coaching principles during short informal conversations about an issue raised by a colleague. This models a professional learning dialogue and supports the development of reflective thinking and practice.
- **Specialist coaching** – this utilises specialist knowledge with a coachee to develop their practice in a specific area, e.g. SEN, or in a subject specialism or pedagogy. The coach will also have effective practice in coaching skills, qualities and principles.
- **Collaborative peer co-coaching** – partner teachers provide non-judgemental support to each other based on evidence from their own practice. Co-coaches each take on the role of coach and professional learner.
- **Team coaching** – is usually led by an external specialist coach or an internal experienced coach, and is focused on improvement in pedagogy, a particular subject/aspect, e.g. SEN, or a phase (primary or secondary).
- **Expert coaching** – entails an expert external coach or a leading teacher working to develop coaching skills across the school.
- **Self-coaching** – coaching principles and protocols are utilised by an individual on issues of professional concern to them.
- **Pupil coaching** – the promotion of pupil-to-pupil coaching, led by skilled teacher coaches within school.

Models of coaching

There are a number of different coaching models available which the SENCO can utilise. Table 4.1 provides an overview of the key features of each model. All these coaching models offer the SENCO a framework for a coaching assignment with a coachee.

Table 4.1 Coaching models

Coaching Model	Model features
STRIDE	**Strengths** of the coachee
	Target – what the coachee wants to achieve as a result of the coaching
	Reality – current situation and any barriers to not achieving the target
	Ideas – the coachee identifies what they can do to address the problem
	Decision – action and next steps for the coachee
	Evaluation – coachee commitment to take action
FLOW	**Find** – the challenge, what the coachee wants to addresss
	Look – at reality, current state of play
	Open – possibilities, what the coachee could do
	Win – commitment, what the coachee is going to do and when
GROW	**Goal** – desired outcome established
	Reality – current situation and obstacle to the coachee reaching their goal
	Options – the coachee has for reaching their goal
	Will & Wrap up – coachee commits to action (What, Where, Why, When and How)
CLEAR	**Contracting** – setting the scope, agreeing ground rules, and establishing desired outcomes
	Listening – by coach, who offers ideas
	Exploring – coachee considers the impact a situation is having on them and their practice, and with the coach identifies future action to resolve the situation/problem
	Action – ways forward and next steps
	Review – coachee feedback on what worked and what was useful and what they would do differently next time
OSKAR	**Outcome** – objective the coachee hopes to achieve at the end of the session
	Scaling – to enable the coach to judge how bad the situation/problem is on a scale of: 0 = worst to 10 = excellent
	'Know how' – and resources to improve the situation or problem
	Affirm – and action, what's going well for the coachee and what the next small step is to take
	Review – what's improved, what the coachee did to make the change happen, what have been the effects of the change
HILDA	**Highlight** – the issue, i.e. what the coachee wants to change in their practice
	Identify – the strengths of the coachee's practice, and how can these strengths/skills be used to address the issue/problem
	Look – at the possibilities, obstacles, what the coachee has already done, i.e. what worked and what it didn't work, and what could be done next to overcome the issue
	Decide – when the coachee commits to action, e.g. what, how, when
	Analyse – and evaluate the impact, i.e. how will the coachee know they have been successful in addressing the issue, and what the success or good practice will look like.

Key skills for SENCOs as coaches

SENCOs make good coaches because coaching is a natural continuation of what they already do informally with staff, SEN pupils and their parents/carers, i.e. they are attentive, easy to talk to and relate to, and they put others at their ease.

The SENCO acts as a catalyst, bringing fresh perspectives and different ideas to the coaching experience.

There are 10 essential key skills that SENCOs as a coach will require. These are outlined below:

- **Relate sensitively** to the coachee, to build up trust, confidence and rapport.
- **Model expertise** in practice through professional dialogue.
- **Facilitate access to research** and evidence to support the development of the coachee's pedagogic practice.
- **Tailor activities** in partnership and agreement with the coachee.
- **Observe, analyse and reflect** on the coachee's practice and make this explicit, giving them the chance to share their perceptions.
- **Provide information** that enables learning from mistakes and success.
- **Facilitate a growing independence** in professional learning.
- **Use open questions** which are clear, concise, neutral, purposeful, non-judgemental. The questions asked by the SENCO as coach will raise awareness, explore beliefs, help the coachee to understand the problems and to develop their own solutions.
- **Listen actively**, building in periods of silence to develop thinking and suggestions from the coachee.
- **Establish buffer zones** between coaching and other formal relationships with the coachee in school.

Figure 4.3 illustrates the four main stages to coaching.

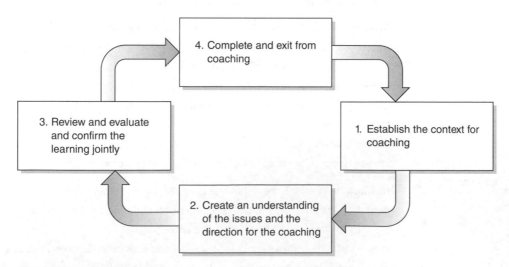

Figure 4.3   Four stages of coaching

Organising a coaching assignment

The following points will help a SENCO new to the coaching experience to organise a coaching assignment (a series of coaching sessions), agreed with the coachee, over a period of time.

1. Get some background information on the coachee, e.g. do a 360 degree feedback with the coachee, and two or three other colleagues who are familiar with their classroom practice and/or role. Ask all parties the same five questions:

   o What is this person (coachee) good at?
   o What do you value most about them (or about yourself, as coachee)?
   o What do they (or you as coachee) need to get better at?
   o What do they (or you as coachee) need to do to be successful in their (your) current role?
   o Do you have any other messages for the coachee, about their current role or professional practice?

2. Prepare an initial proposed timetable which outlines when, where and for how long the coaching sessions will take place.
3. Ensure you book the coaching venue in advance, as well as keep all coaching sessions protected from other competing priorities. To cancel a coaching session or to move a session gives a negative message to the coachee.
4. Select the most appropriate coaching model to use with the coachee.
5. Draw up a coaching agreement with the coachee, and emphasise confidentiality throughout the coaching process.
6. Agree with the coachee when you will observe them in action, prior to each coaching session, to see if they are putting into practice what has been discussed during the coaching conversation.
7. Always allow quality time to write up the notes from a coaching session, preferably as soon after the session as possible.
8. Ensure that if you have promised to send coaching notes and feedback to the coachee by a certain date, this happens on time.
9. Have a bank of open coaching questions available to use with the coachee during a coaching conversation.

Table 4.2 offers the SENCO, as coach, a bank of questions to use in a coaching conversation with a coachee. They are organised according to the purpose and type of questioning approach or strategy.

Figure 4.4 provides a model template for the SENCO as coach, to record the coaching activity taking place during each session in a coaching assignment.

Giving feedback to a coachee

The SENCO should offer constructive, timely, insightful feedback, based on facts and from observations of the coachee in action. The main purpose of any coaching feedback is to help the coachee to learn something new, to reach their goal or objective, to help them overcome an issue in their role or practice, and to make them feel valued, as a professional. When giving feedback to a coachee the SENCO may find the BOOST model a helpful framework.

Balanced – feedback, which focuses on the coachee's strengths and areas for, development, i.e. delivers a positive statement with a difficult message

Observed – feedback is based on the coachee's observed behaviour

Objective – unbiased feedback, not influenced by the coach's own emotions

Specific – feedback comments are supported by real examples

Timely – feedback is given as soon as possible at the end of, or after, the coaching session.

Table 4.2 Coaching conversation model questions

Clarifying questions	Reflective questions
These questions help to clarify the issue to make way for deeper thinking.	These questions encourage the coachee to reflect on their practice.
• Tell me more about ... • What aspect of this do you want to discuss today? • Tell me more about when you have had success in this aspect. • I am interested to hear about ... • You are saying this about ... is that always the case? • What makes you think this is an issue for improvement?	• What factors do you take into account when you ...? • What did you want to happen in your lesson today? • What would have to change in order for ...? • What do you wish ...? • What is another way you might ...? • What would it look like if you ...? • What do you think would happen if you ...? • What sort of impact do you think...? • What might you see happening if ...? • What is your 'gut' feeling about ...? • What was your intention when ...?
Summarising questions	**Outcome questions**
These questions are useful to get a coaching conversation back on track and focused, and for the coach to check their understanding of what the coachee has said.	These questions are useful to adopt at the end of a coaching session.
• So in summary, you are saying ...? • So, you are saying the key issue is ...? • So, in order to address this, you are saying you are going to ...?	• What is the first step to achieving this ...? • What will you do next? • What support do you need? • How much do you want to make this improvement or change? • What will it look like when you are successful?

Source: Allison and Harbour, 2009.

The SENCO as mentor

The SENCO is most likely to act as a mentor for induction to a newly qualified teacher or to a new member of staff joining their team or department who is new to the school. A mentoring partnership is a very rewarding, enriching experience in terms of helping others to develop professionally and become more effective in their job. Mentoring, like coaching, will bring an added time commitment for the SENCO, who must be certain that they will be able to protect this allocated time in order to carry out this important role.

What mentoring involves

Mentoring will involve the SENCO as a mentor in the following activities:

• identifying learning goals and supporting the teacher's progression
• developing the mentee's control over their learning
• active listening
• modelling good practice in the inclusion of SEN pupils, observing the mentee teaching, articulating and discussing practice to raise awareness
• engaging in shared learning experiences, e.g. team teaching, lesson observation, or watching video clips of lessons

Name of coachee: _____
Name of coach: _____
Date of coaching session: _____

Focus 1:

Information recorded	Comments, observations and questions for feedback

Focus 2:

Information recorded	Comments, observations and questions for feedback

Focus 3:

Information recorded	Comments, observations and questions for feedback

Figure 4.4   Recording sheet for a coaching session

- providing guidance, feedback and direction to the mentee
- reviewing the mentee's progress and supporting action planning
- contributing to the assessment and appraisal of the mentee
- brokering access to further professional development opportunities, e.g. visiting other schools, including a special school.

The SENCO may find it useful to ask the mentee at the end of the year to reflect on the following questions:

- How do you feel the year has gone in relation to teaching pupils with SEN?
- What do you consider have been your most significant achievements in SEN this year?
- Which, if any, aspects of your work teaching SEN pupils have you found most challenging?
- Which aspects of your work with SEN pupils would you wish to develop further?

The effective development and deployment of teaching assistants

The effective professional development and deployment of teaching assistants (TAs) is crucial, in relation to having the maximum impact on the progress of the pupils they support and work with. There has been extensive research in recent years exploring teaching assistant deployment, training and effectiveness. Some of the key findings from this research are highlighted below.

In 2004, OFSTED commented on the deployment of teaching assistants:

> Support by teaching assistants can be vital, but the organisation of it can mean pupils have insufficient opportunity to improve their understanding, skills and independence. (OFSTED, 2004: 5)

Later, in 2010, OFSTED published their SEND review, which found that:

> Where additional adult support was provided in the classroom for individuals, this was sometimes a barrier to including them successfully and enabling them to participate. ... When a child or young person was supported closely by an adult, the adult focused on the completion of the task rather than on the actual learning. Adults intervened too quickly, so preventing children and young people from having time to think or to learn from their mistakes. (OFSTED, 2010: 46, para. 99)

and

> When children and young people's learning was least successful:
>
> - the roles of additional staff were not planned well or additional staff were not trained well and the support provided was not monitored sufficiently. (OFSTED, 2010: 47, para. 104)

The DfE in their White Paper *Support and Aspiration: A New Approach to Special Educational Needs and Disability. A Consultation* (2011a) remarked:

> Within schools, support staff can make a real difference to the achievement of pupils with SEN, but they need to be deployed and used effectively in order to do so. However, teaching assistant time should never be a substitute for teaching from a qualified teacher. Too often the most vulnerable pupils are supported almost exclusively by teaching assistants. (DfE, 2011a: 3.26)

Similarly, the Sutton Trust (2012) in their *Teaching and Learning Toolkit*, which referred to evidence-based research, found that low attaining pupils did less well with a teaching assistant. They commented:

> Most studies have consistently found very small or no effect on supported pupils' attainment.

> There is however some evidence that there is greater impact when teaching assistants are given a particular pedagogical role or responsibility in specific curriculum interventions where the effect appears to be greater, particularly with training and support. Impact in these instances is only half the gains compared with qualified teachers. (The Sutton Trust, 2012: 28)

Peter Blatchford et al.'s research report (2009), on the deployment and impact of support staff in schools, confirmed OFSTED's, the DfE's and the Sutton Trust's findings:

> Overall, it is worrying that extra support does not have a positive relationship with pupil progress. (Blatchford et al., 2009: 132)

Blatchford et al. gave the following reasons, as to why teaching assistants may be having little impact on pupil progress:

- lack of preparation for support staff and teachers on effective joint working, i.e. having time before and after a lesson to plan and feedback
- lack of sufficient training for teachers on how best to deploy TAs, in relation to pedagogy and the curriculum
- teaching assistants not knowing how children learn, why some children fail to learn, and which strategies are the most useful to help SEN children learn
- lack of understanding regarding TA support impact, whether delivered within or outside the mainstream classroom, e.g. how it can isolate the supported pupil from teacher interaction, reduce the supported pupil's curriculum coverage and challenge, and isolate them from their peers, all of which impact on the lack of supported pupil's progress
- the informal relationship between the TA and the supported pupil, resulting in more frequent incidental chatter, and less of a focus on pedagogy and talking about learning
- lower expectations about what SEN pupils can achieve, due to not understanding smaller stepped assessment for learning and rates of progress, as well as not knowing what good and adequate progress looks like for a diversity of pupils with SEN.

The effectiveness of teaching assistants

The role of TAs is more effective when they work in partnership with the teacher on joint planning for the inclusion and engagement of SEN pupils in lessons. In order to maximise the full potential of the TA, teachers need to inform them of the expected learning objectives, outcomes and the activities and tasks planned, well in advance of the lesson.

The effectiveness of additional TA support is dependent on good two-way open communication between the teacher and the teaching assistant, who keep the SENCO informed both about the progress of SEN pupils and of any barriers to learning and participation they may face.

OFSTED (2010) commented:

> The best learning occurred in all types of provision when teachers or other lead adults had a thorough and detailed knowledge of the children and young people; a thorough

knowledge and understanding of teaching and learning strategies and techniques, as well as the subject or areas of learning being taught; and a sound understanding of child development and how different learning difficulties and disabilities influence this. (OFSTED, 2010: 11)

The role of the SENCO in coordinating the effective deployment of teaching assistants

The SENCO's role in coordinating the effective deployment of learning support entails:

- producing a clear, up-to-date job description for TAs
- recruiting, inducting, training and managing the team of TAs, with the support of the senior leadership team
- planning the allocation of in-class TA support across the school and the curriculum to meet the needs of SEN pupils, in light of the SEN budget available
- identifying the TAs and other additional supporting adults e.g. SEN teachers, and the learning mentor, following provision mapping, who will deliver additional intervention programmes and SEN support
- devising timetables for TAs and other support staff, and keeping these under review
- planning the annual programme for learning support team meetings
- negotiating non-contact time for TAs to enable them to differentiate curriculum materials in school time, and also to liaise with subject/class teachers and other professionals from external agencies
- providing access to relevant ongoing professional development for TAs via the local teaching school alliance, as well as in-house
- providing coaching and mentoring to newly appointed TAs
- monitoring and evaluating the effectiveness and impact of TA support and interventions, and involving TAs in the process
- undertaking annual appraisals and professional development reviews with TAs.

Figure 4.5 provides a model job description for a teaching assistant, working in a twenty-first century school. This can be customised to suit the context of the school or other educational setting.

There are two excellent resources for SENCOs in relation to coordinating, managing and monitoring the effectiveness of TAs (or learning support assistants in the secondary phase). These were National Strategy resources, some or all of which have been archived and can be accessed via the DfE website, some local authority websites and via NASEN's website (www. nasen.org.uk):

Secondary National Strategy (2006) *Effective Leadership: Ensuring the Progress of Pupils with SEN and/or Disabilities. Section B: Managing the Deployment of Additional Adults*, pp. 11–13 and 24: www.teachfind.com/national-strategies/effective-leadership-ensuring-progress-pupils-sen-andor-disabilities

Key Stage 3 National Strategy (2005) in *Maximising Progress: Ensuring the Attainment of pupils with SEN, Part 3: Managing the Learning Process for Pupils with SEN*, pp. 19–22: www. teachfind.com/national-strategies/maximising-progress-ensuring-attainment-pupils-SEN. There is an excellent monitoring table on page 21 which the SENCO could download and either use themselves to monitor TAs working in the classroom, or give to senior leadership staff when they have a focus on monitoring the impact of additional supporting adults.

Job title: Teaching assistant supporting teaching and learning

Responsible to: SEN coordinator

Main purpose: To work with individual and small groups of SEN pupils to deliver additional interventions, and under the direction of class/subject teachers, to provide in-class support for learning.

Main duties:

Supporting and extending SEN pupils' learning

- Support pupils' learning across the curriculum, tailoring support to match learners' needs
- Support pupils in learning how to learn and to develop their thinking skills
- Support pupils to become independent, cooperative and collaborative learners
- Support pupils' access to learning through the effective use of ICT
- Contribute to assessing pupils' progress, and support them in reviewing their own learning
- Identify and remove barriers to pupils' learning and make reasonable adjustments
- Adapt and customise curriculum materials
- Support teacher planning

Meeting pupils' wider well-being needs

- Support the emotional well-being and mental health of a diversity of SEN pupils
- Enhance SEN pupils' social and personal development
- Contribute to the management of SEN pupils' behaviour
- Support the delivery of additional interventions for improving pupils' well-being
- Support pupils with SEN and/or disabilities to access extra-curricular activities

Providing pastoral support

- Promote SEN pupils' resilience
- Safeguard the welfare of SEN pupils
- Support the transition and transfer of SEN pupils
- Act as a 'champion' and advocate for pupils with SEN and disability

Supporting the wider work of the school

- Comply with school policies and procedures related to child protection and safeguarding, health and safety, equal opportunities, and whistle blowing
- Contribute to the school's improvement planning and self-evaluation processes, through monitoring the impact of additional interventions and in-class support
- Support teachers in the administration of examinations and tests
- Contribute to maintaining pupils' records
- Assist teachers with the display of pupils' work and achievements
- Support the running of lunchtime and after-school clubs for pupils
- Escort and supervise SEN pupils on educational visits and out-of-school activities
- Contribute to, and support, the review of EHC plans

Working with colleagues

- Support and maintain collaborative, productive working relationships with school staff and professionals from external agencies
- Contribute to, and support, the work of other supporting adults in school, e.g. bilingual assistants, pupil counsellors and personal coaches
- Liaise with pupils, their parents/carers, teachers and practitioners from external agencies, to support pupils' learning and well-being
- Take responsibility in developing your own continuing professional development
- Undertake any other duties commensurate with the post, as allocated by the headteacher.

Figure 4.5 Teaching assistant model job description

In effectively supported lessons, TAs ensure that SEN pupils are clear about:

- what is to be learned
- how this links with what they already know and with their targets
- what they are expected to do as an independent learner in the lesson
- what they should know they have learned by the end of the lesson
- what the next steps in their learning will be.

SENCO evaluation on the deployment of teaching assistants

SENCOs may find Table 4.3 helpful in making judgements about the effective deployment of TAs. It mirrors the type of criteria that OFSTED would make judgements against.

SENCOs will need to gather the views of SEN pupils, teachers receiving in-class support from teaching assistants, and from the TA themselves, on their learning support work in the academic year. Figure 4.6 provides a generic survey that can be completed by all three stakeholders. The findings can help to inform whether the SENCO needs to make any necessary changes to the deployment of TAs.

SENCOs need to consider the following questions:

- How are TAs being actively engaged in an SEN policy review, SEN development planning and provision mapping?
- How will you ensure that class and subject teachers support TAs in enabling SEN pupils to transfer what they have learned in targeted intervention programmes across the curriculum?
- How are TAs actively engaged in monitoring the impact of their support and interventions?

Table 4.3 Evaluating the deployment of teaching assistants

Grade	Evidence descriptor
Outstanding (1)	• Teaching assistants are well-directed to support learning • They make a significant contribution in very effectively supporting SEN pupils' learning and well-being • They understand the next steps SEN pupils need to take, and provide a wide range of learning support activities
Good (2)	• Teaching assistants are well-deployed and are effective in what they do • Teaching assistants relate well to the SEN pupils they support and expect them to work hard
Requires improvement (3)	• Teaching assistants are utilised adequately • They are not effective in supporting learning because they have an incomplete understanding of expectations, and accept SEN pupils' efforts too readily, without a sufficient level of challenge
Inadequate (4)	• Teaching assistants are utilised inadequately due to poor management • Teaching assistants lack the necessary knowledge, skills and understanding, thus contributing little to lessons, SEN pupils' learning and well-being

ANNUAL SURVEY OF TEACHING ASSISTANT SUPPORT

Teacher: _____ Teaching assistant: _____

Pupil: _____ Date: _____

QUESTIONS:

1. When is teaching assistant support most helpful and useful?

2. What is the best type of teaching assistant support from your point of view/for you?

    In-class support ☐   Work outside ☐   ICT support/ ☐   Other: (please specify)
                          the classroom   computer   _____

                                                                       _____

3. What makes teaching assistant support effective and work well?

4. Do you like being with the same teaching assistant/teacher all year?

    YES ☐   NO ☐

5. What has been the best and greatest teaching assistant achievement this year?

6. When is teaching assistant support least helpful, least effective or most challenging?

7. What would make teaching assistant support even better?

8. Any further comments on teaching assistant support you wish to make:

Thank you for doing this survey.
Please return to the SEN Coordinator, Mrs Black

Figure 4.6 Annual survey on teaching assistant support

Managing conflict and staff resistance to SEN changes

There may arise at some point in time conflicts of interests among some staff, e.g. teacher and TA, in moving from an existing SEN system over to the new SEN framework. It has to be recognised that conflict is an inevitable consequence of working with others, and that it does help to stop stagnation. In order to ensure these differences do not lead to a breakdown or disruption in working relationships, the SENCO will need to have an understanding of the basics of managing conflict and conflict resolution.

Conflict management styles

Different conflict management styles are useful in different situations, and the SENCO needs to be able to identify which style they should adopt when conflict arises. The five styles described below were first identified by Kenneth Thomas and Ralph Kilmann in the 1970s, and they are still relevant today:

Competitive – using formal authority and a position of power, a firm stand is taken to make a fast decision, usually when an emergency arises.

Collaborative – being assertive at the same time as being cooperative and understanding while acknowledging the concerns of others. This style is used for handling conflicts over very important issues, or to bring a variety of viewpoints together to get the best solution, or when there have been previous conflicts in the group.

Compromising – trying to find a solution that will partially satisfy everyone. Everyone, including the compromiser, is expected to relinquish something. It is an appropriate style to use when dealing with moderately important issues.

Accommodating – having a willingness to meet the needs of others at the expense of the person's own needs, i.e. being highly cooperative rather than assertive. It is a useful approach to use when the issue matters more to the other person, and when keeping the peace is more important than winning.

Avoiding – evading conflict entirely, in order not to hurt anyone's feelings. It is a weak approach to take, and is often an approach taken when the controversy is trivial, or someone else is in a better position to solve the problem.

Conflict resolution strategy

This approach to resolving conflict will entail the SENCO following six key principles:

- Ensure that good relationships are the first priority: build mutual respect, remain calm, constructive and be polite.
- Separate the problem from the person: engage in professional debate without damaging working relationships, and acknowledging that the other person is not really being 'difficult'
- Pay attention to the views or interests being presented: engage in active listening to better understand why the person feels that way, or holds that particular viewpoint.
- Listen first, and then speak: listen to the other person to understand where they are coming from before defending your own or another's position.
- Set out the facts: agree and establish the objective, observable elements that will impact on the decision.
- Explore options jointly: be open and receptive to a 'third way', enabling both parties to reach an amicable position.

Putting conflict resolution into practice

By adopting the following five-stepped approach, the SENCO will be able to resolve any conflict existing between other staff in the school, between parents and staff, and between SEN pupils and staff.

> **Step 1: Setting the scene** – Begin by clarifying that the aim is to resolve the problem amicably through discussion, and summarise what the problem, issue or disagreement is about.
>
> **Step 2: Gather information** – Listen to both viewpoints, and clarify feelings in an attempt to understand the thinking, motivation and reasons behind each view. Establish whether the conflict is affecting the work performance of those involved, if it is disrupting team work, or impeding decision-making, or affecting the delivery of additional provision to SEN pupils.
>
> **Step 3: Agree the problem** – Endeavour to reach a common perception of the problem or issue, or at least understand what both parties see as being the problem.
>
> **Step 4: Brainstorm possible solutions** – Engage both parties in generating possible solutions to the problem, and be open to suggestions and ideas.
>
> **Step 5: Negotiate a solution** – Look for 'trade-offs', a common goal or compromise and a win-win situation. Remain detached and impartial and be patient. Eventually the conflict will be resolved at this final step.

Research and development to inform evidence-based practice

The SENCO, as teacher-researcher, is an active change agent and innovator who aims through action research to identify any gaps in SEN practice, and to check out the impact of an additional intervention programme in improving SEN pupil outcomes.

Action research also entails investigating an idea, issue or problem relating to current SEN policy, practice or provision which requires further explanation, in order to reach a conclusion or solution, based on the evidence gathered.

The action research process

The SENCO is advised to:

- Choose an aspect of SEN that is relevant and important to them in the context of where they work, and which will extend the understanding of other colleagues as well as themselves, i.e. be grounded in evidence-based practice.
- Check that there is sufficient recent literature in existence on the SEN topic, to provide guidance to and steer the research.
- Formulate a clear and concise research question or hypothesis on what exactly you, as SENCO, want to find out.
- Plan a series of manageable actions which use appropriate research methods, to investigate the question or hypothesis.
- Analyse the evidence and findings from the research undertaken, to reach an overall conclusion, and make recommendations for the next steps leading to improvement.

Figure 4.7 illustrates the action research process.

Ideally, the SENCO's action research must show a development of influence, or a new understanding, and/or an improvement in practice in relation to SEN. Change as an outcome of action research will take time and the SENCO must not expect to change everything at once in their own school in relation to SEN. However, they can lead by example, by changing an aspect of their own practice, which will help other colleagues to learn from their research experience.

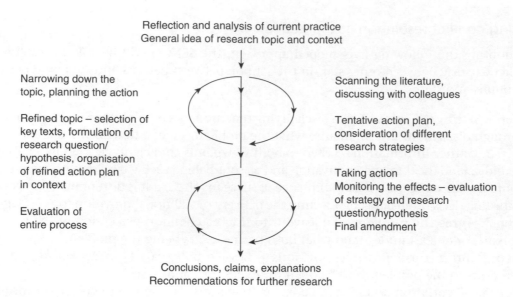

Reflection and analysis of current practice
General idea of research topic and context

Narrowing down the
topic, planning the action

Refined topic – selection of
key texts, formulation of
research question/
hypothesis, organisation
of refined action plan
in context

Evaluation of
entire process

Scanning the literature,
discussing with colleagues

Tentative action plan,
consideration of different
research strategies

Taking action
Monitoring the effects – evaluation
of strategy and research
question/hypothesis
Final amendment

Conclusions, claims, explanations
Recommendations for further research

Figure 4.7   The action research cycle

Source: Koshy, 2009.

The SENCO will need to pilot some research methods initially, particularly if they are new to using them. It is useful for the SENCO to have a 'critical friend' to act as a sounding board, to share thoughts and action research findings with, and who can also offer impartial advice and guidance. This may be a senior colleague within the school, or a skilled and experienced SENCO from another school, or a professional from the local authority or a higher education institution. In addition, other staff, parents and pupils can be involved in school-based research relating to SEN and/or disability, as they can offer valuable insights which help to inform improvements in SEN policy and provision.

The benefits of undertaking small-scale action research

The benefits of undertaking small-scale action research are as follows:

- The SENCO has the autonomy to decide what to investigate.
- Action research enables the SENCO to check their perceptions of what is happening against those of others in the school, in relation to SEN.
- Action research can help the SENCO and others to have a better understanding about an aspect of SEN.
- A developed understanding about SEN helps the SENCO and others to evaluate their practice, and change it as necessary.
- The SENCO's new and improved way of working can influence others to change.
- The school becomes a learning community of 'enquirers' who share their learning and experiences in SEN.

Two hypotheses or issues that the SENCO may wish to explore further, as part of research and development, to support evidence-based practice, could focus on:

1. The additional literacy interventions used in school with SEN pupils that are demonstrating little impact and poor added value; and/or:
2. The current deployment of teaching assistants in school is not making a significant difference to the achievement and attainment of SEN pupils.

Figure 4.8 provides a template for an action research project.

The EEF *DIY Evaluation Guide* may be of interest to SENCOs, and can be downloaded at: www.educationendowmentfoundation.org.uk

Evidence-based practice

Evidence-based practice is a combination of practitioner expertise and knowledge of the best external research and evaluation-based evidence. It involves a careful, clear and thoughtful use of up-to-date evidence when making decisions about how to work with individuals.

The features of evidence-based practice

Evidence-based practice:

- includes steps which a professional or service can use, to ensure everything they do is evidence-based
- entails finding out what works, and ensuring that the additional interventions the SENCO and other professionals make in children and young people's lives are as good as they possibly can be
- involves professionals and practitioners bringing their own knowledge and skills together with best quality evaluation research, to make a decision about selecting the most appropriate intervention or programme to use with the SEN pupil and their family.

Factors to consider when engaging with evidence-based practice

There are five factors that a SENCO needs to consider when they are engaging with evidence-based practice. These are:

- **Applying evidence-based theory** – having an understanding as to why a particular intervention or approach works and is effective in improving pupil progress and achievements.
- **Having the right skills, qualities and knowledge** – to engage in evidence-based practice, e.g. self-awareness, clear communication, power sharing, effective partnership working.
- **Having professional fidelity** – following the right procedures and the key 'ingredients' essential to delivering an effective intervention or approach, and keeping to these.
- **Using clear eligibility criteria** – choosing the best appropriate intervention to match the pupil's needs, in order to ensure maximum impact.
- **Referring to the best research evidence base** – intervention validity has been tested out via research, e.g. a sample of SEN pupils with low reading ages who engage with an intervention programme to boost reading capabilities show a significant increase in reading age, post intervention programme.

SENCOs may find the 2014 Education Endowment Foundation (EEF) *Teaching and Learning Toolkit* (Higgins et al., 2014) a useful point of reference as to which mainstream approaches have the greatest impact on pupil premium children and young people, which includes those with SEN.

Name:	School/Setting:
Project title/hypothesis:	
Introduction and rationale:	
Research project aims:	
Research methodology:	
Research findings:	
Key recommendations:	
Conclusion:	

Figure 4.8 Template for a small-scale action research evidence-based project

SENCO building capacity for SEN in other education settings as an SLE

Specialist leaders of education in SEN

The DfE in its Green Paper *Support and Aspiration: A New Approach to Special Educational Needs and Disabilities* (2011a) stated:

> We will create a new designation of Specialist Leaders of Education. These will be serving middle and senior leaders who are outstanding at what they do and who are able to play a role beyond their school, supporting others, including those who work with children with SEN and disabilities. (DfE, 2011a: 3.22)

SENCOs who take on the role of a specialist leader of education (SLE) in SEN, with at least two years' successful leadership experience and a proven track record in working effectively with other schools to improve SEN, are brokered and commissioned by teaching schools, working as part of a teaching school alliance. The SENCO as an SLE can come from any type and OFSTED category of school.

The SENCO as a specialist leader of education in SEN will undertake several key roles in supporting another school requiring improvement in SEN:

- providing one-to-one support, e.g. coaching or mentoring a new SENCO
- offering facilitated group support, e.g. working with a key stage, subject department, or a team of TAs
- supporting targeted staff in using and analysing SEN pupil-level attainment data to inform planning and progress
- diagnosing strengths and areas for development in SEN, e.g. undertaking a whole school SEN audit to support action planning for improvement
- modelling best practice in teaching pupils with SEN
- working with the SEN governor to clarify their role, particularly in relation to monitoring SEN policy and provision
- undertaking paired lesson observations and classroom walkthroughs with the senior leadership team, to quality assure teaching and provision for SEN pupils.

Teaching schools and their alliances

The concept of teaching schools was proposed in the DfE White Paper *The Importance of Teaching* (2010a), which stated:

> The network of Teaching Schools will include the very best schools with outstanding and innovative practice, in teaching and learning and significant experience developing teachers' professional practice. These schools are best placed to lead system-wide improvement in an area. (DfE, 2010a: 7.8)

Teaching schools perform a number of important roles, by coordinating expertise from their alliance (partners), and utilising the best leaders and teachers, to:

- play a greater role in initial teacher training
- lead peer-to-peer professional and leadership development
- identify and develop leadership potential
- provide support for other schools who are inadequate, requiring improvement and performing below floor standard
- designate and broker specialist leaders of education (SLE)
- engage in research and development.

A teaching school alliance is a group of schools and other partners who commit to working collaboratively, supported by one or more teaching schools. These other partners may include professionals from higher education, a private sector education organisation, or an academy chain. The teaching school alliance may be cross-phase and cross-sector, with partners delivering particular aspects of the alliance activity. A teaching school alliance may choose to work together across alliances (a teaching school network), in order to share services, knowledge and resources.

The following three reports published by the National College for School Leadership (now renamed the National College for Teaching and Leadership), may be of interest to SENCOs:

NCSL (2012) *How Teaching Schools are Already Starting to Make a Difference*

NCSL (2013) *How Teaching Schools are Making a Difference: Part 2*

Matthews and Berwick (2013) *Teaching Schools: First Among Equals?*

Points to remember

- Use one PowerPoint slide per minute with a maximum of four short points per slide, in an SEN INSET.
- Coaching and mentoring help to develop staff confidence in SEN.
- Conflict is an inevitable consequence of working with colleagues to build SEN capacity.
- Every teacher is responsible and accountable for the pupils with SEN in their lessons.
- Evidence-based practice through action research supports SENCO decision-making on how best to work with individuals.
- An SLE in SEN does not have to come from an outstanding school.

Further activities

The following questions, focused on aspects covered in this chapter, meet the requirements of the National Award for Special Educational Needs Coordination, and support reflection and the professional development of experienced and newly appointed SENCOs.

1. Identify the evidence you would collect to demonstrate the impact of any SEN INSET you have delivered to staff in school, in relation to improving their classroom practice in meeting the needs of SEN pupils.
2. Some school staff indicate that they haven't got time to work through the advanced SEN training resources. Describe the action you would take to address this issue.
3. Identify an aspect of coaching which you wish to develop further, and outline the next steps you will take in acquiring the required skill.
4. In confidence, a teaching assistant informs you that a teacher they support is struggling to teach the SEN pupils in their mixed ability class. As SENCO, how would you address this issue?
5. A teacher in school asks for a change of teaching assistant in their classroom. Working relationships appear to have broken down, despite the teaching assistant being knowledgeable and effective in supporting the pupil with autistic spectrum in the teacher's class. Outline the action you would take to resolve the situation.

 ## Online materials

To access electronic versions of the material in this chapter visit: www.sagepub.co.uk/cheminais2e

5

Working in partnership to promote a family centred approach

This chapter covers:

- developing a family centred approach to partnership working
- effective joint commissioning to meet the needs of SEN pupils and their families
- the concept and development of a one-page profile
- Education, Health and Care plans
- using a person centred approach for the annual EHC plan review
- using the structured conversation to empower parents of SEN pupils
- making best use of personal budgets for SEN
- getting to grips with the 'Local Offer'
- signposting families to impartial information, advice and support.

Developing a family centred approach to partnership working

Understanding a family centred approach to partnership working, is reliant on being clear about the concept of the family in the twenty-first century. The family of today includes as parents and carers of children and young people with or without SEN: biological mothers and fathers; adoptive parents; step-parents; same-sex parents; foster carers; legal guardians; grandparents; extended family members such as aunts, uncles and cousins.

The greater diversity in family patterns in the twenty-first century can be contributed to there being more divorce, separation, cohabitation, childbirth outside marriage, marriage and childbearing happening on average later in life, and fertility treatment being made available.

The state and its services have not always kept pace with or understood the reality of modern family life, from changes in family structure and relationships, to economic pressures, and maintaining a healthy work–life balance.

What occurs within the family, whatever its composition, has more impact on a child's learning, development and well-being than any other single factor. What families do is far more important than the structure of the family, particularly as they are the first prime educators of their children. On average, children spend 87% of their time at home with their parents and other family members. Parents are usually the best judges of what children need. They understand their children better than anyone else, and have important insights into what children want.

Partnership, in relation to joint working with families, is a collaborative relationship, that is designed primarily to produce positive educational and social effects on the child or young person with SEN, while being mutually beneficial to all the parties involved. It refers to a state of 'being', that the parents, carers, family of SEN children and young people are viewed as an 'authentic' partner, a 'sharer', an associate of equal worth, whose contributions are valued and respected by other professionals.

Family engagement, through the EHC plan process, for example, has the greatest impact when it is directly linked to supporting the SEN child's learning and development. Approaches such as: the one-page profile, person centred planning, the structured conversation, personal budgets for SEN and the 'Local Offer', as part of the EHC plan process, are all designed to empower and strengthen family participation, by giving parents and carers of SEN children more choice and a 'voice' about SEN provision. Enabling parents to share their knowledge about their child, and engage in positive discussion, helps to give them confidence that their views and contributions are valued, and will be acted upon.

Joint family partnership working, through the SEN Support graduated approach, and the EHC integrated assessment and planning process, is designed to:

- help and support the families of SEN children and young people in an 'enabling' way, i.e. to help them to develop their own sustainable solutions in supporting their child at home
- genuinely support families early, and throughout the SEN journey, and not rescue them, or do crisis management, when it is too late
- work 'with' families of children and young people with SEN, rather than 'do things to' families.

Families of children and young people with SEN and/or a disability want the professionals who work with them to adopt a more positive tone that recognises and appreciates the strengths that exist within the family. They also want professionals to understand their family life context, to keep their promises to help and to deliver the provision and support they say they will.

The families of children and young people with SEN and/or disabilities will want to be reassured that the education setting and its staff:

- accept and value their child for their uniqueness and difference
- focus on their child's strengths and 'hidden' talents
- understand the needs of the child's family and seek support for them during times of stress, and increased pressure
- understand fully the child's special educational needs and/or disabilities, medical needs, or special dietary needs
- can offer the appropriate facilities and care for the SEND child, when they are feeling unwell, or require medication administering
- are tolerant, sensitive and positive about the child's SEND.

A family centred system is based upon local authorities ensuring that parents, children and young people with SEN are involved in discussions and decisions about:

- every aspect of their SEN, including planning outcomes and making provision, to meet those outcomes
- planning and reviewing the Local Offer
- reviewing special educational provision and social care provision
- drawing up individual EHC plans, reviews and reassessments.

The Draft SEND Code of Practice (0–25) 2014 reinforces the fact that families are at the 'heart' of the new coordinated EHC assessment and planning process.

Effective joint commissioning to meet the needs of SEN pupils and their families

In order to enable SENCOs to gain a better understanding of joint commissioning at a local authority level, in securing SEN provision, this section of the chapter will clarify what the term joint commissioning means; it will identify those involved in commissioning SEN provision; and explain what the commissioning process entails.

The concept of joint commissioning

Commissioning is all about change for delivering an improved SEN system. Joint commissioning, as an ongoing process, is a strategic approach to planning and delivering services, in a holistic joined-up way. It enables partners to agree upon how they will work together to deliver personalised integrated support, resulting in positive outcomes across education, health and social care. It also offers partners an opportunity to redesign local systems, making best possible use of local resources and intelligence, so that they can operate more efficiently, and effectively, particularly in helping to improve the experiences of service users, and to meet the outcomes specified in children and young people's EHC plans. Joint commissioning aims to:

- secure education, health and care (EHC) assessments
- secure EHC provision as set out in EHC plans
- agree personal budgets.

Joint commissioning involves families and providers in decisions about integrated SEN provision, ensuring that commissioning is more responsive to local needs.

The Draft SEND Code of Practice (0–25) 2014 commented:

> Local authorities **must** review their provision, taking into consideration the experiences of children, young people and families (including through representative groups such as Parent Carer Forums) or voluntary and community sector providers and local Healthwatch. Information from such reviews will contribute to future arrangements and the effectiveness of local joint working. (DfE, 2014e: 3.28)

Those involved in commissioning SEN provision

The Children and Families Act 2014, Part 3, places a duty on local authorities (LAs) and clinical commissioning groups (CCGs), which are comprised of local consortia of general practitioners (GPs), to work together to commission education, health and social care services for children and young people with SEN, in order to help them achieve their outcomes and ambitions.

Examples of other commissioners in addition to the LA and CCGs include:

- parents, carers and young people with SEN who have personal budgets
- schools, academies, post-16 provisions
- LA services which include public health, education, social care, housing
- NHS Commissioning Board
- Department for Work and Pensions.

Further partners are also consulted by the LA when reviewing SEN provision. These include: governing bodies, proprietors or principals of maintained and non-maintained education settings from early years up to age 25, including the proprietors of academies and free schools, within and beyond the local authority, where SEN children and young people are educated; advisory boards of local children's centres; and other local services, including voluntary organisations contributing to SEN provision.

LAs are required to exercise their functions to promote integration between special educational provision, health and social care provision. The LA and their partner CCGs have to make arrangements for agreeing:

- how local service budgets are used
- the education, health and social care provision reasonably required by local children and young people with SEN
- which education, health and social care provision will be secured by whom
- what advice and information are to be provided about the education, health and care provision and by whom, and to whom these are to be provided
- how complaints about education, health and social care provision can be made, and how they are dealt with
- the procedures for ensuring that any disputes between local authorities and CCGs are resolved as quickly as possible.

What the commissioning process entails

Commissioning is the process of identifying, through a Joint Strategic Needs Assessment (JSNA) and analysis, which health care services are required, and then, arranging and procuring these services from providers. The Health and Social Care Act 2012 requires local Health and Wellbeing Boards to develop Joint Strategic Needs Assessments and joint Health and Wellbeing strategies.

Both processes support prevention, identification, assessment and early intervention, and a joined-up approach, from those providing services. There is a commitment to extend personalisation (i.e. putting more commissioning in the hands of those at individual and operational commissioning levels), co-production (placing equal value on participants'/service users' contributions) and self-directed support, clarifying the outcomes and benefits of commissioning.

Each local authority area's Health and Wellbeing Board includes representatives from the local Healthwatch, from the local CCGs, from the local authority Directors of Adult Social Services, Children's Services and Public Health. It has a strategic influence over local commissioning decisions. The Health and Wellbeing Board considers the needs of vulnerable groups, including those with SEN and/or disabilities, those needing palliative care and looked after children. SENCOs may wish to view their local authority's Child Health Profile at: www.chimat.org.uk

The three levels of commissioning are:

- **Individual level** – e.g. co-production between parents/carers, young people with EHC plan personal budgets and support brokers.
- **Operational/community level** – e.g. groups of parents/carers and SEN young people with EHC plans, pooling budgets; self-directed support and community support to develop local approaches; also includes targeted commissioning for groups or areas.
- **Strategic level** – e.g. the strategic direction is set through co-produced strategic plans, which agree the pace of change, and inform resource allocation. A common

infrastructure is developed, i.e. agreed systems and processes, which endorse self-directed support.

Figure 5.1 illustrates the joint commissioning cycle, which provides a common basic framework for education, health and care (EHC) assessment and planning.

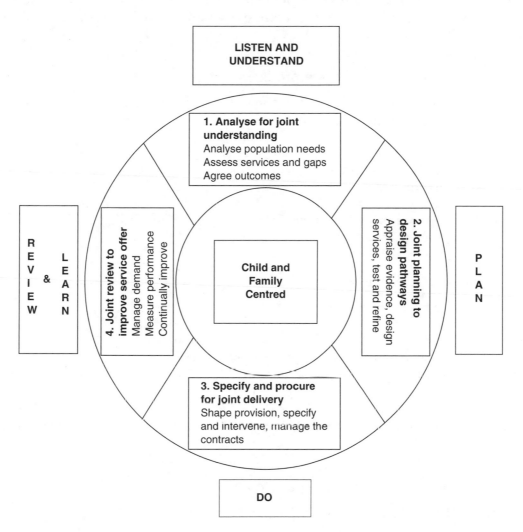

Figure 5.1   The joint commissioning cycle

Key features of effective and successful commissioning

- co-produced with parents, carers and children and young people with SEN
- transparent and objective
- evidence based on what works
- encourages new ways of thinking, resourcing, challenging
- encourages diversity in provision
- stands up to scrutiny.

Further information about commissioning of services for children and young people with SEN can be found in an excellent publication from the South East 7 (SE7) SEND pathfinder entitled: *Joint Commissioning for Children and Young People with SEND*, available from: www.se7pathfinder.co.uk

The concept and development of a one-page profile

The use of a one-page profile acts as a positive starting point in gathering person centred information about the SEN pupil's needs and desires. It gives a short introduction about the individual pupil, from their own perspective, which captures key information on a single page, offering others an understanding of the pupil with SEN, and how best to support them. A one-page profile is also a record of thinking about what is important to the individual pupil.

The components of the one-page profile

The one-page profile consists of a photograph of the child or young person with SEN, followed by three headings/questions, which ask them:

- What is important to me?
- What do others like or admire about me?
- How best to support me?

Figure 5.2 gives an example of a template for a one-page profile, which includes guidance notes for completing each section.

How the one-page profile can be used

The one-page profile can be used to:

- share information about an SEN pupil in a new situation
- be the beginning of a more detailed person centred description
- act as a basis for further action, e.g. asking what is working well and what isn't working from different perspectives, and acting on this
- complement the person centred approach, which supports the EHC plan review
- support an SEN pupil's transition from one phase of education to another, or from college into employment.

The advantages of using the one-page profile

One-page profiles for SEN pupils on SEN Support, or with an EHC plan:

- offer class and subject teachers an at-a-glance overview of how best they can enable the pupil to access learning, by maximising on the child's or young person's strengths and interests
- inform lesson planning, target setting and support needs
- provide parents and carers of the SEN pupil with a means to share their knowledge and expertise on how best their child can be supported in the classroom, and around school
- enable supply teachers to know how best to meet the needs of the SEN pupil, when they are covering another teacher's lesson
- help to ensure continuity in provision for the SEN pupil, across the curriculum
- promote best practice in the delivery of personalised high quality teaching
- provide a 'living' organic document, which can be updated each term, throughout the academic year
- consolidate partnership working between the SEN pupil, their parents or carers, their friends, teachers and teaching assistants, as each contributes information to the one-page profile
- empower the individual SEN pupil by giving them a 'voice'.

Photograph of the child or young person	**Like and admire** – lists the positive qualities, strengths and talents of the child or young person

What is important to me

This is a bullet point list of what really matters to the child or young person from their viewpoint.

It needs to be as detailed and specific as possible.

Who are the important people in the child's or young person's life, and when and how do they spend time together?

Favourite hobbies and activities the child or young person enjoys doing, when, where and how often.

Any routines, which are important, to the child or young person, when they are at school or college.

Favourite lessons, and other school or college activities the child or young person enjoys.

What should be avoided? Things that may annoy or upset the child or young person.

The support I need

List of how the child or young person would like to be supported at school or college.

What is helpful?

What is not helpful?

What do staff need to know?

What do staff need to do?

What do other pupils/students need to know?

Figure 5.2   One-page profile

Top tips or compiling a one-page profile

- The language used on the one-page profile should be 'child-friendly'.
- The one-page profile should be specific, e.g. who, what and when, and avoid using generalisations.
- Positive language giving sufficient detail is important to use.
- Provide support from a teaching assistant or other supportive adult of the child's choice, who can help to upload photographs, graphics, or symbols such as PECS or Makaton, and type up text, where necessary, on the one-page profile.

Further information about the one-page profile can be found at: www.helensandersonas sociates.co.uk

The following website offers a good range of downloadable attractive child-friendly blank templates for SEN pupils to create their own one-page profile: www.sheffkids.co.uk/ adultssite/pages/onepageprofiles

Education, Health and Care plans

The concept of the EHC plan

The SEN Code of Practice acknowledges that ECH plans are based on a coordinated assessment and planning process, which places the child, young person and their family at the centre of decision-making. EHC plans are outcome focused, favouring a person centred approach to planning and review.

The features of a high quality EHC plan

The following features result in the production of a high quality EHC plan:

- children, young people and their parents' carers' views are reflected in the plan, and they inform decision making about the content
- positively describes what the child/young person can do and has achieved
- jargon-free, clear, concise, written in parent/child-friendly language
- evidence-based, focused on how best to achieve short-term outcomes and longer-term aspirations
- indicates clearly how the provision and support will enable the child or young person to achieve the outcomes
- indicates clearly how a personal budget will procure alternative provision and support services
- indicates clearly how education, health and social care provision will be integrated to support the child/young person in achieving the outcomes
- future focused, anticipatory in relation to transfer and transition, and the provision and support required for adulthood, the world of work, independent living and community participation
- clear about how the family, community and statutory agencies will all help the child or young person,to achieve the agreed outcomes.

While the format of the EHC plan will vary from local authority to local authority, the content must include specific sections. These are illustrated in Table 5.1, which gives brief details about what information goes in each section.

Table 5.1   Sections in an EHC plan

Section	
A.	**The views, interests and aspirations of the child, or young person and their parents** – details about play, health, schooling, independence, friendships, FE and future plans for employment; summary of how best to communicate with the child/young person; child's/young person's history.
B.	**The child's or young person's SEN** – primary and secondary needs; health and care needs.
C.	**The child's or young person's health needs which are related to their SEN.**
D.	**The child's or young person's social care needs which are related to their SEN.**
E.	**The outcomes sought for the child or young person** – including outcomes for adult life. The EHC plan identifies the arrangements for setting shorter-term targets by the early years provider, school, college, or other education or training provider.
F.	**The special educational provision required by the child or young person** – including the provision required by the young person to assist in preparation for adulthood and independent living, in finding employment, housing or for participation in society, where they are beyond Year 9 (age 14).
G.	**Any health provision reasonably required by the learning difficulties or disabilities which result in the child or young person having SEN** – and where an Individual Health Care Plan is made for them. Provision detailed, specific and quantifiable; how provision supports outcomes; how advice and information gathered inform the provision. **Health care provision** may include: specialist support and therapies, OT, physiotherapy, nursing support, specialist equipment, wheelchairs, continence supplies, medical treatments and delivery of medications, augmentative and alternative communication systems, or provision for young offenders.
H1.	**Any social care provision which must be made for a child or young person under 18 resulting from section 2 of the Chronically Sick and Disabled Persons Act 1970**
H2.	**Any other social care provision reasonably required by the learning difficulties or disabilities which result in the child or young person having SEN** – includes any adult social care provision being provided to meet a young person's eligible needs (through a statutory care and support plan) under the Care Act 2014.
I.	**The name, and the type of school, maintained nursery school, post-16 institution or other institution, or the type of school or other institution to be attended by the child or young person** where no such institution is named on the EHC plan.
J.	**Resourcing – the Personal Budget,** details of how the personal budget will support particular outcomes, the provision it will be used for including any flexibility in its usage and the arrangements for any direct payments for education, health and social care.
K.	**Appendices** – a list of advice and information gathered during the EHC needs assessment, which is attached to the EHC plan in the appendices.

Source: DfE, 2014e: 9.60.

Reviewing EHC plans

- The EHC plan is reviewed annually, 12 months on from the date of issue.
- Reviews focus on the child's or young person's progress towards achieving the outcomes specified on the EHC plan, and whether the outcomes remain appropriate.
- Reviews are undertaken in partnership with the child/young person and their parents, and take into account their views, wishes and feelings.

- Reviews are undertaken in full consultation with the education setting/early years setting.
- The personal budget or direct payment arrangements are reviewed, where appropriate.
- EHC plans for children under five are reviewed more frequently, e.g. at least every three to six months, to ensure provision continues to be appropriate.
- The reviews for children and young people moving between key phases of education have to be completed by the 15 February in the calendar year of transfer.
- Person centred planning is an effective approach to support the EHC plan review process.

Ceasing an EHC plan

The LA may cease to maintain an EHC plan when any of the following conditions apply:

- the LA is no longer responsible for the child or young person, if they have moved to another LA area
- special educational provision is no longer needed
- a young person aged 16 or over takes up paid employment (including employment with training, but excluding apprenticeships)
- the young person enters higher education
- the young person aged 18 or over leaves education and no longer wishes to engage in further learning.

Good practice in EHC planning and review

The SEND pathfinder project on coordinated assessment and EHC plans identified some really good practice occurring in the pilot local authorities which may be of interest to SENCOs. The eight participating local authorities included: Cornwall, East Sussex, Greenwich, Hartlepool, Hertfordshire, Northamptonshire, Nottinghamshire, and Southampton. The following list captures the best of the good practice, as well as lessons learned:

- **Nottinghamshire** developed a very clear EHC pathway, comprising of seven stages, which gives parents a comprehensive overview of the EHC process. The seven stages comprised of:

  Stage 1 – looking at the services available in the LA Local Offer
  Stage 2 – making a referral for an EHC assessment to the LA
  Stage 3 – one-page profile produced on the child/young person
  Stage 4 – draft EHC plan produced from evidence, reports and views
  Stage 5 – personal budget agreed, where applicable
  Stage 6 – EHC plan finalised, resources agreed, plan to be put in action
  Stage 7 – annual review of the EHC plan.

- **Hartlepool** developed a simple three-stage EHC process:

  Stage 1 – referral/request for an EHC assessment
  Stage 2 – EHC integrated assessment takes place
  Stage 3 – planning.

- **Hertfordshire** created a website page which had information and downloadable tools and resources to trial back in school when doing an EHC review meeting:

  o The LA published a newsletter for parents, and one for schools, to enable the sharing of good practice in the EHC process to occur.
  o A Family Day was held over a weekend, to give information and gain feedback from families of SEND children and young people on the EHC plan process.

- o The LA produced, in partnership with parents and multi-agency professionals, an at-a-glance guide and a checklist for use during EHC assessments and EHC plan reviews.
- o Training was delivered for parents, SENCOs, HLTAs, TAs and teachers on person centred planning, the one-page profile and the structured conversation.

- **Cornwall** clarified the difference between 'outcomes' and a 'solution' in the EHC process, as there was some confusion. An outcome is a personal goal and a solution is the resource the SEN pupil needs to achieve their outcomes.

  - o The LA produced a parent-friendly model to illustrate the core principles of the EHC assessment and planning processes. This is illustrated in Figure 5.3.

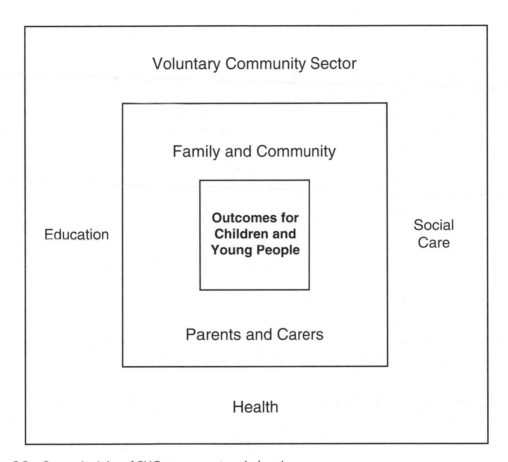

Figure 5.3 Core principles of EHC assessment and planning

- **Bromley** and **Cornwall** piloted the use of a mobile app to reinforce person centred planning and the personalisation of service provision, by turning text messages from families, young people with SEN and practitioners into action.

- **Greenwich** piloted person centred planning and multi-media advocacy with sample families in the learning disability community. iPads were given to nine families to seek their views and experiences on interacting with services virtually, via the Local Offer webpages to inform them about the EHC assessment and planning processes. They also used the iPad to capture their child's behaviour at home, so professionals could have first-hand evidence to inform the EHC assessment and planning processes. Conducting meetings remotely and virtually with young people, their family and professionals using video telephony, i.e. 'Facetime', is not only convenient, but also empowering for the young person.

Lessons learned from the SEND pathfinder project on the EHC process

- The EHC plan assessment meetings are a positive experience, as they are outcomes focused, adopt a solution-focused approach and take a wider, holistic approach to meeting the needs of the whole child, beyond just education, e.g. health and well-being needs.
- The EHC process aligns closely with the local offer, thus there need to be clear links between them.
- It can be challenging combining person centred planning principles with statutory requirements, in that it is very time consuming to administer.
- Key skills are required by those leading the EHC process, at LA and school level. The skills required include: the ability to run quality person centred planning focused meetings; being able to engage with a range of professionals; writing high quality notes during EHC plan meetings; time management; active listening; prioritisation; influencing and negotiating.
- The SENCO is likely to be identified by parents and carers of children and young people with SEN as being the ideal lead professional, leading and coordinating the EHC process in schools and other education settings.
- The use of technology to capture the behaviour of children in the home context, using the video facility on an iPad, did cause some concerns among some professionals, in relation to confidentiality, data sharing and safeguarding protocols.
- Parents choosing to use iPads to communicate information about their child's needs and behaviour at home do require pre-training in how to use this technology.

SENCOs may find Table 5.2 useful for evaluating an EHC plan meeting.

SENCOs may also wish to read the *SEND Pathfinder Information Pack Version 3 December 2013 – Coordinated Assessment and Education, Health and Care Plan*, which gives further information about the pilot local authorities' experiences of the EHC assessment and planning process. This can be accessed at: www.sendpathfinder.co.uk/infopacks/

There is also a valuable appendix, which offers model EHC plans from some of the pilot local authorities. This document is called *Coordinated Assessment and EHC Plan (December 2013) Appendix 1 – CDC EHC Plan Checklist and Example Plan*.

Using a person centred approach for the annual EHC plan review

The concept and features of an effective person centred approach

The person centred approach is a process of continual listening and learning, focusing on what is important to the child or young person with SEN now and in the future, and acting upon this information, in alliance with their family and friends. A person centred approach encourages the participation of the child, young person and their parents, in a less formal way, in the EHC plan review process. The person centred approach can help to facilitate and support the EHC plan process.

The term person centred review is also used in relation to a person centred approach. This utilises person centred thinking tools, to explore what is working and what is not, from the child or young person's perspective, the parents' perspective and the school's perspective, and to agree on actions for change, to address what is not working.

The Draft SEND Code of Practice (0–25) 2014 commented in relation to a person centred approach:

Table 5.2 Feedback questionnaire on the EHC plan review meeting

Please answer all the questions as best you can about the EHC plan meeting today.

Name: _____ Date of meeting:_____

Venue for meeting:_____

√ **one** box for each question below that matches your thoughts about today's meeting.

1. Was the purpose of the EHC plan meeting made clear to you?   YES ☐ NO ☐

2. Did you feel able to give your views at the EHC plan meeting?   YES ☐ NO ☐

3. Did you feel your views were listened to today at the meeting?   YES ☐ NO ☐

4. Were your views written down and taken seriously at the meeting?   YES ☐ NO ☐

5. Do you think the EHC plan meeting was well led and managed?   YES ☐ NO ☐

6. Do you feel OK about what the EHC plan's next steps are?   YES ☐ NO ☐

7. Were you happy with the venue for the meeting today?   YES ☐ NO ☐

8. Did you feel there was enough time for the meeting today?   YES ☐ NO ☐

9. What could be done to make the next EHC plan review meeting better?

_____

_____

_____

10. Is there anything else you wish to say about the EHC plan review meeting today?

_____

_____

_____

Thank you for taking the time to answer this questionnaire

Rita Cheminais' Handbook for SENCOs Second Edition, SAGE Publications Ltd © Rita Cheminais, 2015

By using this approach within a family context, professionals and local authorities can ensure that children, young people and parents are involved in all aspects of planning and decision-making. (DfE, 2014e: 9.21)

The SEND Code of Practice identifies the features of an effective person centred approach as being that which:

- focuses on the child or young person as an individual, and not on their SEN label
- enables children and young people and their parents to express their views, wishes and feelings
- enables children and young people and their parents to be part of the decision-making process
- is easy for children, young people and their parents or carers to understand, and uses clear ordinary language and images, rather than professional jargon
- highlights the child's or young person's strengths and capacities
- enables the child or young person and those who know them best to say what they have done, what they are interested in and what outcomes they are seeking in the future
- tailors support to the needs of the individual
- organises assessments to minimise demands on families
- brings together relevant professionals to discuss and agree together the overall approach
- delivers an outcomes-focused and coordinated plan for the child or young person and their parents (DfE, 2014e: 9.20).

An effective person centred approach starts with the individual child or young person, and takes into account their wishes and aspirations, the outcomes they seek and the support they need to achieve them.

The person centred approach enables the SEN child or young person to identify:

- what is working well and should stay the same in their additional provision
- what is not working in the provision, and therefore needs to change
- what really matters and is important to them and to their family and others
- how each person and professional who cares about them can help them to achieve their goals and aspirations, i.e. the support and help they need.

Five key features of an EHC plan person centred approach

- **The child or young person is at the centre** – they choose who to invite to their review meeting, the venue and the date for the meeting.
- **Family members and friends are partners in the planning** – they add richness of detail to the child's or young person's story, while providing possible clues for change in provision.
- **The plan reflects what is important** – to the child or young person, their capacities and what support they require, i.e. what they can do, their talents and strengths, what is important to them.
- **The plan results in actions** – what is possible now and in later life, e.g. to feel included in school, in the community, and later, when working.
- **The plan results in ongoing listening, learning and further action** – learning through shared action to create change for the better in the child's and young person's life.

The person centred approach, like the structured conversation, is empowering to use with parents and their child, as it gives ownership of both the EHC planning and review process. However, although both processes are time consuming, it is time well spent, in ensuring the child, young person and their parents feel valued for the contributions they make.

Research has revealed that a person centred approach may be less effective in some instances, as it does not suit every child or young person, particularly those with mental health issues, autism, or restricted mobility, as they may find it more difficult to lead and control the process themselves. However, technology can overcome such a difficulty. Through the use of multi-media website software, i.e. Wiki, or a mobile application, combined with a symbol system like PECS or Makaton, the child or young person is able to create their own personalised single plan, with accompanying information, for their annual EHC plan review.

Good practice cameos

Multi-media advocacy and person centred planning (Greenwich)

The young person with intellectual and communication difficulties uses an 'Easy Build Wiki Website' tool for person centred planning in school. It is password-protected for security, and the young person can log into Wiki with Makaton symbols, if typing is problematic.

Wiki utilises a multi-media approach using words, pictures, video clips and sound as ways of conveying the young person's preferences and viewpoints. The aim of using Wiki is to build, compile and develop a personal multi-media centred portfolio for the young person to utilise as part of the EHC plan review process.

The opening page of the Wiki resembles a visual mind map, for the single plan, which has a number of sections that are important to the young person. For example, family, communication, mobility and care, school, social, having fun. Clicking on any of these sections opens another Wiki webpage for viewing or adding information to.

Parents can upload and store photographs, videos and documents on Wiki to support the EHC plan review process. The parents can control who has access to this information.

The Wiki also enables the young person with support to produce a two-minute training video for any new staff who work with him to view how to correctly fit his splints.

Wiki has enabled greater consistency in practice to be maintained between home and school, in relation to the young person's development and learning.

There is a short version and a longer version of this model of good practice to view on YouTube at: www.youtube.com/watch?v=76q1U31ihw0&feature=youtu.be or: bit.ly/sc214-53

It can also be accessed from within the SEND pathfinder information pack.

Mobile application to support person centred planning and personalised service provision (Bromley and Cornwall)

The mobile application is designed as a tool to support the person centred framework, and turn messages from families, young people and practitioners into action. It is for use by parents of disabled children and young people. The information gathered is then shared with professionals, e.g. doctors, nurses, teachers and the young person's employers.

The app provides a single plan format which has the potential to form the basis of the new EHC plan. Information entered can be in the form of a text message, photographs, films, resources or documents. Each of the sections on the single plan has separate sharing permissions attached to them. Examples of the sections on the app include: (1) Your associated people – all those the user has access to information

(Continued)

(Continued)

about. (2) Home page – which leads to a series of sections, including templates that the individual can complete and can share with others. (3) My plan – accessed through the home page and has a number of different optional sections that enable the user to build their own plan, e.g. one-page profile, important people, what's working, support plan, communication preferences, decision-making; a chart to explore how to present choices to support the young person's decision-making and learning preferences. (4) Developmental journal to log achievements, upload pictures and videos. (5) Timeline – ability to write entries, upload films, documents and photographs. (6) Information about conditions and disabilities (7) Documents – assessments, e-books, reports, articles. (8) Local offer – links to all the local offers across England. (9) Contacts database. (10) Diary – to keep track of appointments. (11) Messaging.

More information is available at: www.ncb.org.uk/early-support

The previous Labour government's three-year strategy for people with learning disabilities, Valuing People Now, promoted person centred reviews at transition, which focused on future employment as an outcome for young people.

Learning disability services have led the way in person centred planning for some time.

The component parts of the person centred approach

Basically, the person centred approach and review process is organised into two main parts:

Part 1 – gathers information about what everyone concerned likes and admires about the SEN pupil, identifies what is important to them and for them, what help and support they need, and what is currently working and not working for them at school.
Part 2 – reviews the information and agrees subsequent actions.

The component parts of the person centred approach to support EHC plan reviews are described and illustrated in Figure 5.4.

Further information and downloadable resources about the use of the person centred approach in schools can be found at: www.helensandersonassociates.co.uk

SENCOs working with more complex SEN pupils may wish to explore Wiki at: www.rixcentre.org Multi-media advocacy video case studies can be viewed at: www.multimediaadvocacy.com and Talking Mats at www.talkingmats.com

Multi-media advocacy enables pupils with more complex SEN to organise their thinking, prompt their memory and communicate their views and wishes.

Using the structured conversation to empower parents of SEN pupils

The origin and concept of the structured conversation

The structured conversation originated as one of the strands from the previous Labour government's Achievement for All (AfA) initiative, which was piloted in 454 maintained schools, from September 2009 to September 2011. The structured conversation in AfA was designed to foster greater and more constructive involvement of parents of SEN pupils, and to improve parental relationships with the school, particularly among those parents who were considered to be 'harder to reach'.

The structured conversation is a listening conversation, designed to improve parental engagement and to change the nature of the dialogue between parents and the school; i.e. it is open, supportive and allows for the free exchange of information and views between parents, the school and the teacher/SENCO.

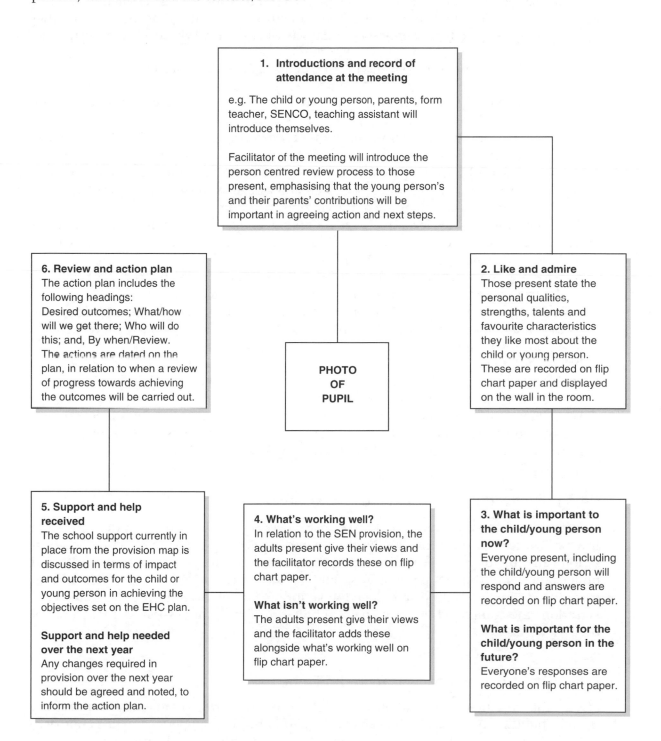

1. Introductions and record of attendance at the meeting

e.g. The child or young person, parents, form teacher, SENCO, teaching assistant will introduce themselves.

Facilitator of the meeting will introduce the person centred review process to those present, emphasising that the young person's and their parents' contributions will be important in agreeing action and next steps.

6. Review and action plan
The action plan includes the following headings:
Desired outcomes; What/how will we get there; Who will do this; and, By when/Review.
The actions are dated on the plan, in relation to when a review of progress towards achieving the outcomes will be carried out.

PHOTO
OF
PUPIL

2. Like and admire
Those present state the personal qualities, strengths, talents and favourite characteristics they like most about the child or young person. These are recorded on flip chart paper and displayed on the wall in the room.

5. Support and help received
The school support currently in place from the provision map is discussed in terms of impact and outcomes for the child or young person in achieving the objectives set on the EHC plan.

Support and help needed over the next year
Any changes required in provision over the next year should be agreed and noted, to inform the action plan.

4. What's working well?
In relation to the SEN provision, the adults present give their views and the facilitator records these on flip chart paper.

What isn't working well?
The adults present give their views and the facilitator adds these alongside what's working well on flip chart paper.

3. What is important to the child/young person now?
Everyone present, including the child/young person will respond and answers are recorded on flip chart paper.

What is important for the child/young person in the future?
Everyone's responses are recorded on flip chart paper.

Figure 5.4 Overview of the person centred review

The structured conversation is recommended to form part of the EHC plan review process, accompanying the one-page profile and person centred planning.

The aims and purpose of the structured conversation

The approach the structured conversation takes focuses on listening to the views of parents and the SEN pupil, in order to better understand what they identify as the main barriers to learning and participation. It also enables both parties to identify what they consider has worked well in relation to SEN provision, and to say what else they would wish to see in place.

Undertaking a structured conversation with parents of SEN pupils aims to:

- facilitate a more positive relationship that has a shared purpose of improving the educational achievement of the pupil with SEN
- promote ongoing two-way communication between parents, the child and the teacher/ SENCO, and clarify the most effective means for parental communication
- provide a means by which parents can make their contribution heard and understood, and feel reassured that any concerns or views they have expressed will be acted upon
- build up a greater understanding of the child in their home context
- draw upon the knowledge parents have about their child, i.e. their child's strengths, what they enjoy and can do well, and the barriers that can get in the way of them making progress and feeling good about themselves
- help to raise the aspirations of the parents and the school about what the SEN pupil can attain, through a focus on progress and achieving better outcomes for them
- develop a genuine trusting collaborative partnership which makes the parents feel more confident about engaging with their child's school and teachers, and taking a greater part in supporting their child's learning and development at home
- help to clarify the responsibilities of the parents, the SEN pupil and the school
- enable parents to participate in identifying the support their child needs in order to meet the agreed set targets and expected outcomes
- keep parents well informed about their child's progress and the next steps in learning
- use the outcomes from the structured conversation with parents to help improve the learning, teaching and SEN provision for the pupil.

Who is involved in the structured conversation

The structured conversation usually takes place between the parent(s) and the class/form teacher, with or without the SENCO. Too many people attending the structured conversation can stifle discussion. Where appropriate, and depending on the age, maturity and understanding of the SEN pupil, they should have a chance to join in the structured conversation, at some point. Where the pupil is not directly involved in the structured conversation, the completed one-page pupil profile can support discussion and take note of their views.

When the structured conversation should be held

Ideally, the structured conversation should take place each term, to coincide with reviewing the SEN pupil's progress and achievements, as part of the SEN Support graduated approach, or the EHC plan process. It can also be aligned with the school's regular cycle of discussions with parents and carers, e.g. parents' evenings, or 'meet the teacher' days.

The framework for the structured conversation

The conversation is structured around four key stages. These are: Explore, Focus, Plan and Review. Each stage is intended to open the conversation, in order that general issues may be understood properly, and then the discussion is narrowed down and focuses on key issues and points for subsequent future action, target setting and the review and summing up of what has been discussed and agreed at the meeting.

Figure 5.5 illustrates the four stages in the structured conversation framework.

Each stage of the structured conversation is explored in more depth in Table 5.3, which can act as an aide memoire to the process for teachers.

The SENCO and the teacher leading the structured conversation may also find Table 5.4 equally useful, for making notes and recording key points arising from the discussion with parents.

Those involved in leading the structured conversation with parents need to remember that there has to be a balance between celebratory positive comments and constructive critical feedback during the conversation. For example, best practice is to make a positive comment, then a constructive critical comment, followed by another positive celebratory comment. This strategy is referred to as the 'sandwich' approach.

Figure 5.5 Structured conversation framework

Table 5.3   At-a-glance guide to the structured conversation

1. EXPLORE – Opening up to explore and understand	2. FOCUS – Narrowing the point of focus on key issues
Key features: • Non-verbal cues of the teacher put parents at ease • Teacher is attentive, listens actively • Silence is used to allow parents thinking time • Teacher paraphrases what a parent has said to check understanding • Teacher shows empathy • Teacher asks questions to gain parents' hopes and aspirations for their child. **Suggested questions:** • What do you consider are the needs of your child? • What do you want for your child in school? • What have been the barriers to your child achieving? • What has worked well in the past to help your child learn? • What do you feel are the limits to your child's potential?	**Key features:** • Being explicit about the nature of aspiration and need • Teacher summarising to draw themes and key points together, to prevent the discussion straying from the focus • Enabling parents to raise an issue or topic (prioritising) • Teacher avoiding using 'How' and 'Why' questions at this stage • Teacher phrasing questions as positive statements, to get key information from parents **Suggested questions:** • Can you tell me something more about when your child ...? • What could you do differently at home with your child next time ...? • Have you any idea why the approach you suggest might work better?
3. PLAN – Actions to address key issues and priorities	4. REVIEW – Summary of key points and clarify next steps

Key features:
 	
 • Teacher gives parents information on their child's provision, progress and achievements to enable them to make a decision as to whether the SEN provision is OK or needs changing
 • Agreed targets set which have a level of challenge
 • Parents consulted on how they feel they can help their child at home
 • Teacher clarifies what strategies and interventions are being put in place at school
 • Parents consulted on timescales and success criteria to evaluate impact of provision
 • Teacher clarifies the ongoing assessment of the child's progress
 • A plan is produced as an outcome of the conversation, which is clear, concise and includes long-term and short-term goals.
	Key features:
	
	 • Teacher summarises the main points:
	   – We have talked about these things today
	   – We've identified the areas we agree are important to target for improvement
	   – This is the agreed plan to put in place
	   – Do you feel the plan will work?
	   – Can you see a difference in your child?
	 • Teacher agrees on how a parent wishes to communicate for follow-up
	 • Dates for next meetings are agreed
	 • Named contact in school provided
	 • Teacher seeks parents' feedback on how they felt the discussion went today.
	
	 Suggested questions
	 • How well do you feel today's meeting has gone?
	 • Is there anything else you want to tell me or add?
	 • Have we missed anything important?
	 • Do you feel we have listened well enough, understood and appreciated the issues you raised?
	 • Is there anything else you want to ask about the next steps or the outcomes from today's meeting?

Table 5.4 Model template for recording key points arising from a structured conversation

Structured conversation stage	Parents' views, concerns, issues, comments Key points	Teacher/SENCO comments Key points
Explore		
Focus		
Plan		
Review		

It was recommended in the AfA initiative that a contract of agreement should be drawn up with the parents at the first initial structured conversation, to agree:

- the aims of the conversation
- the time available for the conversation
- the number of meetings required
- confidentiality.

It is a matter of personal choice for the SENCO and teacher leading the structured conversation as to whether they impose the formality of a contract of agreement for structured conversations, as some parents may find the formality somewhat off-putting, particularly if they have had little or no previous engagement with the school.

Subsequent structured conversations, following the initial discussion, will focus on: the progress the SEN pupil has made against the agreed targets and if the SEN provision and plan of action need amending.

The best source of reference for the structured conversation can be found in a previous DCSF (2009) publication, which has been archived and is entitled: *Achievement for All: The Structured Conversation. Handbook to Support Training.*

Making best use of personal budgets for SEN

The origin and concept of the personal budget

Personal budgets evolved from social care funding originally. A personal budget is an amount of money identified by the local authority to deliver all or some of the provision set out in a child's or young person's EHC plan. Young people and parents of children who have EHC plans have the right to request the local authority to prepare a personal budget, which may contain elements of education, social care and health funding. Education funding for personal budgets comes from the local authority's High Needs Block, and it also may incorporate the school's notional SEN budget, providing the school is agreeable to permitting the £6,000 to contribute to the SEN child's personal budget.

Figure 5.6 provides an example of an extract from a young person's EHC plan, which identifies how the personal budget has been allocated across education, health and social care.

The types of provision a personal budget may secure

The main advantage of personal budgets is that they offer greater control and choice to families with children and young people who have more complex needs which require additional provision, beyond the school day.

Table 5.5 provides an illustrative example of the range of different provisions a personal budget may purchase, with approximate costs.

How much money does a personal budget offer?

Personal budgets allocated to families or young people with SEND vary, according to the complexity and severity of the needs of the individual child or young person. However, a personal budget to secure additional provision can be in the range of £1,700 to £16,500 per year, with £10,200 being the average.

PERSONAL BUDGET

Allocated provision supported by the personal budget
(Please tick the appropriate boxes)

Does the family/young person wish to take a personal budget this year?

YES ☐   NO ☐

Personal budget source(s)

Notional SEN budget ☐	Notional SEN budget & ☑	Direct payment ☐
(Element 2)	High Needs Block	
	(Element 3)	

The total personal budget allocation for the year is: | £13,019.50 |

Description of the personal budget provision		Annual Cost
EDUCATION	Teaching assistant support for 25 hours per week over 12 months (Element 2)	£6,545.50
	Teacher direct work and advice from the Sensory Impairment Service for 1 hour per week over 12 months (Element 3)	£1,710.00
HEALTH	Speech and language therapist delivering an intensive SaLT programme for 1 hour per week over 12 months (Element 3)	£1,020.00
SOCIAL CARE	Support from a personal assistant for 6 hours per week over 52 weeks a year, to enable Paul's engagement in a range of leisure & social activities in the community (Element 3)	£3,744.00
OTHER, e.g. Voluntary sector		
Total personal budget spent		**£13,019.50**

Figure 5.6   Example of a personal budget page from an EHC plan

Personal budget funding can be pooled across health, education and social care, or it can remain as separate funding sources, per service.

How a personal budget may be delivered

The SEND pathfinder on personal budgets found the following options existing in the participating local authorities for delivery:

- **Notional arrangement** – where the LA keeps the funding but the parent or carer or young person directs its use.
- **Third party arrangement** – where the personal budget funds are paid to a named representative/organisation, on behalf of the parent/carer and young person, and they manage the funds for them.

Table 5.5 Services a personal budget for SEN may purchase

Education	Health	Social care
Transport to take a young person to work placement for 2 weeks @ £200 Electronic communication tools and supportive software @ £415	Speech and language therapist for 12 months @ £1,020 Modifications to child's home – ramp for wheelchair access	Holiday respite for 2 days a week over 12 weeks @ £2,700 Holiday placement at a camp for a week @ £225 Personal assistant support for 3 hours per week for 13 weeks over school holidays @ £409.50 Family break additional costs @ £301 Attendance at sessions and events at a day centre over a year @ £1,160 2 x 4 hour sessions per week at a childminder during school holidays (13 weeks per year) @ £5 per hour (total £520) Transport to special school play scheme during summer holidays @ £10 per travel journey (total £60) Family break – additional costs @ £301

- **Direct payments** – where the parents/carers and young person receive the money directly to purchase the services themselves.
- **A Trust** – this is established to act on behalf of the disabled child and their family and holds and manages the money for them.
- **A service provider** – is paid the personal budget directly and they manage the money through an Individual Service Fund (ISF), which stipulates that the personal budget funding is ring-fenced, and can only be spent on behalf of the SEND young person and their family.
- **The LA Care Manager** – acts on behalf of the child, young person and their family, and then organises service provision based on their allocated budget.

The list above for managing and spending the personal budget appears to be a fairly mixed model. However, over time, the best and most efficient model that suits the preferences of families and young people will emerge as best practice.

Learning from the SEND pathfinder on personal budgets

What appears to have been learned among the local authorities participating in the personal budget SEND pathfinder is as follows:

- Personal budgets have helped to reinforce the importance of a person centred approach, focused on outcomes for the child or young person, rather than on provision, i.e. hours of support at so many £s.
- Personal budgets require a family centred approach, whereby there is effective partnership working and good integrated delivery between providers from health, education and social care.
- Clear communication from an early stage with families is essential in relation to informing them about the different ways a personal budget can be offered. The local authority's

'Local Offer' should also explain this, along with information about who may be eligible for a personal budget and how it can be accessed.

- A phased approach to the deployment of personal budget funds should be offered to families, with accompanying managerial support, until they feel they are equipped to take on the management of the personal budget themselves.

Local authorities and other independent parent advisers will play a major role initially in guiding and advising families and young people with SEND on how to make best use of their personal budget. SENCOs should not find themselves being too embroiled in the financial aspects of provision on the EHC plan, as the focus is on outcomes for the child or young person with SEND. SENCOs may find the following resources a useful point of further reference regarding personal budgets for SEN:

SEND Pathfinder Information Pack. Version 3 (December 2013) – *Personal Budgets* (Mott-MacDonald, 2013b; accessed at: www.sendpathfinder.co.uk
DfE (2011b) *Individual Budgets for Families with Disabled Children: Final Evaluation Report: The IB Process*. DfE-RR145

Getting to grips with the 'Local Offer'

Concept and origin of the Local Offer

The Draft SEN Code of Practice (0–25) commented:

Local authorities **must** publish a Local Offer, setting out in one place information about provision they expect to be available across education, health and social care for children and young people in their area who have SEN or are disabled, including those who do not have Education, Health and Care (EHC) plans. (DfE, 2014e: 4.1)

The Local Offer has come about in response to concerns from parents and others that they find it hard to access information about what support is available for them and their child in the local area. All local authorities in England have to publish a Local Offer in accordance with the Special Educational Needs and Disability Regulations 2014 (Part 4), which provide a common framework for the Local Offer.

The key aims of the Local Offer

The local authority's Local Offer has three key aims:

- to provide clear, comprehensive and accessible information about the provision available
- to make provision more responsive to local needs and aspirations by directly involving children and young people with SEN, their parents and carers and the service provider in its development and review
- to help the local authority and their health partners to improve provision for children and young people with SEN and their families.

A local authority can have over 2,000 services and providers contributing to the Local Offer. The challenge for local authorities therefore is to keep this information up-to-date, and not just produce a directory of existing services.

What the Local Offer must include

The Special Educational Needs and Disability Regulations 2014 (Part 4) and the SEND Code of Practice (0–25) 2014 both provide a common framework for the Local Offer, and specify clearly who the local authority should consult with when they are preparing, developing, publishing and reviewing their Local Offer.

The local authority Local Offer must include:

- special educational, health and social care provision for children and young people with SEN or disabilities
- arrangements for the identification of SEN and assessing children's and young people's SEN, including arrangements for EHC needs assessments
- details of how parents and young people can request an assessment for an EHC plan and the education, health and social care provision available locally from universal, targeted and specialist services, including that from other providers, e.g. the voluntary community sector
- other educational provision such as sports or arts provision
- the provision available from outside the local authority which is likely to be used, e.g. cross-border provision, residential special school provision
- the provision available in local early years settings, maintained and non-maintained special schools and mainstream schools – with and without separate special units, academies – pupil referral units (PRUs) and 16+ institutions
- post-16 education and training provision
- details about the support for young people with SEN preparing for adulthood, including preparation for employment, independent living and participation in the community
- information about apprenticeships, traineeships and supported internships
- transport travel arrangements to and from schools, post-16 institutions and early years providers
- support for children and young people with SEN, moving between phases in education (transfer and transition)
- where to get information, advice and support for families with children and young people with SEND, e.g. support groups, parents and carers forums, Parent Partnership Service
- information about leisure activities for children and young people with SEN and their families
- information about child care, including suitable provision for disabled children and those with SEN
- details about the support available to young people in higher education, particularly on the Disabled Students Allowance (DSA) and the process and timescales for making an application for DSA
- information on what to do if parents, children and young people are not happy about their provision, e.g. how to make a complaint, how to seek mediation support for resolving any disagreements; and the right to appeal to the First-Tier Tribunal (SEN and disability)
- the arrangements for providing top-up funding and how parents and young people with an EHC plan can access, use and manage a personal budget
- published comments from service users on the content of the local authority's Local Offer, the accessibility of the information in the Local Offer and how involved parents, SEN children and young people have felt in developing and reviewing the Local Offer.

The local authority Local Offer has to be widely accessible and published on their website. The local authority must consult children and young people with SEN, and their parents/carers, on what should be included in the Local Offer; how the Local Offer information should be set out, when published; and how it will be made available to those families without internet access, and to those who require the information in different formats and languages.

What should be included in an education setting's Local Offer

The SEND pathfinder on the Local Offer signposts readers to an example of a school's Local Offer website area. This provides a useful model for a SENCO to consider when producing their own unique Local Offer information for the education setting's website.

The following information needs to be included in an education setting's Local Offer:

- The home page should briefly describe the school's vision for SEN, accompanied by a statement of intent relating to their Local Offer, both of which will indicate that these have been co-produced with parents, SEN pupils and governors.
- A summary of the school's overall strengths in SEN provision should be highlighted, supported by testimonials, e.g. OFSTED inspection evidence, parents' and SEN pupils' comments.
- An overview/menu of the additional and different SEN provision available at the school is then listed, under the headings of the four areas of SEN: e.g. provision for pupils with cognition and learning needs; provision for pupils with communication and interaction needs; provision for pupils with sensory/physical needs; provision for pupils with social, emotional and mental health difficulties, with each area being subdivided into provision at SEN Support and at EHC plan stage.
- Information should be included about the point of contact for SEN – SENCO contact details, accompanied by staffing for SEN provision, with relevant qualifications/areas of SEN expertise.
- Information is given about how the school manages and reviews its SEN Support and EHC plans.
- A 'Frequently Asked Questions' page is included, which offers answers to commonly asked parent and pupil questions on SEN provision.
- Signposting and links to further information are also included, e.g. local and national organisations, advice and support available in school and locally from the Parent Partnership Service.
- There must also be details about when and how the school's Local Offer will be reviewed, and how parents, SEN pupils, service providers, governors are involved in this process and help to inform the ongoing development of the Local Offer in school.

SENCOs may find it useful to undertake an internet search to view other education settings' websites on how they have published their Local Offer.

The *SEND Pathfinder Information Pack. Version 3* (December 2013) provides a webpage link to a school's Local Offer, which may be of interest: www.send pathfinder.co.uk

What has been learned from the SEND pathfinder on the Local Offer

A number of local authorities were involved in the Local Offer SEND pathfinder. These included: Darlington, East Sussex, Hampshire, Hartlepool, North Yorkshire County Council, Oldham, Solihull and Oldham.

The following points have arisen from their experiences of preparing, developing and publishing an initial Local Offer:

- Focus groups and user testing with parents/carers, children and young people with SEN help the development and refining of the Local Offer, e.g. views on website design templates, the use of interactive route maps to support filtering of information, the ease of navigation and the presentation of Local Offer content.

- Don't forget to consider the other ways for families to access the Local Offer on the internet, e.g. information brokers and Local Offer 'tourist guides' within public libraries, school and college libraries, community centres, children's centres, who can support those families who don't have internet access at home to use the facility in those public locations.
- It is useful to produce a short paper version of the Local Offer containing key information.
- A user-led approach has helped to ensure that the Local Offer is designed in a way that those using it can easily understand and use it to meet their requirements.
- Building upon the good practice existing in the local authority Family Information Service, the Parent Partnership Service and the Parent Carer Forum help to develop a comprehensive Local Offer.
- Engagement with service providers early on helps to clarify the Local Offer and shape it, particularly if it aligns with commissioning, personalisation and personal budgets.
- Developing a large Local Offer is daunting, therefore it is helpful to break it down into component parts, and develop it over time.
- Offering support to schools and other education settings at a collective meeting has helped to develop a consistent approach in producing Local Offers.

SENCOs may find the local authorities' learning experiences useful in relation to informing the publication of their own education setting's Local Offer.

What works well in relation to a Local Offer

The SEND pathfinder project on the Local Offer has identified what works well in relation to developing, producing and publishing a Local Offer, at local authority level. This good practice readily transfers to developing a Local Offer at school level.

What works well is:

- Having a single point of contact for families at different stages in their SEN provision journey in using the Local Offer is helpful, particularly for signposting; e.g. having a 'Local Offer champion' to provide impartial advice, support and guidance on the services available.
- Having someone families can talk things through with regarding services available in the Local Offer is useful, e.g. which is best, to suit needs.
- Having the facility to talk to other parents/families with SEN children and young people who have accessed or used a particular service is also helpful.
- Having the Local Offer on the local authority website was daunting and overwhelming, in relation to the amount of information it held. Summary leaflets and booklets for parents were welcome which provided a comprehensive overview of the services available and how to make best use and navigate the local authority Local Offer website pages.
- Taking into consideration cross-border services to include in the Local Offer.
- Organising services under different headings on the local authority Local Offer website was helpful. One local authority listed services according to whether they were universal, targeted or specialist. Another local authority organised their services on the website according to the four areas of SEN. Another local authority organised their local offer under Health, Social Care, Education, Community and Leisure headings, and then for each service area, the provision available was graduated according to the age of the service user.
- Producing fact sheets for parents which cover specific topics relating to the EHC plan process, e.g. personal budgets, commissioning, person centred planning, the structured conversation, the role of decision-making organisations such as the CCG, Healthwatch, the Health and Wellbeing Boards.
- Incorporating a star rating/service user feedback facility on the Local Offer website, which can help to provide a quality assurance check on services.

- Having a 'Frequently Asked Questions' section on the Local Offer website area proved to be popular with families and young people.
- Holding a provision mapping workshop for SENCOs in the local authority enabled schools to map their additional and different SEN provision, for inclusion on the school's and local authority's Local Offer webpages.

Figure 5.7 provides a model template for SENCOs to use to map the additional and different SEN provision in their Local Offer.

Signposting families to impartial information, advice and support

There are a number of local and national organisations that provide information, advice and support to parents and carers of children and young people with special educational needs and/or disabilities (SEND). SENCOs are likely to be familiar with those organisations and services operating locally. National organisations have many useful resources to sign-post parents and carers to.

Parent Partnership Service

The Parent Partnership Service (PPS) is a statutory service. There is one in every local authority. It is a free, impartial and confidential service, offering advice and support to parents and carers of children and young people with SEN. The aim of the PPS is to provide a menu of flexible services which aim to help parents and carers to play an active and informed role in relation to their child's SEN provision.

The PPS activities include:

- a confidential helpline
- support in preparing for and attending meetings
- help with filling in forms and writing letters and reports
- support for parents and carers in resolving disagreements with the LA and school
- signposting parents and carers to other statutory and voluntary services
- links to local parent support groups and forums
- ensuring that parents' and carers' views help to inform local SEN policy and practice
- training opportunities for parents and professionals
- working with the families of children and young people who have been excluded from school.

The National Parent Partnership Network

The National Parent Partnership Network (NPPN) is funded by the DfE to:

- promote the work of PPSs across the country
- provide a national network for PPSs to learn from each other and to share information and good practice
- provide support and information to local PPSs
- provide training for PPS workers
- work with the PPS, LAs and others to ensure parents have access to high quality parent partnership services at a local level.

The NPPN is based in London at the Council for Disabled Children, which sits with the National Children's Bureau (NCB).

THE SCHOOL'S LOCAL OFFER FOR SEN PROVISION

SEN threshold	Cognition and learning	Communication and interaction	Social, emotional and mental health difficulties	Physical and/or sensory needs
SEN Support				
EHC plan				

The school's Local Offer is updated, to reflect the full diversity of pupils with SEN, as they join the school, throughout the year.

The additional and different SEN provision reflects reasonable adjustments, which have required additional resourcing.

It also includes provision from the voluntary community sector, in addition to that provided by Education, Health and Social Care Services.

Figure 5.7   Template for mapping an education setting's Local Offer

Contact a Family

Contact a Family is a national charity which supports the families of disabled children. They have 30 years' experience of working with these families. Their vision is to empower families with disabled children to live the lives they want and to achieve their full potential in the community and society as a whole.

Contact a Family offers support, information and advice to over 340,000 families per year. This organisation is the delivery partner for the DfE, supporting the development of parent carer participation and parent carer forums across England. In addition to this important role they also:

- campaign for the rights and justice of all families with disabled children
- offer a freephone helpline for parents and professionals across the UK
- produce a wide range of publications, newsletters, parent guides and research reports
- put families who have children with similar needs in touch with each other via their 'Linking Families' service and through their online social networking site
- produce the Contact a Family Directory which gives information on a range of medical conditions and disabilities, and the support groups available
- offer one-to-one practical and emotional support to families of disabled children, via their Family Support Service, their local offices and through their volunteer parent representatives.

SENCOs may signpost parents and carers to their website (www.cafamily.org.uk) to explore the free downloadable resources available, including a YouTube video on the work of Contact a Family, which can be viewed at: www.youtube.com/cafamily Publications include *How to Guide to Parent Participation and Parent Carer Participation: An Overview*, which can be accessed at: www.cafamily.org.uk/families/parentparticipation/index.html

Contact a Family also works in partnership with the National Network of Parent Carer Forums (NNPCF).

National Network of Parent Carer Forums

The NNPCF links all the parent carer forums across England. They ensure that local parent carer forums are aware of national developments, and promote opportunities for parent carers' 'voice' to influence decision-making at a national level. They work closely with the DfE and the DoH and other partner organisations to improve outcomes for children and young people with SEND and their families. SENCOs may signpost parents and carers of SEND children to the YouTube video on parent partnership entitled: *Working Together: Our Experience of Co-Production,* which can be accessed at: www.youtube.com/watch?v=Ze gFplpKFw

This video, produced by the NNPCF and the SE7 SEND pathfinder, in collaboration with the DfE, provides examples from parent carer forums of parents and carers of disabled children working in partnership with local authority officers, to inform decision-making at a strategic level and to provide appropriate services for families and their children and young people with disabilities.

Parent carer forums

Local parent carer forums (PCFs) were first introduced in 2008, under the then Labour government. They have subsequently developed with the help of government funding, in most local authorities. The DfE has made a commitment to continue to support parent carer forums until April 2015.

Parent carer forums are supported by Parent Partnership Services at the local level, to develop as parent carer led organisations. A PCF is a constituted group made up of parents and carers of disabled children and young people, and/or those with SEN, who work with LAs, education, health and social care services and other providers to make sure the services they plan and deliver really do meet the needs of disabled children and their families. Through its parent representatives the parent carer forum ensures that a common understanding about effective services for disabled children and young people is reached, at a local level.

There are three essential elements for successful parent carer participation:

- good, relevant and timely information
- honest consultation, which promotes two-way communication
- effective participation requiring commitment from parents and professionals.

There are six principles underpinning good joint working for parent carer forums and the PPS:

- a shared belief in raising the quality of life, improving outcomes and opportunities for all SEND children and their families
- clarity over each other's respective roles and responsibilities
- commitment to partnership working to support, train and empower parents to have a 'voice'
- acknowledging the development of each other's practice
- open and solution focused communication
- public support of and championing each other's contributions.

These six principles were part of the Together is Better agreement, which can found in Appendix 1 of the NPPN/Contact a Family publication *Together is Better. A Report. April 2013.*

Independent supporters

On 7 January 2014 the DfE announced a new Independent Support Fund of £30 million, managed by the Council for Disabled Children (CDC) as the DfE's strategic reform partner, to recruit and train 1,800 independent supporters (SEN Champions), who would be drawn from independent, voluntary, community and private organisations. It is envisaged there will be 12 independent supporters in each local authority in England.

The role of the independent supporter is to spend one-to-one time with families who have a child or young person with SEN, to give them the independent help and advice they need to progress through the new SEN system. They will offer support to any families who have a disagreement about assessment and the EHC plan process, to ensure local authorities understand what families want.

The independent supporters will also support the PPS and local authorities, as the implementation of the new SEN system rolls out from September 2014.

Points to remember

- Parents are equal partners in having a say about their child's SEN provision.
- Effective joint commissioning is informed by the experiences of children, young people with SEN and their families.
- The one-page profile acts as a starting point to gather person centred information.
- EHC plans are outcomes focused, favouring a person centred approach to planning and review.
- The person centred approach takes into account the wishes and aspirations of the SEN child or young person, the outcomes they seek and the support they need to achieve these.
- The structured conversation is designed to improve parental engagement with the school, through the free exchange of information and views between parents and teachers.
- A personal budget is an amount of money identified by the LA to deliver all or some of the provision set out in a child's or young person's EHC plan.
- The Local Offer sets out in one place information about the provision the LA expects to be available for SEND children and young people in the area.
- Families of children and young people with SEND are entitled to impartial information, advice and support.

Further activities

The following questions, focused on aspects covered in this chapter, meet the requirements of the National Award for Special Educational Needs Coordination, and support reflection and the professional development of experienced and newly appointed SENCOs.

1. How will you go about enhancing the participation of parents and carers of SEN pupils in relation to informing decision-making about SEN provision in your educational setting?
2. You have been asked by the headteacher to give a presentation to the governors on the value of using the one-page profile and the structured conversation as part of the EHC plan review process. Produce a PowerPoint presentation for this meeting.
3. A class teacher is not feeling confident about using the person centred approach. Describe the strategies you would use with them to address this issue.
4. A parent of one of your SEN pupils with an EHC plan would like to have a personal budget, following her child's annual review. What advice would you give to them in relation to making best use of this High Needs Block funding?
5. You are in the process of updating the SEN webpages on the school's website. Draft a couple of new pages which will reflect your school's Local Offer for SEN, in light of the new SEND system.

 Online materials

To access electronic versions of the material in this chapter visit: www.sagepub.co.uk/cheminais2e

Figure 5.2 One-page profile
Figure 5.4 Overview of the person centred approach
Figure 5.6 Example of a personal budget page from an EHC plan
Figure 5.7 Template for mapping an education setting's Local Offer
Table 5.1 Sections in an EHC plan
Table 5.2 Feedback questionnaire on the EHC plan review meeting
Table 5.3 At-a-glance guide to the structured conversation
Table 5.4 Model template for recording key points arising from a structured conversation
Table 5.5 Services a personal budget for SEN may purchase

6

Accountability for SEN

> **This chapter covers:**
>
> - accountability for SEN provision
> - gathering evidence through classroom walkthroughs
> - undertaking an SEN learning walk to collect evidence
> - monitoring SEN provision through lesson observations
> - undertaking the scrutiny of SEN pupils' work
> - appreciative inquiry and focused discussions with key stakeholders
> - evaluating the impact of integrated working
> - external accountability – OFSTED inspections and SEND.

Accountability for SEN provision

The term accountability refers to the obligation of an individual or organisation to account for their activities, accept responsibility for them, and to disclose the results in a transparent manner. It also ensures the school is answerable and held to account for the effectiveness of the SEN provision it offers, in respect of how the school's SEN funding has been effectively allocated and used.

The new 2014 national SEND statutory framework strengthens schools' accountability for SEN in a number of ways:

- through an enhanced focus on SEN pupil outcomes via the EHC plan annual review process
- through SEN reforms, i.e. the legal requirements in Part 3 of the Children and Families Act 2014, the Special Educational Needs and Disability Regulations 2014, the Special Educational Needs (Personal Budgets and Direct Payments) Regulations Section 49 and the SEND Code of Practice (0–25) 2014
- through the SEN funding arrangements for schools and academies in respect of the impact the SEN provision it has commissioned and procured with the money has had on SEN pupils' progress and achievements
- through enhanced parent and SEN pupil voice, in them having a say about the provision offered, via the structured conversation and person centred planning processes, as part of the graduated approach to SEN
- through the requirement on schools to publicise SEN information on their website, e.g. reporting on the school's Local Offer, the effectiveness of its additional provision and engaging parents/SEN pupils in consultation about what should be included in the school's SEN offer

- through the schools' performance management and appraisal systems for teachers and teaching assistants, i.e. every teacher and TA has a performance management objective set, which relates to SEN pupil achievement
- through the schools' governance system, i.e. the governing body are the responsible body for ensuring that the necessary SEN provision is made for all SEN pupils in the school
- through the school's own 'Parent Charter for SEN', which provides a checklist of what parents and carers of SEN pupils can expect in relation to SEN provision
- through the OFSTED inspection process, where there is a focus on the extent to which the education provided by the school meets the needs of disabled pupils and those with SEN
- through the local authority's Local Offer, where parents and SEN children and young people have had the opportunity, through consultation, to shape and influence the SEN provision, at a local level.

The SENCO needs to be aware of all these forms of accountability when they undertake their ongoing and annual monitoring and evaluation of SEN policy and provision.

This chapter outlines the strategies and approaches the SENCO can utilise, in partnership with the senior leadership team and the SEN governor, in order to meet the internal and external accountability requirements for SEN.

Gathering evidence through classroom walkthroughs

Regular focused classroom walkthroughs every half term offer the SENCO valuable information about what's working, or not working, in SEN policy and practice, across the school.

Concept of the classroom walkthrough

The concept of the classroom walkthrough is that it offers short, focused, informal observation of the teaching and learning taking place in classrooms. It is a brief, structured, non-evaluative classroom observation. Classroom walkthroughs are a monitoring tool, which drives a cycle of continuous improvement in SEN by focusing on the effects of teaching on SEN pupils' learning. It is a strategy for providing the school, not individual teachers, with general feedback on what is going well, and what is not going as well for SEN pupils in the school.

Classroom walkthroughs assume a positive role in reflective practice, by making it clear to teachers and teaching assistants that the teaching and learning of SEN pupils are a top priority for the SENCO.

Classroom walkthroughs are not intrusive, invasive or formal. They are not part of teachers' performance management or TAs' appraisal. The classroom walkthrough is not a bureaucratic or paper-laden exercise. The recommended time period in each classroom on the walkthrough is between three and five minutes.

The benefits and purpose of the classroom walkthrough

The benefits and purpose of the classroom walkthrough are many and include:

- helping the SENCO to identify the strengths and areas for further development in SEN
- gathering first-hand information to facilitate reflective thinking about provision in practice
- providing a school-wide snapshot of practice to meet the needs of SEN pupils
- helping to inform whole school SEN training required by staff in the school
- identifying where additional teaching assistant support could be better deployed

- offering a flexible approach in focusing on specific and different aspects of SEN policy and provision, each half term
- identifying 'Look-fors' (conditions that when present in the classroom enable SEN pupils to improve their achievement and skills as independent learners)
- providing a powerful, collaborative opportunity for the SENCO, teachers and school leaders to have productive learning conversations about 'What constitutes good practice for SEN pupils'
- helping the SENCO to gain new insights and understandings
- enabling SEN best practice to be disseminated and shared;
- providing useful evidence to external bodies, e.g. OFSTED, the LA, to show that the SENCO undertakes regular monitoring of SEN policy and provision, across the school.

Five steps to the classroom walkthrough

There are five steps in the classroom walkthrough process. These are:

1. **SEN pupil engagement in learning** – are they motivated, on task, oriented to work, enjoying their learning?
2. **Lesson and learning objectives** – are the curriculum lesson and learning objectives appropriate for SEN pupils, and what are their responses? Is the content of the lesson sufficiently challenging for SEN pupils?
3. **Learning approaches/pedagogy** – teaching approaches used, meta-cognition, assessment for learning, learning arrangements, i.e. pair, group, whole class and independent learning.
4. **'Walk the walls'/learning environment** – clues as to what has been taught previously, how do displays support SEN pupils' learning, the quality of SEN pupils' work displayed, if the classroom is a safe, healthy place to learn.
5. **Reflection** – what is the SENCO's response to what has been seen, heard and felt? What single reflective question would the SENCO like to explore further?

Table 6.1 offers a model template for undertaking a classroom walkthrough, with a focus on SEN pupils' learning. This can be customised to suit the focus of the walkthrough.

Organising classroom walkthroughs

- It is recommended that the SENCO undertakes paired classroom walkthroughs with another colleague. For example, the headteacher, deputy or assistant headteacher, the SEN governor, or another SENCO or SLE for SEN from another school.
- Prior to commencing the classroom walkthroughs, the focus should be agreed.
- The SENCO may be assigned a particular focus, e.g. the deployment of teaching assistants in the classroom, and the headteacher or other colleague may focus on what the SEN pupils are learning.
- After completing the classroom walkthroughs, both observers need to meet together on the same day, for 45 minutes or so, to discuss the evidence they have collected and to agree upon one or two priorities for further action and development.
- The SENCO will share the general headlines from the classroom walkthroughs collectively with staff, ideally at the following morning's staff briefing.

Follow-up reflective questions for the SENCO

- What is your initial response about SEN in the school?
- What is the evidence gathered telling you about the strengths and weaknesses in SEN policy and provision in the school?
- What is the reflective experience telling you about staff CPD needs in SEN?

Table 6.1 Classroom walkthrough template

Observation guidance	Comments
Step 1: Pupil engagement To what extent are the pupils engaged with learning; what behaviours are observable; what habits for learning have they developed; are all learners engaged (particularly pupils with SEND, or FSMs, LAC, summer births)?	
Step 2: Purpose – desired learning outcomes/objectives What is the teacher's purpose (objectives): what are the desired learning outcomes; are they age appropriate; how do they meet the needs of this group of learners? How are the pupils responding to the learning opportunities being created?	
Step 3: Learning approaches How are the actions of the teacher developing the learning of the pupils? What are the decisions the teacher is making in responding to the responses of pupils to the learning approach? How do the actions and reactions of the teacher move pupils' learning forward?	
Step 4: Learning environment 'Walk the Walls' How is the classroom environment contributing to pupils' learning? Are there scaffolds and prompts for learning in the classroom? Do the pupils actively make use of these? What is the quality of pupils' work displayed on classroom walls? Is the classroom an emotionally safe learning environment where children can take risks and make mistakes in their learning? Is equipment being used safely? Is there sufficient lighting and ventilation? Can pupils move around the classroom safely?	
Step 5: Reflection What is your reflective response to what you have observed? What opportunity might this observation offer in terms of generating a reflective question for the teacher/TA to explore further?	

Rita Cheminais' Handbook for SENCOs Second Edition, SAGE Publications Ltd © Rita Cheminais, 2015

SENCOs can find out more about classroom walkthroughs from the following two books:

The Three-Minute Classroom Walk-Through: Changing School Supervisory Practice One Teacher at a Time (Downey et al., 2004)
Advancing the Three-Minute Walk-Through: Mastering Reflective Practice (Downey et al., 2010).

Undertaking an SEN learning walk to collect evidence

Concept of a learning walk

A learning walk offers a snapshot of the learning and teaching taking place at the school. It is a very structured, collaborative approach for gathering evidence of progress against a clearly defined issue, and subsequently planning ways forward.

A learning walk should take approximately one hour and 45 minutes on average.

The purpose of a learning walk

A learning walk can have a number of different purposes. These include:

- to monitor or audit an aspect of SEN practice throughout the school
- to share good practice in SEN
- to promote consistency in SEN policy and practice across the school
- to raise awareness about an aspect of SEN policy or provision
- to check for progression in SEN pupils' learning
- to support staff CPD
- to stimulate reflective professional discussions between teachers.

Organising and setting up a learning walk for SEN

- Establish a set focus for the SEN learning walk. Ideally the chosen focus should be linked to the priorities on the SEN development plan. Evidence of the SEN focus should be observable in classrooms.
- Form a learning walk team comprising of three or four 'walkers'. The SENCO will be the lead walker, plus a member of the senior leadership team, the SEN governor and a SENCO or SLE for SEN from another local school.
- The number of classrooms to be visited needs to be agreed by the team, in a particular key stage or year group. Ten minutes will be spent in each classroom.
- A timetable for the half day learning walk will be produced and publicised to the staff.
- The learning walk team will be provided with the necessary observation tools and templates for gathering and recording evidence.
- The learning walk process, purpose and protocols will be confirmed with team members.
- Learning walk team members will be allocated a role in the process. For example, the SENCO will focus on pedagogy for SEN pupils; the senior leader will scrutinise SEN pupils' work; the SEN governor will focus on the learning environment; and the SLE for SEN/other SENCO will talk to SEN pupils about their learning.
- On completion of the learning walk, the team will meet for 30 minutes to reflect upon the evidence gathered and share findings.
- The school's SENCO as 'lead walker' will compile a report from the team's evidence, to be presented to the headteacher and the chair of governors.
- Highlights from the report will be fed back to the whole staff in a briefing or at a staff meeting.

Dependent on the focus of future SEN learning walks, the SENCO may invite a parent of an SEN child, an SEN pupil and an external professional to join the next learning walk team.

The outcomes from the SEN learning walk

- Good practice in classroom provision for SEN pupils will be shared across the school.
- The strengths and areas for further development in SEN will be clarified.
- Any changes or amendments to SEN policy and practice will be confirmed.

Table 6.2 and 6.3 are practical tools for SENCOs to utilise on a SEN learning walk. They have been adapted from the archived Primary National Strategy resource *Learning Walks: Tools and Templates for Getting Started* (DCSF, 2007).

Monitoring SEN provision through lesson observations

The SEND Code of Practice (0–25) 2014 identifies some of the key roles of the SENCO, in relation to monitoring provision for pupils who have SEN:

- monitoring the effectiveness of any special educational provision
- promoting the pupils' access to the school's curriculum
- advising teachers at the school about differentiated teaching methods appropriate for individual pupils with SEN.

Lesson observations enable the SENCO to check on these three aspects. In addition, they also deepen the SENCO's understanding about the impact of high quality personalised teaching on SEN pupils' learning and achievement. Lesson observations also help the SENCO to identify any barriers to pupils' learning, and whether reasonable adjustments are being made to ensure SEN pupils' active participation in the learning.

Lesson observations are time consuming, and if time is short, the SENCO may request the headteacher and the senior leadership team to focus on SEN in one of their termly formal lesson observations, across the school. The SENCO may be selective in their lesson observations, only undertaking these in the lessons which have been identified through evidence gathered previously in learning walks, five-minute classroom walkthroughs, work scrutiny and/or feedback from SEN pupils, that there is a particular curriculum subject or a particular teacher where it would be useful to observe teaching and learning. A class or subject teacher may also nominate themselves for a lesson observation by the SENCO where they are finding it a challenge to meet the needs of an individual SEN pupil with more complex needs.

Dependent on the SENCO's previous experience in undertaking lesson observations, it would be useful to undertake at least the first one with a member of the senior leadership team (SLT).

Possible areas of focus for SENCO lesson observations

Any of the following aspects may be a focus for SEN lesson observations:

- the deployment and effectiveness of teaching assistants (TAs) in lessons
- access to learning for SEN pupils with physical and/or sensory needs
- whether SEN pupils are transferring learning from additional interventions to their mainstream lessons
- SEN pupil progress in lessons
- SEN pupils developing learning skills to become independent learners;
- SEN pupils reviewing and assessing their own learning and progress.

Table 6.2 Record sheet to capture observations on an SEN learning walk

SEN learning walk focus: High quality teaching for SEN pupils
Classroom displays support learning
Work in pupils' books showed evidence of progress
Discussion with pupils about their learning:
What do you already know about this topic?
What new things have you learnt about the topic today?
Was there anything in the lesson you found hard, and if so what would have helped you learn better?
The range of teaching approaches used by the teacher:
Teacher discussion: How is the teacher supporting SEN pupils to become effective learners?
How the TA is supporting SEN pupils to become effective learners

Table 6.3 Reflection following the SEN learning walk

Overall findings from your learning walk observation sheets
What I have learnt from undertaking this SEN learning walk?
List the evidence of strengths and what is working well in the teaching and learning of SEN pupils
List of areas requiring further improvement in the teaching and learning of SEN pupils
Questions you would wish to explore further with the headteacher, as an outcome of undertaking the SEN learning walk

Preparing and planning for lesson observations

- Agree the lessons you wish to observe with the headteacher, and the SLT.
- Clarify the focus and reasons for undertaking lesson observations with the headteacher, the SLT and with the teacher being observed.
- Prepare lesson observation tools, e.g. recording forms, checklists and any observation schedules, in advance.
- Plan the timetable for lesson observations, and check with the respective teachers that the time and date are convenient.
- Request a copy in advance of the teachers' lesson plans, to check for curriculum differentiation, reasonable adjustments and TA deployment.

Activities during the lesson observations

The SENCO will look for the following evidence during lesson observations:

- whether SEN pupils are learning effectively, and if they are making good enough progress
- identifying how the teacher makes reasonable adjustments and differentiates the curriculum for SEN pupils, to match their learning needs
- observing the teacher's repertoire of teaching and learning styles
- observing SEN pupils' behaviour for learning, e.g. on task, motivated
- talking to SEN pupils about their learning, e.g. what they already know about the topic being covered, what new learning they have gained in the lesson
- looking at SEN pupils' work in their exercise books or folders
- taking note of any teaching and learning resources being used in the lesson, which help to scaffold, reinforce or extend SEN pupils' learning, including the use and application of multi-media technology
- observing how the teaching assistant in the lesson supports and extends SEN pupils' learning
- summarising the strengths and areas for further development on the lesson observation form
- making a note of SEN pupils absent from the lesson, and following up on the reasons for non-attendance.

Feedback after the lesson observation

- Thank the teacher for allowing you to observe their lesson.
- Ask the teacher how they felt the lesson went.
- Provide verbal feedback on the strengths and areas for further development, which are factual, non-judgemental, based on observations.
- Give the teacher an opportunity to comment on what you have fed back.
- Enable the teacher to identify for themself how they can address the areas for further development, and offer further support as appropriate.
- Give the teacher, their line manager and the headteacher a copy of the lesson observation form.

The SENCO will be likely to use the education setting's own lesson observation form, however Table 6.4 offers a model lesson observation record sheet, along with Table 6.5 which provides a model SEN pupil survey on learning, and Table 6.6, which offers a useful proforma for the SEN governor to utilise on a monitoring visit to the education setting.

Table 6.4 Lesson observation form

Teacher:	Lesson/Subject:		Term:
			Date: Time:
Observer: SENCO	**Class:**	**No. SEN**	**TA:**

Focus of lesson observation:

Lesson objectives:

Evidence of effective teaching:	**Evidence of less effective teaching:**

Evidence of effective learning:	**Evidence of less effective learning:**

Effectiveness of support for learning: (TA support)	**Evidence of behaviour for learning and pupil progress in lesson:**

Strengths:	**Areas for further development:**

Table 6.5 SEN pupil survey on learning

Things that help me learn in lessons	√ relevant boxes	Pupil comment
The teacher telling me how to do something		
The teacher showing me what to do		
The teacher explaining something new		
The teacher asking me to copy from the whiteboard		
Watching a video clip/YouTube of how to do the task		
Doing practical work, making things		
Hot seating, role play, acting out something		
Telling a friend in class how I did the task		
Writing down how I did the task in my own words		
Copying notes out of a textbook		
Using a mind map to get my ideas down on paper		
Talking to other pupils, or to the teacher or teaching assistant, about ideas on how to do the task		
Asking questions if I don't understand something		
Answering the teacher's/teaching assistant's questions		
Being given thinking time when asked a question		
Having a break between learning tasks		
Working with another pupil in a pair		
Working in a small group with other pupils		
Working as part of the whole class		
Working and learning on my own sometimes		
Using the computer/internet, iPad in lessons		
The teacher telling you how to make your work better		

When is learning fun and most enjoyable?

If you find work difficult, or don't understand what to do in class, what do you do?

When the teacher gives you homework do you follow what you have to do?

Pupil name:	Date:

Rita Cheminais' Handbook for SENCOs Second Edition, SAGE Publications Ltd © Rita Cheminais, 2015

Table 6.6   SEN governor visit recording form

SEN governor:	Date of visit
Visit focus	**Lessons/staff visited**

Summary of SEN governor activities on visit:
(e.g. lunch with SEN pupils; viewing new SEN learning resources; paired lesson observation; talking to SENCO, teachers/TAs and SEN pupils)

-
-
-
-

What I have learned from today's visit: (Positive comments)	**What I need to know more about:** (Areas for further exploration)
<ul><li></li><li></li><li></li><li></li></ul>	<ul><li></li><li></li><li></li><li></li></ul>
Questions I would like answered: • • •	**SEN aspects needing clarification:** • • •

Suggestions for the focus of future SEN governor visits:

-
-
-

Any further comments about today's visit:

Signature: _____   SENCO: _____
(SEN governor)

Undertaking the scrutiny of SEN pupils' work

The scrutiny of a sample of SEN pupils' work across the curriculum can help the SENCO identify strengths and weaknesses in performance. This in turn will inform the SENCO's lesson observations in curriculum subject areas, where there is an identified area for improvement, e.g. curriculum differentiation, teacher expectations.

The purpose of work scrutiny

There are a number of purposes and reasons for undertaking a scrutiny of SEN pupils' work. These are as follows:

- to identify how teachers' marking and assessment on work help SEN pupils to know how to improve their learning and work
- to see if SEN pupils respond to the teachers' marking comments in the next and subsequent pieces of written work, by correcting or improving their work
- to judge whether written tasks set provide an appropriate level of challenge for SEN pupils, and do not rely on too many worksheets with a low level of challenge
- to evaluate whether there is evidence of pupils having made progress over time, from the written work presented
- to judge whether the standard of work presented is good enough in relation to presentation and accuracy
- to check whether SEN pupils are transferring their learning from extra literacy interventions across the curriculum
- to check whether SEN pupils are experiencing any barriers to learning in relation to recording their written responses to tasks set by the teacher
- to identify curriculum subjects or curriculum aspects which will require SEN pupils to benefit from pre-tutoring, or to have further intensive literacy support and interventions
- to identify whether teachers are using scaffolding to support SEN pupils' writing, e.g. mind maps, writing frames
- to identify any emerging trends arising from the work scrutiny, e.g. any significant causes for concern, relating to specific SEN pupils, e.g. those on FSMs, or who have summer birthdays, gender differences, or who have a particular type of special educational need
- to identify areas for further training and CPD for teachers, e.g. differentiation of the curriculum to match reading ages, making reasonable adjustments to enhance curriculum access, use of alternative methods of recording

Organising a work scrutiny.

The following points offer a guide to SENCOs in how best to prepare for and organise a purposeful SEN pupil work scrutiny, across the curriculum:

- Give teachers two weeks' notice, regarding when the SEN pupils' written work will be required for sampling.
- Share with the teachers what the focus of the work scrutiny will be, e.g. evidence of SEN pupils' progress in learning.
- Select the sample of SEN pupils who you wish to sample work from, e.g. attainment tracking data will have informed which pupils to choose.
- Prepare evaluation tools in advance for the work scrutiny, e.g. checklists, recording sheets.
- Inform the sample of SEN pupils that you will be looking at their work across the curriculum to see how they are progressing in their learning.
- Allow half a day to undertake the work scrutiny.

- If possible, undertake the work scrutiny with a member of the SLT, especially if this aspect of monitoring is a new role.
- Make notes during the work scrutiny process, recording individual SEN pupil findings, and general findings, using the model templates provided.

Follow-up to the work scrutiny

- In discussion with the colleague who undertook the work scrutiny with you draw out the main findings, e.g. strengths, general areas for improvement. Identify if any common trends or patterns are occurring, e.g. in a specific curriculum subject area, or among a particular cohort of SEN pupils.
- Identify where there is evidence of SEN pupil underachievement and lack of sufficient progress, and where this is the case, follow up with a lesson observation.
- Write up the findings in a report, feed back general headlines in a staff briefing or staff meeting, and give a copy to the headteacher.
- Provide any follow-up SEN CPD for staff who would benefit from a refresher session in curriculum differentiation and making reasonable adjustments to enhance curriculum access.
- File the work scrutiny report in the SENCO monitoring file, to retain as evidence of ongoing monitoring of SEN policy and provision.

The SENCO may find Tables 6.7 and 6.8 useful tools to support the written recording of evidence from the SEN pupil work scrutiny, at an individual pupil level, and at a more general level.

Appreciative inquiry and focused discussions with key stakeholders

The concept of appreciative inquiry

Appreciative inquiry is an evaluative technique with the main purpose of introducing and implementing a successful change. For example, developing the school's SEN local offer, and implementing a whole school new SEN system.

Appreciation is about recognition, valuing others' contributions and attributes, enhancing value, affirming past and present strengths and potentials. Inquiry refers to exploration and discovery, asking questions and learning, seeking to better understand, and being open to new possibilities.

Appreciative inquiry uses positive experiences to bring about change for the better. It enhances self-esteem and self-expression, by giving staff, parents and SEN pupils a chance to be heard and to make a positive contribution in shaping and informing SEN provision. Appreciative inquiry is designed to make things better by exploring what is working well in SEN within the school, why it is working well and then doing more of it. The concept of appreciative inquiry requires a commitment to continuous learning in a reflective organisation.

The overall aim of appreciative inquiry is to help the school to build upon what it already does best in relation to meeting the needs of SEN pupils as learners, by focusing on what is going right.

The advantages of using appreciative inquiry

The advantages of using appreciative inquiry as part of internal accountability are as follows:

- It supports a new outlook on SEN.
- It empowers participants, staff, parents, SEN pupils.

Table 6.7 Model work scrutiny SEN pupil monitoring feedback sheet

Pupil name: _____ Nature of SEN: _____

Form/Class: _____ Date of work scrutiny: _____

	Outstanding High quality marking improves pupil's learning; persistently high level of challenges over time; pupil response to marking comments shows marked improvement in learning	Good Good use of marking improves pupil's learning; level of challenge over time ensures good progress; pupil acts appropriately on feedback from teacher comments in marking	Requires improvement Written work requires improvement because it doesn't meet the criteria for good	Inadequate Pupil can't write as well as they should; too much work is missing or incomplete; presentation is consistently poor and untidy; work is not marked regularly or informs improvement
Work matches the ability and reading age of SEN pupil				
Work set offers a good level of challenge				
Evidence of teacher marking informing improvement				
Evidence of AfA pupil/peer assessment				
Presentation, layout and completion of pupil's work				
Evidence of transfer of learning from extra literacy intervention, across the curriculum				
Strengths				
Points for development				

Rita Cheminais' Handbook for SENCOs Second Edition, SAGE Publications Ltd © Rita Cheminais, 2015

Table 6.8 Model recording sheet for general findings from work scrutiny

Curriculum subject	Strengths	Areas for improvement

- It helps to identify best practice in SEN.
- It addresses any SEN and disability stereotyping by valuing diversity.

Four stages to appreciative inquiry

There are four stages in the collaborative and participative appreciative inquiry process. It is reliant on group discussions and reflective questioning to energise participants, and accelerate positive change. Figure 6.1 illustrates the four-stage appreciative inquiry cycle.

> **Stage 1: Discovery** – finding out and understanding, through questioning and focused discussion, the best of 'what is' and the best of 'what has been' in SEN within the education setting. Real success stories are shared about what works well.
> **Stage 2: Dream** – creative thinking about the future of SEN in the education setting, i.e. 'what might be' under a new SEN system.
> **Stage 3: Design** – planning for the future changes in SEN (transformation), which reflect the views of key stakeholders in respect of good practice and vision. Making choices about 'what should be' in place for SEN pupils in the education setting, under a reformed SEN system.
> **Stage 4: Deliver** – working out what will need to happen to make the change in implementing a new SEN system, and in producing a good quality school SEN local offer, i.e. 'what will be', the actions to take that will support ongoing learning and innovation and continuous improvement in SEN.

SENCOs can find further information about appreciative inquiry in the resource:

The Power of Appreciative Inquiry: A Practical Guide to Positive Change, 2nd edn (Whitney and Trosten-Bloom, 2012).

Focused discussions with parents, SEN pupils and staff

Focused discussions with parents, SEN pupils and staff in separate focus groups are an excellent way of capturing views about SEN provision first hand. The information gathered from discussion can be explored in greater depth later by the SENCO, who acts as facilitator for the focus group discussions. The SENCO will be looking for common themes and emerging issues.

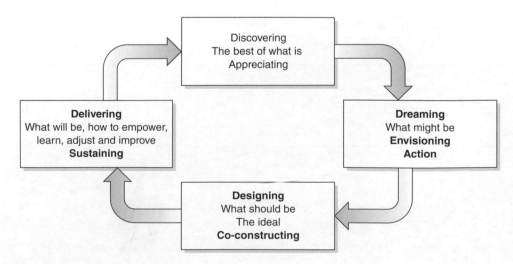

Figure 6.1 Appreciative inquiry process

A focus group is a semi-structured information gathering method in which a sample of participants gather to discuss a given topic, based on a list of key themes. Focus groups complement the appreciative inquiry process.

The aim of any focus group is to gain further and deeper understanding of issues, concerns and positive comments relating to SEN pupil provision in the education setting, which in turn can inform the setting's SEN Local Offer.

The SENCO as facilitator of the focus group discussions needs to lead and manage a group discussion with confidence, allowing time for participants to listen to each other's views and reflect upon what has been said. Questions used in focus group discussions need to move from initial general questions onto more specific questions. The SENCO as facilitator will clarify and summarise the main points emerging from the focus group discussion. These will be written up and circulated to those participating in each focus group, for checking. The information gathered will inform future planning and the education setting's SEN Local Offer.

Top tips for using focus groups for internal accountability

- Focus groups need to be carefully planned, ensuring that a good representation of participants are invited to contribute.
- Limit the size of each focus group to a maximum of six to eight participants.
- Plan a small number of clear topics or themes relating to SEN for discussion.
- Set an agreed timeframe for the focus group to meet for the discussion.
- Use an interview or discussion schedule to guide and keep the focus group on track.
- Provide an emotionally intelligent environment for the focus group to meet in and to promote open discussion.
- Ensure each member of the focus group is given sufficient opportunity to give their views.

Table 6.9 provides the SENCO with a model template for recording the collective views of participants in a focus group.

Evaluating the impact of integrated working

The SEND Code of Practice (0–25) 2014 emphasises the need for well-coordinated and coherent support across education, health and social care (integrated services), to help SEN children and young people achieve their agreed outcomes. Joint working between these services achieves far more for these children and young people than separate working.

The NHS Act 2006 and the Health and Social Care Act 2012 make clear that NHS England, the Clinical Commissioning Groups (CCGs) and the Health and Wellbeing Boards in local authorities must promote the integration of services, e.g. the integration of SEN provision with health and social care provision, in order to promote the well-being of children and young people with SEN, and improve the quality of special educational provision.

The concept of integrated working is difficult to define because of the number of different terms used to describe it, e.g. partnership working, joint working, multi- and inter-disciplinary working. Integrated working (integration) is defined as agencies working together within a single, new organisational structure. Multi-agency working is where services are provided by more than one agency working together and drawing on pooled resources or budgets.

The SEND Code of Practice (0–25) 2014 identifies the measures for monitoring and evaluating the outcomes (the impact and consequences of help received) that integrated services

Table 6.9 Model record sheet to gather collective views from a focus group

SEN Focus Group Record Sheet of Discussion		
Focus group participants		Date of discussion:
Topic/Theme	Key questions	Points arising from the discussion

hope to achieve, e.g. improved educational progress and outcomes for SEN pupils; improved family well-being; increased early identification of children with SEN prior to school entry; reductions in health inequalities; and positive family/service user experience feedback.

Effective, collaborative, integrated services should add value to the existing work and efforts of the education setting.

The key role of integrated working with SEN pupils is to contribute to removing barriers to learning and participation by providing universal, targeted and specialist services, as part of the LA's and the education setting's local offers, and as a total package of provision for SEN pupils on EHC plans, or on SEN Support, as appropriate.

Gathering evidence on the impact of integrated services for SEN

The SENCO will be gathering evidence of the impact of integrated service provision in improving outcomes for SEN pupils from a range of qualitative and quantitative sources.

Qualitative sources of evidence will largely include feedback from practitioners, from staff in the education setting, from parents/carers' and from SEN pupils where appropriate. The views of service users are particularly important, and the SENCO will gain this feedback from EHC plan reviews, from the reviews of those pupils on SEN Support, who have direct inputs from health and social care services, and also from focus group discussions and responses to surveys and questionnaires. The SENCO would also be advised to build up a portfolio of successful case studies, which would demonstrate the positive impact of integrated service provision, for a diversity of pupils with SEN and/or disability.

In relation to quantitative evidence, the SENCO will collect SEN pupil-level attainment and attendance data, behaviour and well-being data, e.g. Pupil Attitude to Self and School (PASS) and the Health Related Behaviour Questionnaire (HRBQ).

The information gathered from both sources will not only inform provision at individual SEN pupil level, it will also inform the provision made available through the local authority and through the education setting's Local Offer.

The SENCO will find Figure 6.2 and Table 6.10 two valuable accountability tools for gathering evidence on the effectiveness of integrated service provision.

Previous research studies into the impact of integrated working on children and young people with learning difficulties, disabilities and/or mental health difficulties, found that this way of working did make a difference in the areas of attainment and support, but less so in relation to emotional needs. Further information about integrated services and multi-agency working can be found in the following resources:

Cheminais, R. (2009) *Effective Multi-Agency Partnerships: Putting Every Child Matters into Practice*. London: Sage.

CWDC research report (2010) *Integrated Working: A Review of the Evidence*.

OFSTED (2014f) *Inspecting the Effectiveness of Partnerships: Briefing for Section 5 Inspection*.

External accountability – OFSTED inspections and SEND

OFSTED updated their inspection framework, inspection handbook and subsidiary guidance in January 2014, to reflect the changes required by the Secretary of State for Education,

ANNUAL INTEGRATED SERVICE USER SURVEY

Please indicate who you are: SEN pupil ☐   Parent/carer ☐

1. Which services have you used at the school?

2. Have you found the services easy to access?

   YES ☐   NO ☐

3. Do you feel the services used have been helpful in meeting your needs?

   YES ☐   NO ☐

   If no, please state how the service(s) could be improved:

4. Do you feel the staff who worked with you from the integrated services listened to your views, understood your needs, and respected confidentiality?

   YES ☐   NO ☐

   If no, state what the integrated services could do to improve this situation:

5. Do you consider the facilities and environment where you receive your service provision to be good?

   YES ☐   NO ☐

   If no, please state how these could be improved:

6. Is there anything else you wish to say in relation to integrated service provision?

   Thank you for taking the time to complete this short survey.
   Your answers will help to inform the improvement of the local offer.

Figure 6.2   Model integrated service user survey

Table 6.10 Evaluating the effectiveness of integrated services

Aspect of partnership working	RAG rating	Evidence and comments	Action and next steps for development/improvement
1. Accessibility of service			
2. Quality and usefulness of information/publicity materials			
3. Procedures and protocols for referral, assessment and provision			
4. Joined-up integrated working, team work			
5. Communication and information sharing			
6. Seeking the views and feedback on service provision from service users			
7. Practitioner's skills, knowledge, attitudes and values			
8. Inter-professional training and development			
9. Quality of monitoring and evaluation of service impact			
10. Any other aspect of partnership working (please specify)			

Rita Cheminais' Handbook for SENCOs Second Edition, SAGE Publications Ltd © Rita Cheminais, 2015

in relation to teaching and behaviour. The inspection framework, handbook and the subsidiary guidance offer the SENCO a valuable insight into what the OFSTED inspectors will expect to find in relation to SEND. In a nutshell, OFSTED inspections of schools and academies focus on how well individual pupils benefit from their education, and how well they are helped to make progress and fulfil their potential.

OFSTED make four key judgements about:

- the achievement of pupils
- the quality of teaching
- the behaviour and safety of pupils
- the quality of leadership and management.

In addition, OFSTED inspectors also consider:

- the spiritual, moral, social and cultural development of pupils
- the extent to which the education provided meets the needs of the range of pupils, and in particular the needs of pupils who have a disability as defined by the Equality Act 2010 and pupils who have special educational needs.

What is new in the updated January 2014 OFSTED guidance

- A clearer government definition of what expected progress is at different key stages is provided. Expected progress is defined by the government as two National Curriculum levels of progress between Key Stages 1 and 2, for example, from Level 2a to Level 4, Level 2c to Level 4 or Level 3 to 5, and three National Curriculum levels of progress between Key Stage 2 and 4, for example, from Level 3 to grade D, Level 4a to grade C, or Level 4c to grade C. However, SENCOs need to be aware that this will change, with the government's assessment reforms, which encourage schools to move away from solely judging pupil progress in terms of NC levels.

Inspectors will balance evidence about previous cohorts of pupils with evidence about the progress being made by the pupils being taught in the school currently (OFSTED, 2014a: 35).

- Expected progress for pupils attaining below Level 1 of the National Curriculum at the end of Key Stages 1 or 2 should be judged using the Transition Matrices, as part of RAISEonline, and the data sets 2–3 of the DfE Progression materials 2010–11.
- Where pupils' cognitive ability is such that their attainment is unlikely to ever rise above 'low', judgement on achievement is based on an evaluation of the pupils' learning and progress relative to their starting points at particular ages, and using the school's assessment measures.

In this instance evaluation is not compared with national benchmarks.

- A particular method or approach to teaching or planning lessons or a particular preference towards a specific lesson structure will not be advocated by inspectors, as it is for the school to determine how best to teach and engage pupils to secure their good learning.
- In relation to behaviour, inspectors will judge the extent to which pupils' attitudes to learning help or hinder their progress in lessons. For example, how quickly children settle at the start of lessons, whether they have the right equipment, their willingness to answer questions, whether they remain focused when working on their own, the tidiness of their work and the pride they show in its presentation, and the overall effort that they make.
- The prevalence of low level disruption will be noted by inspectors.
- Pupils' contribution to the culture of the school; how they conduct themselves, including their respect, courtesy and good manners towards each other and adults; and the pupils'

respect for the school's learning environments, facilities and equipment (including by not dropping litter), and adhering to school uniform policies.

- The extent to which schools engage their pupils in extra-curricular activity and volunteering within their local community is a new addition to leadership and management.
- How well leaders, managers and governors create a culture of high expectations and aspirations, academically and socially for *all* pupils, and establish an orderly and hard-working school community.
- How well senior leaders in the school work to promote improvement across the wider system. (This will include the SENCO as a member of the senior leadership team.)

OFSTED specific guidance in relation to SEN pupils

OFSTED's latest version of *Subsidiary Guidance* (January 2014) is an essential read for all SENCOs. Pages 16–18 relate to the achievement of SEND pupils; pages 22–3 relate to the behaviour of SEND pupils; and pages 47–8 relate to mainstream schools' specially resourced provision for SEND pupils.

SENCOs would be well advised to share this information with teaching staff, teaching assistants and the SEN governor.

Briefly, some of the important points to note from this guidance include:

- SEN pupils receiving an additional intervention should be demonstrating accelerated or sustained progress, indicating that the intervention has been effective.
- Rigorous moderation within the school and across a group of schools takes place, to ensure the accuracy of the progress data being used by the school, e.g. P levels, in order to validate teacher assessment.
- There should be evidence of the school's analysis of outcomes for the different groups of SEN pupils with a particular need or disability, which should note patterns over time (e.g. three-year trends).
- Where a pupil is achieving below the level expected for their age or making slower progress than anticipated, the effectiveness of generic teaching and support systems should be analysed first before deciding a pupil has SEN and therefore is in need of increased adult support or additional provision.
- Where a SEN pupil may access alternative provision, offsite, arrangements should be in place to ensure additional tuition is available, to enable them to catch up with any mainstream work missed.
- In relation to teaching, inspectors should not criticise teacher talk for being over-long or bemoan a lack of opportunity for different activities in lessons, or expect all work in lessons to always be matched to the specific needs of each individual pupil, or to expect to see 'independent learning' in all lessons, or to criticise 'passivity' in learners, unless any or all are stopping pupils from learning new knowledge, gaining skills and understanding, or slowing learning over time. In other words, where SEN pupils may not be receiving inspiring or exciting teaching, as long as they make progress in their learning, that is fine.
- How far variations in the behaviour of pupils, between settings, time of day, different subjects, different groupings and different staff, influence learning will be noted by inspectors in respect of whether the school is aware of this, and is taking effective action.
- Whether 'reasonable adjustments' are made for ASD pupils and those with social, emotional and mental health difficulties, to help them be included in school.

OFSTED and best practice in SEN

From their inspection experiences and from their 2010 SEND review, OFSTED identified the following best practice in raising standards in SEN:

- strong teaching and learning
- accurate assessment and identification
- close tracking and rigorous monitoring of progress with interventions quickly put in place
- a well-designed curriculum, matched to reading age and ability
- coaching others to improve the teaching of SEN pupils
- a thorough evaluation of the impact of additional provision
- clear routes to gain specialist support.

OFSTED expectations for SEN

- OFSTED expect subject leaders and class teachers to be responsible for SEN pupils and for them not to be referring to the SENCO as being the responsible member of staff for these children.
- When tracking a cohort of SEN pupils across the school, OFSTED will check that subject lessons reflect the SEN pupils' reading age, in relation to curriculum differentiation and delivery.
- The term 'good pace' used by OFSTED refers to the curriculum being differentiated for different children, it doesn't necessarily mean at a 'faster pace'.
- OFSTED inspectors want to hear quality dialogue about learning taking place between teachers and pupils, and teaching assistants and pupils, as well as the use of open questioning by both adults.
- OFSTED will be interested in the school's 'Local Offer'; how parents and SEN pupils have helped to shape and inform this, and its effectiveness in improving SEN pupils' achievements and progress.

Key questions for SENCOs in preparing for OFSTED visits

1. Do you know all SEN pupils' attainments accurately?
2. Is there close tracking and monitoring of SEN pupils' attainment and progress?
3. Do you know who (which SEN pupils) are making less than expected progress for their age?
4. How well do you monitor the effectiveness of the support for SEN pupils performing below expected levels for their age, and making less than expected progress? How has the progress of these pupils accelerated?
5. Do you take into account the quality of provision when identifying pupils with SEN?
6. Is the information about the quality of SEN provision obtained from lesson observations or by other methods? How is this information used, in order to improve provision?
7. How does the work of SEN pupils in their books compare with what you see in other pupils' exercise books, within the same class group?
8. Is there rigorous tracking of the behaviour and progress of those pupils with social, emotional and mental health difficulties, and if there is, is there convincing improvement in their behaviour and attitude to learning?
9. Is all the above information provided effectively to the SLT and to the governors?

SENCOs undertaking a mini-SEN inspection in school

Some SENCOs undertake a mini-inspection of SEN across the school at the end of an academic year, as a way of evaluating the impact of SEN policy and provision. The good practice

Table 6.11 Meeting the SEND OFSTED requirements – an at-a-glance guide for SENCOs

OFSTED inspection area	OFSTED SEND requirements	Implications for the SENCO
1. Achievement of pupils at the school	• How good the value added progress is for individual SEND pupils, based on their starting point on entry to the school and their age. • How clear the difference is between SEND pupils who have barriers to learning and those pupils who are just simply underachieving (i.e. the correct identification of SEND pupils). • Three-year attainment trends for SEND: expected rates of progress from KS1 to KS2 (2 levels of progress) and KS2 to KS4 (3 levels of progress). • The learning of SEN pupils is consistently good or better, or is generally good.	• The SENCO has a robust moderation system in place for all teacher assessment of SEND pupils' progress. • Moderation shows evidence of working with other schools/partners • The RAISEonline Transition Matrices and the data sets from the DfE's *Progression 2010–11* materials are used, to judge how good SEND pupils' progress is. • The SENCO can justify why some SEND pupils make above average progress, and why others have performed below age related expectations. • The SENCO collects SEND pupils' well-being data, which demonstrate progress in aspects such as attendance, exclusions, behaviour, self-esteem, independence.
2. Quality of teaching in the school	• How well lessons observed are well-planned to offer enough good quality learning opportunities for SEND pupils. • The extent to which teachers secure high quality learning for SEND pupils by setting challenging tasks matched to pupils' specific learning needs. • The quality of teaching and learning support provided for pupils with a range of SEND, aptitudes and needs, to improve their learning. • How effectively teachers use support staff in relation to the planning for their deployment; their briefing; how much time the teacher spends working with SEND pupils across the ability range, and how well small group interventions are taught. • As a result of outstanding or good teaching SEN pupils make rapid, sustained or good progress over time.	• The SENCO has evidence to demonstrate their impact on improving teachers' practice in teaching a diversity of SEND pupils, across the school. • The SENCO has evidence to show how far teachers across the school, take on responsibility for SEND pupils in their classes. • Evidence from SENCO lesson observations across the school, shows how teachers are using assessment information to set high expectations for SEND pupils. • The SENCO has evidence of how they evaluate teachers' monitoring and tracking data relating to SEND pupils' learning, in order to support curriculum differentiation, and make any changes quickly and promptly.

(Continued)

Table 6.11   (Continued)

OFSTED inspection area	OFSTED SEND requirements	Implications for the SENCO
3. The behaviour and safety of pupils at the school	• How many SEND pupils are poor attendees at school, have poor punctuality, experience fixed term and permanent exclusions or internal school exclusions/sent to a withdrawal room, and how many experience or are involved in bullying incidents. • How rigorous the tracking of the behaviour and progress of those pupils who have identified social, emotional and mental health difficulties is, and whether there is robust evidence of improvement in their behaviour and in their attitude to learning. • What the SEND pupils' views are in relation to their attitude to learning and their safety in school, particularly in relation to bullying. • How far SEND pupils' learning is disrupted in lessons across the school.	• The SENCO has evidence of how the behaviour of SEND pupils is tracked and monitored across the school. • The SENCO can show evidence of SEND pupil 'voice' in relation to them having a say about their learning, safety and additional provision, e.g. in EHC plan reviews, or case studies. • Where appropriate, the SENCO can provide details about the composition of lower sets or teaching groups, e.g. how many SEND pupils are in these groups, how often they experience disruption to their learning, because of the poor behaviour of other peers in the same set or group, and the action taken to address this issue. • The SENCO has evidence of 'reasonable adjustments' being made to ensure the inclusion of ASD pupils and those with social, emotional and mental health difficulties.
4. Quality of leadership in, and management of, the school	• How accurate the identification of pupils who have SEND is in the school. • Whether leaders and managers, including the SENCO, have considered thoroughly the quality of teaching and support as part of the identification of SEND pupils. • How effectively the school evaluates the quality of teaching for pupils with SEND, and improves it where necessary. • How thorough the school's evaluation is of the progress made by individual SEND pupils, based on age and prior attainment. • How rigorous the school's arrangements are to moderate assessment of attainment for low attaining pupils, including those with SEND. • How far additional interventions for SEND pupils show that they have made accelerated progress.	• The SENCO has evidence of how they effectively lead SEND whole school, to effect change and improvement. • The SENCO has evidence of how he/she contributes to whole school self-evaluation, in relation to SEND. • The SENCO can provide evidence to show the effectiveness of the SEND governor in providing challenge and acting as a 'critical friend' for SEND. This may be in the form of reports to the governing body, minutes from SENCO meetings with the SEND governor, which take place at least once each term, or from paired learning walks.

OFSTED inspection area	OFSTED SEND requirements	Implications for the SENCO
	• How the school's analysis of additional intervention data has been compared to the national data sets for pupils performing below age expected levels, in order to judge whether progress is good enough. • The quality of the school's provision map. • How thoroughly the SEND governor is aware of the accuracy of the identification of pupils with SEND; the quality of their progress; and the effectiveness of the additional interventions, including the use of the pupil premium, in meeting these pupils needs.	

approach they adopt is to track a critical group of SEN pupils in a particular form or class across a whole school day, to judge their experience, progress and learning. This can be a very revealing exercise, in relation to the type of curriculum tasks SEN pupils are being set, i.e. whether there is over-use of worksheets in every subject area, in the day. The SENCO follows the framework for inspection, using the OFSTED model for an audit trail, and gathers sufficient evidence from a range of methods, to identify why the cohort of SEN pupils may be underachieving and lacking motivation in their learning.

Ideally, it is best if the SENCO undertakes this activity with a member of the senior leadership team, or with another experienced SENCO or an SLE in SEN from another local school.

The outcomes from the SEN mini-inspection are written up as a report, and the findings are shared with the headteacher. The exercise is another excellent example of SENCO monitoring, which can be presented to any external evaluators, such as the local authority or OFSTED.

SENCOs may find Table 6.11 a useful resource to act as an aide memoire when preparing for an OFSTED inspection, or their own mini in-house SEN inspection.

In addition to the OFSTED inspection publications mentioned at the start of this section in Chapter 6, they may wish to read an inspector's SEN briefing paper which appears to have informed much of the content of OFSTED's subsidiary guidance. This resource is entitled: *Special Educational Needs and/or Disabilities in Mainstream Schools: A Briefing Paper for Section 5 Inspectors* (OFSTED, 2011).

> ## Points to remember
>
> - Accountability ensures the school is held to account and is answerable for the effectiveness of the SEN provision it offers.
> - Classroom walkthroughs offer short, informal observations of the teaching and learning taking place across the school.
> - A learning walk offers a snapshot of the learning and teaching taking place at the education setting.
> - Lesson observations offer a deeper insight into identifying any barriers to learning and where reasonable adjustments need to be made.
> - The scrutiny of SEN pupils' work across the curriculum helps to identify progress over time.
> - Appreciative inquiry builds on the positive experiences of others to bring about change for the better.
> - Focused discussions with service users help to capture views first hand, and identify common themes and emerging issues.
> - Effective, collaborative integrated services add value to the work and efforts of the education setting.
> - OFSTED inspections offer an external view about how well SEND pupils benefit from their education, and how the school responds to their needs to ensure they make progress and fulfil their potential.

Further activities

The following questions, focused on aspects covered in this chapter, meet the requirements of the National Award for Special Educational Needs Coordination, and support reflection and the professional development of experienced and newly appointed SENCOs.

1. The SEN officer from the local authority wishes to meet with the SENCO and headteacher to discuss how the school is evaluating the effectiveness of the additional provision it offers to SEN pupils with communication and interaction needs. Describe the range of evidence you would present at this meeting, for accountability purposes.
2. The SEN governor, during a learning walk, notices that there is one classroom where there is no SEN pupils' work on display. As SENCO, what action would you take to discover the reason for this finding?
3. Following the outcome of a work scrutiny, you notice that three SEN pupils in the same English group are failing to complete written tasks on a regular basis, and that teacher marking is not informing improvement. Describe the follow-up actions you will take to address this issue.
4. An outcome from focused discussions about SEN provision in the school reveals a level of uncertainty about whether pupils on SEN Support are receiving sufficient additional interventions to meet their needs. Outline the next steps you would take in exploring this issue further.
5. A small cohort of parents of SEN pupils on EHC plans are unclear about the impact a particular service has had in making a difference to their child's emotional well-being. Describe the steps you would take to check if their perceptions are correct, or otherwise.

 ## Online materials

To access electronic versions of the material in this chapter visit: www.sagepub.co.uk/cheminais2e

Figure 6.2 Model integrated service user survey
Table 6.1 Classroom walkthrough template
Table 6.2 Record sheet to capture observations on a SEN learning walk
Table 6.3 Reflection following the SEN learning walk
Table 6.4 Lesson observation form
Table 6.5 SEN pupil survey on learning
Table 6.6 SEN governor visit recording form
Table 6.7 Model work scrutiny SEN pupil monitoring feedback sheet
Table 6.8 Model recording sheet for general findings from work scrutiny
Table 6.9 Model record sheet to gather collective views from a focus group
Table 6.10 Evaluating the effectiveness of integrated services
Table 6.11 Meeting the SEND OFSTED requirements – an at-a-glance guide for SENCOs

Acronyms and abbreviations

ABA	Anti-Bullying Alliance		DCSF	Department for Children, Schools and Families
ADD	attention deficit disorder		DDA	Disability Discrimination Act
ADHD	attention deficit hyperactivity disorder		DED	Disability Equality Duty
AfA	Achievement for All		DfE	Department for Education
AfL	assessment for learning		DfES	Department for Education and Skills
AHDC	Aiming High for Disabled Children		DH	Department of Health
APF	additional pupil funding		DSA	Disabled Students Allowance
APS	average point score		DOB	date of birth
ASD	autistic spectrum disorder		DVD	digital versatile disc
BAS	British Ability Scales		EAL	English as an additional language
BESD	Behavioural, emotional and social difficulties		ECM	Every Child Matters
BOOST	balanced, observed, objective, specific and timely		EEF	Education Endowment Foundation
BPPE	Basic per Pupil Entitlement		EFA	Education Funding Agency
BPVS	British Picture Vocabulary Scale		EHC	Education, Health and Care
CAMHS	Child and Adolescent Mental Health Service		EHRC	Equality and Human Rights Commission
CAT	cognitive ability test		EYFS	early years foundation stage
CCG	Clinical Commissioning Group		FE	further education
CDC	Council for Disabled Children		FFT	Fischer Family Trust
CEOP	Child Exploitation and Online Protection		FIS	Family Information Service
CFS	chronic fatigue syndrome		FLOW	find, look, open, win
CLEAR	contracting, listening, exploring, action, review		FSD	Family Services Directory
			FSM	free school meals
CPD	continuing professional development		GL	Granada Learning
			GORT	Gray Oral Reading Tests
CRB	Criminal Records Bureau		GP	General practitioner
CVA	contextual value added		GROW	goal, reality, options, will
CWDC	Children's Workforce Development Council		GSRT	Gray Silent Reading Tests
			HE	higher education
DASH	detailed assessment of speed handwriting		HI	hearing impairment

HILDA	highlight, identify, look, decide, analyse	NCLSCS	National College for Leadership of School and Children's Services
HLTA	higher level teaching assistant	NCSL	National College for School Leadership
HMI	Her Majesty's Inspector		
HORT	Hodder Oral Reading Test	NCTL	National College for Teaching and Leadership
HRBQ	Health Related Behaviour Questionnaire	NGA	National Governors' Association
IB	indicative budget, individual budget	NNPCF	National Network of Parent Carer Forums
ICT	information communication technology	NPPN	National Parent Partnership Network
IDP	Inclusion Development Programme	NQT	newly qualified teacher
IEP	individual education plan	OCD	obsessive compulsive disorder
IM	instant messaging	ODD	oppositional defiance disorder
INSET	in-service education and training	OFQUAL	Office of Qualifications and Examinations Regulations
ISEA	International Studies in Educational Administration	OFSTED	Office for Standards in Education, Children's Services and Skills
ISF	Individual Service Fund	OPM	Office for Public Management
ISP	internet service provider	OSKAR	outcome, scaling, know-how, affirm, review
ITT	initial teacher training		
JSNA	joint strategic needs assessment	OT	occupational therapy
KS	Key Stage	PA	personal assistant
LA	local authority	PASS	Pupil Attitude to Self and School
LAC	looked after child		
LDA	learning difficulty assessment	PB	personal budget
LEA	local education authority	PC	personal computer
LSA	learning support assistant	PCF	parent carer forum
LSCB	Local Safeguarding Children's Board	PD	physical disability
ME	myalgic encephalitis	PECS	picture exchange communication system
MLD	moderate learning difficulties	PMLD	profound and multiple learning difficulties
MSI	multi-sensory impairment	PPS	Parent Partnership Service
NAHT	National Association of Headteachers	PRU	pupil referral unit
NASEN	National Association of Special Educational Needs	PSED	public sector equality duty
		QOL	quality of life
NC	National Curriculum	QTS	qualified teacher status
NCB	National Children's Bureau	RAFT	refer, action, file, trash

RAG	red, amber, green	SLD	severe learning difficulties
RAISE	Reporting and analysis for improvement through school	SLE	specialist leader of education
SaLT	speech and language therapy/ speech and language therapist	SLT	senior leadership team
		SpLD	specific learning difficulties
SEAL	social, emotional aspects of learning	STA	Standards and Testing Agency
SEN	special educational needs	STRIDE	strengths, target, reality, ideas, decision, evaluation
SENCO	special educational needs coordinator		
SEND	special educational needs and/or disability	TA	teaching assistant
		TAF	Team around the Family
SENDA	Special Educational Needs and Disability Act	TSO	The Stationery Office
SLC	speech, language and communication	VAK	visual, auditory and kinaesthetic
		VCS	voluntary community sector
SLCN	speech, language and communication needs	VI	visual impairment

Glossary

Accountability is the acknowledgement and assumption of responsibility for actions, decisions and policies, and to report, explain and be answerable for resulting consequences.

Action research is the investigation into a problem, topic or issue, which, on the basis of the information collected, draws conclusions and makes recommendations for improvement in practice, or in resolving a problem.

Appreciative inquiry is a collaborative and evaluative change management approach, focused on the positives in an organisation, building on what is working well, which in turn heightens participants' energy and vision for change.

Assessment uses a range of measures to collect the necessary information about a child or young person's attainment, progress and well-being, in order to inform the next steps in meeting their needs.

Assessment for learning is the process of seeking and interpreting evidence for use by pupils and their teachers, to decide where the child is in their learning, where they need to go next and how to get there.

Bullying is any behaviour by an individual or group of pupils which is repeated over time, that intentionally hurts another individual or group, either physically or emotionally. It is often motivated by prejudice against a particular group, based on race, gender, religion, disability, or sexual orientation.

Change is a developmental process which reassesses existing beliefs, values and assumptions in order to introduce new policies and new ways of working to improve upon current practice.

Classroom walkthroughs offer a short, focused informal observation of the teaching and learning taking place in classrooms across an education setting.

Clinical Commissioning Group comprises a local group of GPs who are responsible for procuring health and care services to meet the needs of children and adults in the local community.

Coaching is a structured sustained process that enables the development of a specific aspect of a professional learner's practice, which is solution focused in its approach.

Commissioning is the term given to the process of identifying what child and adult services are required by local people, and then arranging and procuring these services from providers.

Co-production is a dynamic group process which places equal value on the contributions of service users and service providers, to inform the delivery of services that better fit the needs of those accessing them locally.

Cyber-bullying is the act of using internet and digital (mobile) technologies to upset or humiliate another individual.

Delegation is the process of entrusting somebody else with the appropriate responsibility, for the accomplishment of a particular activity.

Direct payments   are a cash payment made to parents and carers of SEN children and young people with more complex needs, to enable the family to purchase the support their child needs.

Disability   describes the condition of any individual who has a physical or mental impairment which has a substantial and long-term adverse effect on their ability to carry out normal day-to-day activities.

Distributed leadership   refers to the sharing out of aspects of leadership across different levels in a workforce, in order to divide up tasks and responsibilities more equitably.

Education, Health and Care plan   is an outcome focused plan which favours a person centred approach to planning and reviewing additional provision for children and young people with more complex and severe special educational needs, aged 0–25.

Emotional resilience   is being able to cope with and recover 'bounce back' from any setbacks in leading change.

Evaluation   entails judging the quality, effectiveness, strengths and weaknesses of provision, based on robust evidence collected during review and monitoring processes.

Evidence-based practice   involves professionals and practitioners bringing their own knowledge and skills together with best quality evaluation research, in order to make a decision about selecting the most appropriate intervention or course of action which leads to improvement.

Focus group   is a semi-structured information gathering method in which a sample of participants gather to discuss a given topic, based on a list of key themes. The aim is to gain further and deeper insight and understanding about the issues, concerns and positives about the topic under discussion, that in turn inform decision-making and change for the better.

Graduated approach   to meeting the needs of children and young people with SEN comprises of four stages: assess, plan, do and review. It incorporates the use of evidence-based interventions.

HealthWatch England   is a champion for health and adult social care users, and is a statutory committee of the Care Quality Commission. It works with local HealthWatch groups to monitor local health conditions and to raise any concerns.

Health and Wellbeing Boards   integrate approaches to health care in local authority areas, combining representatives of NHS bodies and other local service providers.

High quality teaching   is that which is differentiated and personalised to meet the needs of the majority of pupils, including those with SEN. It is part of the daily repertoire of teaching strategies that ensure pupils' progression in learning.

Independent supporter   is an SEN champion recruited from the independent, voluntary, community and private sector, who offers one-to-one tailored advice and support to families of SEND children and young people as they progress through the 2014 revised SEN system.

Integrated working   is where practitioners work together, adopting common processes to deliver front-line services, coordinated and built around the needs of children, young people and their families.

Joint commissioning   as an ongoing process is a strategic approach to planning and delivering services in a holistic joined-up way. It enables partners to agree upon how they will work together to deliver personalised integrated support, resulting in positive outcomes across education, health and social care.

Lead professional   is a designated professional from health, education or social services who has day-to-day contact with a child or young person, and who coordinates and monitors service provision.

Learning walk   offers a snapshot of the learning and teaching taking place in an education setting. It is a collaborative structured approach to gathering evidence of progress against a clearly defined issue, and subsequently planning ways forward.

Local Offer   sets out in one place information about the range of services and provision the local authority expects to be available in the local area for children and young people with SEND and their families. The Local Offer informs the joint commissioning of services.

Mentoring   refers to the help given by a more experienced professional to another colleague who is less experienced, to enable them make significant transitions in knowledge, work or thinking.

Meta-cognition   refers to learners' automatic awareness of their own knowledge and ability to understand, control and manipulate their own thinking processes. It is part of high quality teaching, and it is about the pupil knowing when and how to use particular learning strategies to solve a problem.

Monitoring   is the systematic checking on progress and the gathering of information to establish the extent to which agreed plans, policies, statutory requirements or intervention programmes are being implemented.

Multi-agency working   is where those professionals from more than one agency or service work together, sharing aims, information, tasks and responsibilities in order to intervene early to prevent a child or young person's difficulties becoming worse.

NHS England   was created through the Health and Social Care Act 2012 and has responsibility for commissioning health care services for people in England. It plays a key role in securing the best possible health outcomes for patients by prioritising them in every decision it makes. NHS England has 27 area teams, which act as its 'local arms' to discharge its responsibilities, which include commissioning.

One-page profile   gives a short introduction to the individual which captures key information on a single page, offering others an understanding of the individual and how best to support them.

Outcomes   are identifiable (positive and negative) impacts of additional interventions and services on children and young people with additional needs. It also refers to what a plan or set of actions must deliver.

Parent carer forum   is a constituted group of parents and carers of SEND children and young people, who work with the local authority, education, health and social care services, and their providers, to ensure the services planned and delivered meet the needs of service users.

P levels   are smaller stepped differentiated performance criteria used for assessing the progress of SEN pupils aged between five and 16 who are working below National Curriculum Level 1.

Personal budget   is an amount of money identified by the local authority to deliver all or some of the provision set out in a child or young person's EHC plan. It enables parents and carers of SEN children and young people, and the young person themselves, where appropriate, to have a greater responsibility for how they spend this budget, in order to secure some or all of the additional provision required. The funding may come from several sources, i.e. health, social care and education.

Personalisation   places the child, young person and their family at the centre of making decisions about what will work best for them. It enables them to make use of their own resources and capacities, as well as drawing on tailored service support as required.

Person centred planning   is a process of continual listening and learning, focusing on what is important to the child or young person now, and in the future, and acting upon this information, in alliance with their family and friends. It is an approach which is recommended to support the Education, Health and Care plan process.

Progress   refers to pupils making at least two levels of progress across a key stage, in relation to their age and prior attainment (starting point).

Provision map   is a strategic management tool which provides a summary and overview of the range of additional and different provision made available to vulnerable pupils, including those with SEND.

Pupil premium   is additional funding targeted at pupils on free school meals, or who are looked after children, or who are children from an armed service family. The money is used by schools to help close the attainment gap between these vulnerable, disadvantaged children and their more socially and economically advantaged peers.

RAISEonline   is a web-based system which contains data about a school's basic characteristics, attainment and progress in the core subjects, to support evaluation and target setting.

Reading age   a pupil's ability to read at a given age is tested and compared with the average reading ability of other children of the same age. The comparison produces a reading age.

Reasonable adjustments   refer to removing barriers to participation and learning for children and young people with disabilities, to prevent them being at a substantial disadvantage compared to other peers without a disability. It relates to ensuring access to the curriculum, to information in different formats and to buildings.

Review   refers to a meeting between key professionals, the child and family to look at how SEN provision and support has been going, whether it is delivering the outcomes as set out in the EHC plan and whether any changes are required to improve the plan, the provision and support. Reviews usually happen at set intervals, e.g. three, six and 12 months.

Risk assessment   is the careful examination of what could cause harm to an individual or group of people, which enables the person in charge to weigh up whether enough precautions have been taken and if any further action needs to be taken to prevent potential harm occurring.

Self-evaluation   is the ongoing formative rigorous evidence gathering process, embedded in the daily work of the classroom and school, which gives an honest assessment of their strengths, weaknesses and effectiveness.

SEN Support   is a school-based single category which adopts a graduated approach to meeting the needs of those children and young people identified with SEN, without an EHC plan, who would have previously been those on Action and Action Plus.

Special educational needs   is where a child is defined as having SEN if they have a learning difficulty that calls for special educational provision to be made for them. A learning difficulty means that the child has significantly greater difficulty in learning than most children of the same age.

Specialist leader of education   is an outstanding middle or senior leader who supports their colleagues in similar positions in other schools to improve a whole school aspect, such as SEN, behaviour, a curriculum subject, or a phase of education such as early years.

Specialist services   are for those who require more specialised longer-term support. They are also referred to as Tier 3 services, as they go over and above universal and targeted services.

Strategic leadership   refers to knowing what you want to achieve, being able to justify the direction and finding the best ways to get there. It entails anticipating change or events, envisioning possibilities and empowering and managing through others to gain consensus and create strategic change.

Structured conversation   supports the greater engagement of parents of SEN children and young people, by enabling them to make their contributions heard and understood by teachers, the SENCO and the wider school.

Targeted services   provide additional short-term support over and above that provided routinely as part of universal services. They are also referred to as Tier 2 services.

Transfer   refers to the move for a child from one school or phase of education to another.

Transition   refers to the move for a child from one year group to the next in the same school, or other education setting.

Underachievement   refers to the mismatch between a child's current levels of attainment and their potential, which results in them not achieving the national expectation at the end of a key stage.

Universal services   are the services that the majority of the population use, for all to access. They are also to referred to as Tier 1 services.

Value added   is a measure that shows the difference a school makes to the educational outcomes of pupils given their starting points.

Voluntary sector   are charities and other organisations outside of the public (state funded) and private (for profit) sectors.

Further reading and references

ABA (2012) *Cyberbullying and Children and Young People with SEN and Disabilities: Guidance for Teachers and Other Professionals. SEN and Disability: Developing Effective Anti-Bullying Practice.* London: Anti-Bullying Alliance.

Allison, S. and Harbour, M. (2009) *The Coaching Toolkit: A Practical Guide for Your School.* London: Sage.

Autism Education Trust (2012) *Do You Have a Child with Autism in your Class? A Guide for Teachers.* Available at www.autismeducationtrust.org.uk

Blatchford, P., Bassett, P., Brown, P., Koutsoubou, M., Martin, P., Russell, A. and Webster, R. with Rubie-Davies, C. (2009) *Deployment and Impact of Support Staff in Schools: The Impact of Support Staff in Schools. Results from Strand 2 Wave 2.* DCSF-RR148. London: Institute of Education, University of London.

CDC (2013) *Coordinated Assessment and EHC Plan (December 2013) Appendix 1 – CDC EHC Plan Checklist and Example Plans.* London: Council for Disabled Children.

Chapman, C., Ainscow, M., Miles, S. and West, M. (2011) *Leadership that Promotes the Achievement of Students with Special Educational Needs and Disabilities: Full Report.* Nottingham: National College for School Leadership, University of Manchester.

Cheminais, R. (2009) *Effective Multi-Agency Partnerships: Putting Every Child Matters into Practice.* London: Sage.

Cheminais, R. (2013) *Promoting and Delivering School-to-School Support for Special Educational Needs: A Practical Guide for SENCOs.* Abingdon: Routledge.

Contact a Family (2012a) *Parent Carer Participation: An Overview.* London: Contact a Family.

Contact a Family (2012b) *How to Guide to Parent Participation.* London: Contact a Family.

CWDC (2010) *Integrated Working: A Review of the Evidence.* Leeds: Children's Workforce Development Council.

Davies, B. and Davies, B.J. (2012a) *The Nature and Dimensions of Strategic Leadership in Schools.* London: Specialist Schools and Academies Trust.

Davies, B., Davies, B.J. and Ellison, L. (2012b) *Success and Sustainability: Developing the Strategically-Focused School.* Nottingham: National College for School Leadership.

DCSF (2005) *Maximising Progress: Ensuring the Attainment of Pupils with SEN.* Annesley: Department for Children, Schools and Families.

DCSF (2006) *Effective Leadership: Ensuring the Progress of Pupils with SEN and/or Disabilities.* Annesley: Department for Children, Schools and Families.

DCSF (2007) *Learning Walks: Tools and Templates for Getting Started.* Primary National Strategy. Annesley: Department for Children, Schools and Families.

DCSF (2008a) *What Makes a Successful Transition from Primary to Secondary School?* DCSF-RR019. Annesley: Department for Children, Schools and Families.

DCSF (2008b) *Bullying Involving Children with Special Educational Needs and Disabilities: Safe to Learn: Embedding Anti-Bullying Work in Schools.* Annesley: Department for Children, Schools and Families.

DCSF (2009a) *Achievement for All: Local Authority Prospectus.* Annesley: Department for Children, Schools and Families.

DCSF (2009b) *Achievement for All: Guidance for Schools.* Annesley: Department for Children, Schools and Families.

DCSF (2009c) *Achievement for All: The Structured Conversation.* Annesley: Department for Children, Schools and Families.

DCSF (2009d) *Identifying and Teaching Children and Young People with Dyslexia and Literacy Difficulties* (Rose Report). Annesley: Department for Children, Schools and Families.

DCSF (2009e) *The Lamb Inquiry: Special Educational Needs and Parental Confidence.* Annesley: Department for Children, Schools and Families.

DCSF (2009f) *Make Them Go Away Resource Pack.* Annesley: Department for Children, Schools and Families.

DfE (2010a) *The Importance of Teaching: The Schools White Paper 2010.* Norwich: The Stationery Office.

DfE (2010b) *Progression 2010–11: Advice on Improving Data to Raise Attainment and Maximise the Progress of Learners with Special Educational Needs.* London: Department for Education.

DfE (2011a) *Support and Aspiration: A New Approach to Special Educational Needs and Disability.* Norwich: The Stationery Office.

DfE (2011b) *Individual Budgets for Families with Disabled Children: Final Evaluation Report: The IB Process.* DfE-RR145. London: Department for Education.

DfE (2012) *Support and Aspiration: A New Approach to Special Educational Needs and Disability. Progress and Next Steps.* London: Department for Education.

DfE (2013a) *Equality Act 2010: Departmental Advice for School Leaders, School Staff, Governing Bodies of Maintained Schools and Academies.* London: Department for Education.

DfE (2013b) *Indicative Draft: The (0–25) Special Educational Needs Code of Practice.* London: Department for Education.

DfE (2013c) *School Funding Reform: Findings from the Review of 2013–2014. Arrangements and Changes for 2014–15.* London: Department for Education.

DfE (2013d) *Preventing and Tackling Bullying: Advice for Headteachers, Staff and Governing Bodies.* London: Department for Education.

DfE (2013e) *Draft Special Educational Needs (SEN) Code of Practice: For 0 to 25 Years. Statutory Guidance for Organisations Who Work with and Support Children and Young People with SEN.* London: Department for Education and the Department of Health.

DfE (2014a) *Governors' Handbook: For Governors in Maintained Schools, Academies and Free Schools.* London: Department for Education and the Department of Health.

DfE (2014b) *Supporting Pupils at School with Medical Conditions: Statutory Guidance for Governing Bodies of Maintained Schools and Proprietors of Academies in England. Draft.* London: Department for Education.

DfE (2014c) *Special Educational Needs and Disability: Research Priorities and Questions.* London: Department for Education.

DfE (2014d) *The SEN and Disability Pathfinder Programme Evaluation: Progress and Indicative Costs of the Reforms. Research Report March 2014.* London: Department for Education.

DfE (2014e) *Draft Special Educational Needs and Disability Code of Practice: 0 to 25 Years. Statutory Guidance for Organisations Who Work with and Support Children and Young People with Special Educational Needs and Disabilities. April 2014.* London: Department for Education and the Department of Health.

DfE (2014f) *Implementing a New 0 to 25 Special Needs System: LAs and Partners. Further Government Advice for Local Authorities and Health Partners. April 2014.* London: Department for Education and the Department of Health.

DfE (2014g) *Keeping Children Safe in Education: Statutory Guidance for Schools and Colleges. April 2014.* London: Department for Education.

DfE (2014h) *Keeping Children Safe in Education: Information for all School and College Staff.* London: Department for Education.

DfE (2014i) *Consultation on Draft Guidance for Supporting Pupils at School with Medical Conditions: Summary of Responses.* London: Department for Education.

DfES (2001a) *Inclusive Schooling: Children with Special Educational Needs.* Annesley: Department for Education and Skills.

DfES (2001b) *Special Educational Needs Code of Practice.* Annesley: Department for Education and Skills.

DfES (2001c) *SEN Toolkit.* Annesley: Department for Education and Skills.

DfES (2001d) *Special Educational Needs and Disability Act.* London: The Stationery Office.

DfES (2002) *Accessible Schools: Summary Guidance.* London: Department for Education and Skills.

DfES (2003a) *The Report of the Special Schools Working Group.* Annesley: Department for Education and Skills.

DfES (2003b) *Every Child Matters.* London: The Stationery Office.

DfES (2004a) *Every Child Matters: Next Steps.* Annesley: Department for Education and Skills.

DfES (2004b) *Every Child Matters: Change for Children in Schools.* Annesley: Department for Education and Skills.

DfES (2004c) *Removing Barriers to Achievement: The Government's Strategy for SEN.* Nottingham: Department for Education and Skills.

DfES (2004d) *The Children Act 2004.* Norwich: HMSO.

DfES (2004e) *Learning and Teaching for Children with Special Educational Needs in the Primary Years.* Norwich: Department for Education and Skills

DfES (2005a) *Promoting Inclusion and Tackling Underperformance. Maximising Progress: Ensuring the Attainment of Pupils with SEN. Part 1: Using Data – Target Setting and Target Getting.* Norwich: Department for Education and Skills.

DfES (2005b) *Promoting Inclusion and Tackling Underperformance: Maximising Progress: Ensuring the Attainment of Pupils with SEN. Part 2: Approaches to Learning and Teaching in the Mainstream Classroom.* Norwich: Department for Education and Skills.

DfES (2005c) *Promoting Inclusion and Tackling Underperformance. Maximising Progress: Ensuring the Attainment of Pupils with SEN. Part 3: Managing the Learning Process for Pupils with SEN.* Norwich: Department for Education and Skills.

DfES (2006a) *Promoting Inclusion and Tackling Underperformance: Effective Leadership: Ensuring the Progress of Pupils with SEN and/or Disabilities.* Norwich: Department for Education and Skills.

DfES (2006b) *Leading on Intervention.* Annesley: Department for Education and Skills.

DH (2010) *Valuing People Now: A New Three Year Strategy for People with Learning Disabilities.* London: Department of Health.

Downey, C.J., Steffy, B.E., English, F.W., Frase, L.E. and Poston, W.K. Jr (2004) *The Three-Minute Classroom Walk-Through: Changing School Supervisory Practice One Teacher at a Time.* Thousand Oaks, CA: Corwin Press.

Downey, C.J., Steffy, B.E., Poston, W.K. Jr and English, F.W. (2010) *Advancing the Three-Minute Walk-Through: Mastering Reflective Practice*. Thousand Oaks, CA: Corwin Press.

EFA (2013a) *2014–2015 Revenue Funding Arrangements: Operational Information for Local Authorities*. London: Education Funding Agency.

EFA (2013b) *Implementing High Needs Place Funding Arrangements for 5–25 Year Olds. 2014–2015*. London: Education Funding Agency.

EHRC (2010a) *New Equality Act Guidance*. Available at www.equalityhumanrights.com/advice-and-guidance/new-equality-act-guidance/

EHRC (2010b) *Equality Act 2010: Education Providers: Schools' Guidance*. Available at www.equalityhumanrights.com/advice-and-guidance/new-equality-act-guidance/

Higgins, S., Katsipataki, M., Kokotsaki, D., Coleman, R., Major, L.E. and Coe, R. (2014) *The Sutton Trust–Education Endowment Foundation Teaching and Learning Toolkit*. London: Education Endowment Foundation.

HM Government (2013) *Working Together to Safeguard Children: A Guide to Inter-Agency Working to Safeguard and Promote the Welfare of Children*. London: Her Majesty's Government.

HM Treasury/DfES (2007) *Aiming High for Disabled Children (AHDC): Better Support for Families*. Norwich: Her Majesty's Treasury and the Department for Education and Skills.

Husbands, C. and Pearce, J. (2012) *What Makes Great Pedagogy? Nine Claims from Research*. Nottingham: National College for School Leadership.

In Control (2012) *Joint Commissioning for Children and Young People with SEND*. Wythall: In Control/East Sussex: SE7.

Koshy, V. (2009) *Action Research for Improving Educational Practice: A Step-by-Step Guide*. London: Sage.

Lazarus, C., Miller, C. and Smyth, J. (2012) *Making it Personal: How to Commission for Personalisation – Guidance for Commissioners and Others*. London: Office for Public Management (OPM).

Learn Together Partnership (2009) *Making Sense of School Performance Data: The Governors' Role in Supporting and Challenging Schools*. Knowsley: Learn Together Partnership.

Macintyre, C. (1991) *Let's Find Why: A Practical Guide to Action Research in Schools*. Edinburgh: Moray House Publications.

Macintyre, C. (2000) *The Art of Action Research in the Classroom*. London: David Fulton.

McLaughlin, C., Byers, R. and Oliver, C. (2012) *Perspectives on Bullying and Difference: Supporting Young People with Special Educational Needs and/or Disabilities in Schools*. London: Anti-Bullying Alliance/National Children's Bureau.

Matthews, P. and Berwick, G. (2013) *Teaching Schools: First among Equals*. Nottingham: National College for Teaching and Leadership.

McAfee (2014) *Digital Deception: The Online Behaviour of Teens*. Santa Clara, CA: McAfee.

Mott-MacDonald (2013a) *SEND Pathfinder Information Pack. Version 3, December 2013 – Local Offer*. Available at www.sendpathfinder.co.uk

Mott-MacDonald (2013b) *SEND Pathfinder Information Pack. Version 3. December 2013–Personal Budgets*. Available at www.sendpathfinder.co.uk

Mott-MacDonald (2013c) *SEND Pathfinder Information Pack. Version 3. December 2013 – Joint Commissioning*. Available at www.sendpathfinder.co.uk

Mott-MacDonald (2013d) *SEND Pathfinder Information Pack. Version 3 December 2013 – Co-ordinated Assessment and Education, Health and Care Plan*. Available at www.sendpathfinder.co.uk

NAHT (2014) *Report of the NAHT Commission on Assessment*. Haywards Heath: National Association of Headteachers.

NASEN (2013a) *Draft Special Educational Needs (SEN) Code of Practice: for 0–25. Summary*. Tamworth: National Association for Special Educational Needs.

NASEN (2013b) *The NASEN Guide to SEN*. Tamworth: National Association for Special Educational Needs.

NCLSCS (2009) *Change Facilitators' Handbook: Using the Bridge Change Leadership Framework*, 1st edn. Nottingham: National College for Leadership of School and Children's Services.

NCSL (2012) *How Teaching Schools Are Already Starting to Make a Difference*. Nottingham: National College for School Leadership.

NCSL (2013) *How Teaching Schools Are Making a Difference: Part 2*. Nottingham: National College for School Leadership.

NGA (2013a) *Knowing your School: The FFT Governor Dashboard for Primary School Governors*. London: National Association for Special Educational Needs.

NGA (2013b) *Knowing your School: The FFT Governor Dashboard for Secondary School Governors*. London: National Association for Special Educational Needs.

NGA (2014a) *Knowing Your School: RAISEonline for Governors of Primary Schools*, 2nd edn. London: National Governors' Association.

NGA (2014b) *Knowing Your School: RAISEonline for Governors of Secondary Schools*, 2nd edn. London: National Governors' Association.

NPPN/Contact a Family (2013) *Together is Better: A Report. April 2013*. London: National Parent Partnership Network and Contact a Family.

OFSTED (2004) *Special Educational Needs and Disability: Towards Inclusive Schools*. London: Office for Standards in Education.

OFSTED (2010) *The Special Educational Needs and Disability Review: A Statement is not Enough*. Manchester: Office for Standards in Education, Children's Services and Skills.

OFSTED (2011) *Special Educational Needs and/or Disabilities in Mainstream Schools: A Briefing Paper for Section 5 Inspectors*. Manchester: Office for Standards in Education, Children's Services and Skills.

OFSTED (2012) *The Pupil Premium: How Schools are Using the Pupil Premium Funding to Raise Attainment for Disadvantaged Pupils*. Manchester: Office for Standards in Education, Children's Services and Skills.

OFSTED (2013a) *The Pupil Premium: How Schools are Spending the Funding Successfully to Maximise Achievement*. Manchester: Office for Standards in Education, Children's Services and Skills.

OFSTED (2013b) *The Pupil Premium: Analysis and Challenge Tools for Schools*. Manchester: Office for Standards in Education, Children's Services and Skills.

OFSTED/DfE (2013c) *RAISEonline 2013 Summary Report Key Stage 1 Key Stage 2*. Manchester: Office for Standards in Education, Children's Services and Skills and the Department for Education.

OFSTED/DfE (2013d) *RAISEonline 2013 Summary Report Key Stage 4*. Manchester: Office for Standards in Education, Children's Services and Skills and the Department for Education.

OFSTED (2014a) *School Inspection Handbook: Handbook for Inspecting Schools in England under Section 5 of the Education Act 2005 (as amended) from September 2012*. Manchester: Office for Standards in Education, Children's Services and Skills.

OFSTED (2014b) *The Framework for School Inspection: The Framework for Inspecting Schools in England under Section 5 of the Education Act 2005 (as amended)*. Manchester: Office for Standards in Education, Children's Services and Skills.

OFSTED (2014c) *Subsidiary Guidance: Supporting the Inspection of Maintained Schools and Academies from January 2014*. Manchester: Office for Standards in Education, Children's Services and Skills.

OFSTED (2014d) *Inspecting Equalities: Briefing for Section 5 Inspection*. Manchester: Office for Standards in Education, Children's Services and Skills.

OFSTED (2014e) *Pupils with Medical Needs: Briefing for Section 5 Inspection*. Manchester: Office for Standards in Education, Children's Services and Skills.

OFSTED (2014f) *Inspecting the Effectiveness of Partnerships: Briefing for Section 5 Inspection*. Manchester: Office for Standards in Education, Children's Services and Skills.

Oliver, C., Mooney, A. and Statham, J. (2010) *Integrated Working: A Review of the Evidence*. Leeds: CDWC, Thomas Coram Research Unit, Institute of Education, University of London.

Quong, T. and Walker, A. (2010) 'Seven principles of strategic leadership', *International Studies in Educational Administration* (ISEA) 38(1): 32–3.

Sanderson, H. (2013a) *One Plan for 0–25 Education, Health and Care*. Stockport: HSA Press.

Sanderson, H. (2013b) *Using Person-Centred Practices in Schools*. Stockport: HSA Press.

Sanderson, H., Smith, T. and Wilson, L. (2010) *One Page Profiles in Schools: A Guide*. Stockport: HSA Press.

Sanderson, H., Thompson, J. and Kilbane, J. (2010) 'The emergence of person-centred planning as evidence-based practice', *Journal of Integrated Care* 14(2): 18–25.

SEN Policy Research Forum (2013) *How Will Accountability Work in the New SEND Legislative System?* SEN Policy Paper. London

STA (2013) *Assessment and Reporting Arrangements*. London: Standards and Testing Agency.

Starr, J. (2011) *The Coaching Manual: The Definitive Guide to the Process, Principles and Skills of Personal Coaching*, 3rd edn. London: Prentice Hall Business/Pearson Education Limited.

The Communication Trust (2012) *Misunderstood: Supporting Children and Young People with Speech, Language and Communication Needs*. London: The Communication Trust/Early Support.

The Sutton Trust – Education Endowment Foundation (2012) *The Teaching and Learning Toolkit*. London: The Sutton Trust – Education Endowment Foundation.

Thomas, K.W. and Kilmann, R.H. (1974) *Thomas–Kilmann Conflict Mode Instrument*. Mountain View, CA: Xicom, a subsidiary of CPP, Inc.

TSO (2008) *The Education (Special Educational Needs Coordinators) (England) Regulations 2008*. London: The Stationery Office.

TSO (2010) *Equality Act 2010*. Norwich: The Stationery Office.

TSO (2012) *Draft Legislation on Reform of Provision for Children and Young People with Special Educational Needs*. Norwich: The Stationery Office.

Warnock, M. (2005) *Special Educational Needs: A New Look*. Paper 11. London: Philosophy of Education Society of Great Britain.

Whitney, D. and Trosten-Bloom, A. (2012) *The Power of Appreciative Inquiry: A Practical Guide to Positive Change*, 2nd edn. San Francisco: Berrett-Koehler Publishers.

Index